Reversin

This book examines the global unfolding of the African Diaspora, the migrations and dispersals of people of Africa, from antiquity to the modern period. Their exploits, challenges, and struggles over a wide expanse of time are discussed in ways that link as well as differentiate past and present circumstances. The experiences of Africans in the Old World, in the Mediterranean and Islamic worlds, is followed by their movement into the New, where their plight in lands claimed by Portuguese, Spanish, Dutch, French, and English colonial powers is analyzed from enslavement through the Cold War. While appropriate mention is made of persons of renown, particular attention is paid to the everyday lives of working class people and their cultural efflorescence. The book also attempts to explain contemporary plights and struggles through the lens of history.

Michael A. Gomez is Professor of History at New York University. He is the author of *Pragmatism in the Age of Jihad: The Precolonial State of Bundu* (Cambridge, 1992) and *Exchanging Our Country Marks: The Transformation of African Identities in the Colonial and Antebellum South* (1998). He currently serves as Director of the Association for the Study of the Worldwide African Diaspora (ASWAD).

*New Approaches to African History*

*Series Editor*
Martin Klein, *University of Toronto*

*New Approaches to African History* is designed to introduce students to current findings and new ideas in African history. Although each book treats a particular case and is able to stand alone, the format allows the studies to be used as modules in general courses on African history and world history. The cases represent a wide range of topics. Each volume summarizes the state of knowledge on a particular subject for a student who is new to the field. However, the aim is not simply to present views of the literature; it is also to introduce debates on historiographical or substantive issues, and it may argue for a particular point of view. The aim of the series is to stimulate debate, to challenge students and general readers. The series is not committed to any particular school of thought.

Other books in the series:

*Africa Since 1940,* by Frederick Cooper
*Muslim Societies in African History,* by David Robinson

# Reversing Sail

## A History of the African Diaspora

**Michael A. Gomez**
*New York University*

CAMBRIDGE
UNIVERSITY PRESS

CAMBRIDGE UNIVERSITY PRESS
Cambridge, New York, Melbourne, Madrid, Cape Town,
Singapore, São Paulo, Delhi, Tokyo, Mexico City

Cambridge University Press
32 Avenue of the Americas, New York, NY 10013-2473, USA

www.cambridge.org
Information on this title: www.cambridge.org/9780521001359

First published 2005
8th printing 2011

A catalog record for this publication is available from the British Library.

Library of Congress Cataloging in Publication Data

Gomez, Michael Angelo, 1955–
Reversing sail : a history of the African diaspora / Michael A. Gomez.
    p.  cm. – (New approaches to African history)
Includes bibliographical references and index.
ISBN 0-521-80662-3 – ISBN 0-521-00135-8 (pb.)
1. African diaspora – History.  2. Blacks – History.  I. Title.  II. Series.
DT16.5.G66    2004
909'.0496–dc22                                        2004051992

ISBN 978-0-521-80662-6 Hardback
ISBN 978-0-521-00135-9 Paperback

*In memory of the love of my mother,*
*Mary Williams Gomez, 1936–1999,*
*the first to make me see*
*the beauty and suffering of the African Diaspora.*

# Contents

# List of Figures and Maps

## Figures

## Maps

ix

# Acknowledgments

I am indebted to a number of persons who gave of their time and expertise to help shape this project. I thank Martin Klein, who approached me with the idea of writing this book, and who patiently read through several drafts. Colin Palmer also read drafts, as did Kathleen Phillips-Lewis. Their comments, suggestions, and criticisms were extremely important. There were other readers whose names were not revealed to me; I thank them as well. Of course, all errors of fact and interpretation are solely mine.

I wish to thank those NYU graduate students who have studied with me, and with whom I have studied. These include Tanya Huelett, Edwina Ashie-Nikoi, Njoroge Njoroge, Aisha Finch, Natasha Lightfoot, Hillina Seife, Seth Markle, Michaela Harrison, Amir al-Islam, Marc Goulding, Alexis Doster, Oghenetoja Okoh, Yuko Miki, and Michelle Thompson; we have enjoyed spirited discussions about the African Diaspora, both in and out of class, and I have been the major benefactor. I look forward to great tomes from each of you, and of a quality that far exceeds my own.

I owe a special debt of gratitude to my Spelman College family, who continue to model the study of the Diaspora, and with whom I share a vital bond.

I also want to acknowledge the friendship and support of Sterling Stuckey. Our continuous dialogue has contributed significantly to my thinking.

My wife Mary and our daughters, Sonya, Candace, and Jamila, remain my principal supporters and dedicated companions along this way. I owe them all my love and appreciation.

As always, I give praise to the Almighty.

# Introduction

The dawn of the twenty-first century finds persons of varying ethnic and racial and religious backgrounds living together in societies all over the globe. The United Kingdom and France in Europe, together with the United States and Brazil in the Americas, are perhaps only the better known of many such societies, a principal dynamic of which concerns how groups maintain their identities while forming new and viable communities with those who do not share their backgrounds or beliefs. To achieve the latter requires a willingness on the part of all to learn about the histories and cultures of everyone in the society.

This book is about people of African descent who found (and find) themselves living either outside of the African continent or in parts of Africa that were territorially quite distant from their lands of birth. It is a history of their experiences, contributions, victories, and struggles, and it is primarily concerned with massive movements and extensive relocations, over long periods of time, resulting in the dispersal of Africans and their descendants throughout much of the world. This phenomenon is referred to as the African Diaspora. Redistributions of European and Asian populations have also marked history, but the African Diaspora is unique in its formation. It is a story, or a collection of stories, like no other.

As an undergraduate text, this book is written at a time of considerable perplexity, ambiguity, and seeming contradiction. People of African descent, or black people, can be found in all walks of life. In ancient and medieval times their achievements were in instances unparalleled; their economic contributions to the modern world have been extensive and foundational, introducing agricultural forms and mining techniques while providing the necessary labor. They have contributed to the sciences and the arts in spectacular ways, but it is their cultural influence, involving literature, theater, painting, sculpture, dance, music, athletics, and religion, that has received greater recognition, with individual artists or athletes achieving extraordinary heights. Jazz, blues, reggae, and hip hop, for example, are global phenomena. Even so, the contemporary contrast between the individual of distinction and the popular perception of blacks as a whole could not be more striking. Blacks as a group are disproportionately associated with crime, poverty, disease, and educational underachievement. This perception is paralleled by the view of Africa itself, a continent brimming with potential but waylaid by war, poverty, disease, and insufficient investment in human capital.

The study of the African Diaspora can be distinguished from the study of African Americans in the United States, or from other groups of African-descended persons in a particular nation-state, in that the African Diaspora is concerned with at least one of two issues (and frequently both): (1) the ways in which preceding African cultural, social, or political forms influence African-descended persons in their new environment, and how such forms change through interaction with non-African cultures (European, Native American, Asian, etc.); and (2) comparisons and relationships between communities of African-descended people who are geographically separated or culturally distinct.

The observation that the African Diaspora is a complex pattern of communities and cultures with differing local and regional histories raises an important question: Why continue to speak of the African Diaspora as a unified experience? There is no easy answer or scholarly consensus, but there are a number of factors that together suggest a related condition. These are (1) Africa as the land of origin; (2) an experience of enslavement; (3) the struggle of adapting to a new environment while preserving as much of the African cultural background as possible; (4) the reification of color and race; (5) a continuing struggle against discrimination; and (6) the ongoing significance of Africa to African-descended population. With these factors in mind, one can state that the African Diaspora consists of the connections of people of African descent around the world, who are linked as much by their common experiences as their genetic makeup, if not more so.

This book is divided into two parts, "Old" World Dimensions and "New" World Realities, with chapters that proceed in more or less chronological fashion. Chapter One, Antiquity, begins with a consideration of ancient Egypt, Nubia, and Greece and Rome. Chapter Two, Africans and the Bible, recognizes the critical role Judeo-Christian traditions have played in the formation of African Diasporic identities and seeks to examine the historical bases for this process. Chapter Three, Africans and the Islamic World, centers on the roles of Africans, subsaharan and otherwise, in the formation and expansion of Islam as a global force. The fourth chapter, Transatlantic Moment, shifts the inquiry away from the Old World to the New and discusses the various dimensions of the transatlantic slave trade. Chapter Five, Enslavement, focuses on the similar and dissimilar experiences of slavery in the Americas. The response of Africans and their descendants to the disorientation of displacement and enslavement, their various strategies of resistance and reconstitution, and the ambiguities of economic, political, and juridical conditions in the postslavery period are the subjects of Asserting the Right to Be, Chapter Six. Chapter Seven, Reconnecting, concerns the first half of the twentieth century and the rise of global capitalism, and it considers migrations of those of African descent, especially involving the Caribbean and the American South. Such developments increased contact between diverse populations, contributing to the rise of Pan-Africanism, the Harlem Renaissance, and négritude. Chapter Eight, Movement People, covers the period from World War II through the 1960s, highlighting the interconnections between decolonization, civil rights, black power, music, sports, and writing.

As an interpretive history, this book is far from an exhaustive treatment of such a vast topic (or set of related topics). As part of a strategy to sufficiently treat the various components of the African Diaspora at some point in time, geographic emphases shift from chapter to chapter. Originally envisioned as part a series of short books introducing African history, the book's scope is necessarily influenced by spatial constraints, and, in keeping with the format for the series, there are no endnotes. But in addition to African history, *Reversing Sail* can also be used for courses examining the African Diaspora as well as African American history. While not intended to serve as a comprehensive reference section, suggested readings following each chapter identify materials of most immediate assistance in the undergraduate search for greater depth.

# I

## "Old" World Dimensions

# CHAPTER 1

# Antiquity

Scholars of American history have long understood that discussions of the African American experience must begin with a consideration of people and cultures and developments in Africa itself, before the rise of American slavery and the transatlantic slave trade, to debilitate the notion that black folk, prior to their experiences in the Americas, had no history worthy of the name.

Long before the rise of professional historians, black men and women had reached a similar conclusion. Facing the withering effects of slavery, black thinkers as early as David Walker and Frederick Douglass were careful to mention the glories of the African past. When circumstances all around suggested otherwise, they found evidence of the potential and ability of black people in the achievements of antiquity. Rather than conforming to divine decree or reflecting the natural order of things, the enslavement of black people, when placed in the context of thousands of years of history in Africa itself, was but an aberration. In this view, there was nothing inevitable about black suffering and subjugation.

These early thinkers, uninformed about the greatness of West and West Central African civilizations, invariably cited those of ancient Egypt, Nubia, and Ethiopia as exemplars of black accomplishment and creativity. In so doing, they anticipated the subsequent writings of scholars like W. E. B. Du Bois, Carter G. Woodson, and St. Clair Drake, who likewise embraced the idea that ancient Egyptian and Nubian societies were related to those toiling in American sugar cane and cotton fields. This view was not limited to black thinkers in the

Americas; the Senegalese scholar Cheikh Anta Diop argued for links between Egypt, Ethiopia, and West Africa. The latest to make such claims have been the "Afrocentrists," but whatever the particular school of thought, certain of their ideas resonate with communities in both West Africa and the African Diaspora, where the notion of a connectedness to either Egypt and Nubia or Ethiopia resides in the cultural expressions of the folk. Whether one accepts their views or finds them extravagant, there is no avoiding the realization that Africans and their descendants have pursued a long and uninterrupted conversation about their relationship to the ancients. Such intergenerational discussion has not been idle chitchat but rather has significantly influenced the unfolding of African American art, music, religion, politics, and societies.

A brief consideration of ancient Africa, especially Egypt, Nubia, and Ethiopia, remains important for at least two reasons: First, it contextualizes the discussion of subsequent developments largely inaugurated with massive trades in African captives. Antiquity reminds us that modernity could not have been predicted, that Africans were not always under the heel but were in fact at the forefront of human civilization. Second, antiquity reminds us that the African Diaspora did not begin with the slave trades. Rather, the dissemination of African ideas and persons actually began long ago. In this first diasporic phase, ideas were arguably more significant than the number of people dispersed. The Mediterranean in particular benefited from Egyptian and Nubian culture and learning. This initial phase was further distinguished by the political standing of the Africans in question; Egypt was a world power that imposed its will on others, rather than the reverse. This was therefore a different kind of African Diaspora than what followed many centuries later.

## Egypt

The study of ancient Egypt is a discipline unto itself, involving majestic monuments, mesmerizing religions, magnificent arts, epic wars, and the like, all of which lie beyond our purpose here. Rather, our deliberations are confined to Egypt's relations with its neighbors, especially to the south, as it is in such relations that the concept of an ancient African Diaspora can be demonstrated.

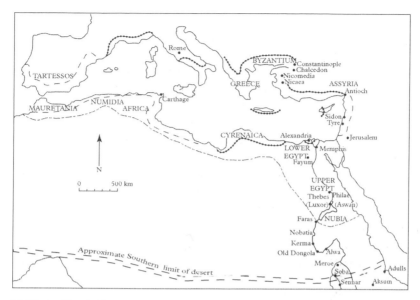

**MAP 1.** North Africa in antiquity.

Ancient Egypt, located along the Nile and divided into Upper and Lower regions, exchanged goods and ideas with Sumer (in Mesopotamia, between the Tigris and Euphrates Rivers) as early as 3500 BCE, and by 1700 BCE it was connected with urban-based civilizations in the Indus valley, the Iranian plateau, and China. Situated in Africa, Egypt was also a global crossroad for various populations and cultures, its participation in this intercontinental zone a major feature of the African Diaspora's opening chapter.

Just who were these ancient Egyptians? While none can reasonably quibble with identifying them as northeastern Africans, the discussion becomes more complex when the subject turns to "race." Race, as it is used currently, lacks scientific value or meaning; it is as a sociopolitical concept that race takes on decided import and gravity. Our understanding of ancient Egypt is complicated by our own conversations about race, and by attempts to relate modern ideas to ancient times. A contemporary preoccupation, race was of scant significance in ancient Egypt, if the concept even existed. For example, while some paintings depict the Egyptians as dark skinned, it is more common to see males painted a dark reddish-brown and females a lighter brown or yellow. Such varying representations were not meant to simply convey physical traits, but social standing as well; a woman portrayed as light brown suggests privilege and exemption from the need to work outdoors, her actual skin tone a matter of conjecture.

Ancient Egyptians were highly ethnocentric, regarding themselves as "the people" and everyone else as uncivilized, a distinction having more to do with land of birth and culture than outward appearance. Foreigners included Bedouins from Arabia, "Asiatics" from Asia Minor, Libyans from the west, and the Nehesi from the area south of Egypt, called *Nehesyu* or *Khent* ("borderland") by the Egyptians, otherwise known as Nubia or Kush. But given Egypt's long history, its gene pool periodically received infusions from Asia Minor, southern Europe, the Arabian peninsula, and, of course, subsaharan Africa. What Egyptians may have looked like in the third millennium BCE is not necessarily how they appeared 1,000 years later, let alone after 4,000 years. Swift and dramatic changes in the North American gene pool between 1500 CE and 2002 caution that sustained and substantial immigration can produce startling transformations.

## Egypt and the South

During the Old and Middle Kingdoms (3400–2180 and 2080–1640 BCE), Egypt sought to militarily control Nubia and parts of Syria and Palestine. Under the New Kingdom (1570–1090 BCE), Egypt repeatedly invaded Palestine and Syria in its competition with Assyria and (subsequently) Babylon for control of the region. Africa was therefore a major foreign power in what would become the Middle East for thousands of years, years that were formative, in lands destined to become sacred for millions of people.

While especially interested in Nubia's gold, Egypt also recruited the Nubians themselves for the Egyptian army, as their military prowess, especially in archery, was highly regarded (Egyptians referred to Nubia as *Ta-Seti*, or the "land of the bow"). Nubians were also sought as laborers, and some were even enslaved. However, with the possible exception of the Hebrews, Egypt's enslaved population was never very large, with slaves from Europe and Asia Minor often more numerous than Nubians or other Africans.

While extending its control over Nubian territory and tapping Nubian labor, Egypt also relocated select Nubians to its capital at Thebes, where an institution called the *Kap* provided a formal, rare Egyptian education. Nubians learned the ways of Egypt, but their presence as elites, workers, and soldiers also led to the spread of Nubian culture in Egypt. This phenomenon was similar to later developments in the Americas, where the convergence of African, European, Asian, and Native American elements led to a flourishing of African-inspired cultures, among others.

One of the more fascinating aspects of the New Kingdom's eighteenth dynasty's involvement with Nubia was the determinant role Nubian women played in the royal court. Indeed, Nubian women became Egyptian royals, wielding tremendous power as queen mothers and royal wives. As wives, they ruled at times with their husbands, at times as regents, and in some instances alone. Ahmose I inaugurated the eighteenth dynasty and ruled with Nefertari, a Nubian who enjoyed tremendous prestige and popularity with native Egyptians. Their great-granddaughter Hatshepsut ruled as both queen and regent from 1503 to 1482 BCE. Ties to Nubia were later strengthened when Amenhotep III married thirteen-year-old Tiye, another Nubian. Their seven children included sons Amenhotep IV and Tutankhamen. Renowned and emulated for her beauty, Tiye was also well educated and quite the political force; funerary sculptures depict her as an equal to Amenhotep III. She may have been responsible for affairs of state under Amenhotep IV, who changed his name to Akhenaton (from *aton*, solar symbol of supreme deity) as part of his promotion of monotheism. As Akhenaton's wife, Nefertiti, was yet another Nubian, we can see that it is not possible to discuss the New Kingdom without acknowledging the Nubian presence and contribution.

## Nubian Ascendancy

Nubia, also located along the Nile, was called *Qevs* by its inhabitants. None of its various names – Nubia, Qevs, Cush, Kush, Ta-Seti, Nehesyu, Khent – refer to skin color; one can surmise that whatever differences existed between Egyptians and Nubians, skin color was not one that elicited elaboration.

Nubia was likewise divided into Lower and Upper regions: The former was associated with bows, shields, and other manufactures as well as raw materials; the latter with gold, semiprecious stones, leopard skins, and cattle. A Nubian state may have existed prior to Egypt's Old Kingdom, and at least one was its contemporary. The three major

Nubian kingdoms came later and are named after their capitals: Kerma (1750–1550 BCE), Napata (750–300 BCE), and Meroë (300 BCE–350 CE).

Scholars point to the distinctiveness of Nubian history and culture, that Nubia was not simply an outpost of Egyptian civilization or an imitation of Egypt on a smaller scale. The history of Napata, however, features Egyptian and Nubian convergence. Under Napata's leadership, the Nubians not only freed themselves of Egyptian domination but also turned and conquered Egypt. Establishing the twenty-fifth dynasty, the Nubians ruled as Egyptian pharaohs, their acceptance by the Egyptians a reflection of the long familiarity of the Egyptian with the Nubian.

The twenty-fifth dynasty was a time of contestation between Egypt and Assyria for control of Palestine. Assyria invaded Egypt in 674 BCE but was defeated. Three years later they were successful, driving the Nubians south where they eventually reestablished their capital at Meroë. Removed from the interminable conflicts in the Near East, neither the Ptolemies nor Rome mounted any serious effort to conquer Meroë, opting instead to maintain trade relations. Commerce and defensible terrain allowed Meroë to flourish and export such commodities as gold, cotton, precious stones, ostrich feathers, ivory, and elephants (the latter for war and amusement), while producing large quantities of iron.

Meroë was a unique civilization, with large stone monuments of stelae and its own system of writing, Meroïtic. Nubian women played major roles in government (Egypt's eighteenth dynasty may reflect this custom); queen mothers were especially powerful, and, together with royal wives, were called *Candaces* (from *Kentakes*). The renown of the Candaces in the ancient Near East was such that they reappear in accounts connected with the Bible; they were a source of dramatic and powerful images reverberating to the present day.

## Africans in the Graeco-Roman World

The ancient Mediterranean world, successively dominated by the Greeks, Phoenicians, and Romans, came to know Africans from a number of places and in varying capacities. Most Africans, especially during the Roman period, entered the Mediterranean from both Egypt and Nubia. They also came from areas south of the Nile, North Africa (from what is now Libya west to Morocco), the southern fringes of the Sahara Desert, and West Africa proper.

In sharp contrast to the impressions that Egyptians and Nubians had of each other for millennia, southern Europeans were completely struck by the African's color; the darker the color, the stronger the impression. Although stunned, southern Europeans generally did not ascribe any intrinsic value or worth to skin color, and, unlike contemporary notions of race and racism, did not equate blackness with inferiority. Modern day racism apparently did not exist in the ancient Mediterranean world. In fact, there is evidence that just the opposite was true, that Africans were viewed favorably.

The Greeks were so taken with the pigmentation of Africans that they invented the term *Ethiopian* (from *Aethiops*). The term means "burnt-faced person" and reflects the European belief that the skin color and hair of the African were caused by the sun. "To wash an Ethiopian white" was a common expression in the Graeco-Roman world, indicating enough familiarity with blackness to use it in conveying the futility of attempting to change the unalterable. The term *Ethiopian* was at times also applied by the Greeks to Arabs, Indians, and others of dark hue, and it is often used inaccurately to refer to Nubians. It should be borne in mind that the ancient state of Ethiopia did not begin until the first century CE.

The combined vocabulary of the Greeks and Romans could include terms of distinction. Color variation was one scheme by which groups (rather than individuals) were categorized, located as they were along a continuum from dark (*fusci*) to very dark (*nigerrimi*). Ptolemy, for example, described the population around Meroë as "deeply black" and "pure Ethiopians," as opposed to those living in the border region between Egypt and Nubia, who, according to Flavius Philostratus, were not as black as the Nubians but darker than the Egyptians. While these classifications are nonscientific and subjective, they demonstrate that blackness varied in the ancient world, much as it does today.

In addition to pigmentation, diet also formed the basis of categorization, so that the work of second-century BCE geographer and historian Agatharchides, as recorded in *On the Erythrean Sea* and surviving in part in the writings of Diodorus (born 100 BCE) and Photius, speaks of the *Struthophagi* or ostrich eaters; the *Spermatophagi*, consumers of nuts and tree fruit; the *Ichthyophagi* or fish eaters; and the *Pamphagi*, who ate everything. Of course, some groups were purely fanciful, as is evident by Pliny the Elder's (born 23 CE) list that includes the

*Trogodytae* (voiceless save for squeaking noises); the *Blemmyae* (head-less, with eyes and mouths in their chests); the *Himantopodes,* who crawled instead of walked; and the three- and four-eyed *Nisicathae* and *Nisitae.*

Greek and Roman attempts to account for unknown parts of Africa represent an acknowledgment of the limitations of the former's knowledge. But what the Greeks and Romans did know of Africa, they tended to admire. Their attitudes toward Africans can be deduced from their accounts of actual encounters, as well as from their literature (such as poetry and drama). Artwork is also a source of information. These views come together in yet another Graeco-Roman division of the African population, this time along lines of civilizational achievement; African societies deemed high in attainment were greatly acclaimed. Egyptians and Nubians had established literate, urban-based, technologically advanced civilizations long before there was a Rome or an Athens, so there was every reason for African achievement to be praised and even emulated. It is not surprising that Homer speaks of the Olympian gods, especially Zeus, feasting with the "blameless" Ethiopians, the most distant of men, who by the time of Xenophanes (d. circa 478 BCE) had been identified as black and flat nosed, and by the fifth century located to the south of Egypt. Herodotus maintained that the Ethiopians were the tallest and most handsome of men, and the most pious. He added that Meroë was a "great city," and that the Nubians had supplied Egypt with eighteen pharaohs. Diodorus wrote that the inhabitants of Meroë were the "first of all men and the first to honor the gods whose favor they enjoyed," and, together with Lucian, who maintained that the "Ethiopians" had invented astrology, claimed that many Nubian practices and institutions were subsequently borrowed by the Egyptians. Meroë was to be distinguished, however, from "primitive" Ethiopians, who went about "filthy" and naked (or nearly so) and who did not believe in the gods. Celebrated sexual encounters in the Greek and Roman imagination are yet another measure of the regard for the Nubian. Examples include Zeus, who may have been portrayed in the *Inachus* of Sophocles (circa 496–406 BCE) as black or dark, and whose child by Io is described by Aeschylus (525–456 BCE) as black and by Hesiod (fl. circa 700 BCE) as the ancestor of the Ethiopians and Libyans. Delphos, the founder of Delphi, was believed to be the son of Poseidon or Apollo and a woman whose name means "the black woman." There is also the example of Perseus, who married the daughter of the king of the Ethiopians, the dark-hued Andromeda.

Just as individuals like Herodotus actually traveled to Africa and gathered information, Africans also entered southern Europe. The context was often one of war, both for and against the Greeks and Romans. Nubians were a part of the Egyptian occupation of Cyprus under Amasis (569–522 BCE), and there is the account of Memnon and his black soldiers coming to the aid of the Greeks in the possibly mythical Trojan Wars. A large number of Nubians fought under Xerxes of Persia in the very real Battle of Marathon in 480–79 BCE. These Nubians experienced liaisons with Greek women, resulting in the "brown babies" of the Persian Wars. Carthage, founded no earlier than 750 BCE by the combination of Phoenician settlers and Berber natives referred to as Numidians, developed a society in which the Berber masses were treated harshly. Although transsaharan trade in the hands of the Garamantes was not very important during Carthaginian ascendancy, a sufficient number of subsaharan Africans made their way to Carthage, where they were inducted into military service. Frontius records the presence of "very black" auxiliaries among the Carthaginian prisoners taken by Gelon of Syracuse in 480 BCE. The Punic Wars (264–241, 218–201, and 149–146 BCE) also saw Maghribian (North African) "Ethiopians," possibly West Africans, employed in the invasion of Italy, serving as *mahouts* aloft elephants. Rome would go on to conquer Egypt and occupy it from the time of Augustus to the sixth century CE. Its relations with Nubia and the south were relatively peaceful until the third century CE, when it incurred difficulties with the Beja of the Red Sea hills, called "Blemmyes" in the Roman sources.

Africans enslaved in the Graeco-Roman world were only a small fraction of the total number of slaves in these territories. Enslaved Africans also only represented a portion of the overall African population living in southern Europe. A number of Africans were attracted to places like Rome for trade and occupational opportunities, and they could be found working as musicians, actors, jugglers, gladiators, wrestlers, boxers, religious specialists, and day laborers. Some became famous, such as the black athlete Olympius described by sixth-century poet Luxorius. In addition to entertaining and fighting the Romans, Africans also served in the Roman armies, as was the case with the elite Moorish cavalry from northwest Africa under Lusius Quietus, himself of possible Moroccan heritage. Black soldiers even served in the Roman army as far north as Britain.

Potentially more far-reaching than the actual presence of Africans in southern Europe was the impact of their cultural influence. Scholars debate the extent to which Egyptian science, engineering, architectural forms, and philosophy influenced developments in Greece. There can be no question, however, that Egyptian and Nubian religion was deeply influential throughout the Mediterranean world for many centuries if not millennia, especially the worship of Isis, adopted and worshiped in many places under several names. Her worshipers made pilgrimage to the island of Philae, near the border of Egypt and Nubia, and Nubian specialists in Isiac worship were welcomed in various centers throughout southern Europe, where the Isiac rites were known as the Eleusianian mysteries.

From all that can be determined, it would appear that the racial attitudes of the ancient Graeco-Roman world differed significantly from the contemporary West. Africans were seen and treated as equals, the representatives of homelands both ancient and respected. Their reception in southern Europe and the Near East underscores the power and prestige of African realms and leaders as a factor that distinguishes this phase of the African Diaspora from what takes place much later. In the ancient world, Africa and Africans were forces to be reckoned with; indeed, for thousands of years, they were the leaders of the ancient world.

## Suggestions for Further Reading

Useful general histories of Africa include Philip Curtin, Steven Feierman, Leonard Thompson, and Jan Vansina, *African History: From Earliest Times to Independence* (London and New York: Longman, 1995, 2nd ed.), and J. Fage and R. Oliver, eds., *The Cambridge History of Africa* (Cambridge: Cambridge U. Press, 1975–86), an eight-volume collection.

Concerning ancient Egypt, works providing general reconstructions include Ian Shaw, ed., *The Oxford History of Ancient Egypt* (Oxford: Oxford University Press, 2000); Karol My'sliwiec, *The Twilight of Ancient Egypt: First Millennium B.C.E.*, trans. David Lorton (Ithaca, NY: Cornell U. Press, 2000); and Sergio Donadoni, ed., *The Egyptians*, trans. Robert Bianchi et al. (Chicago: U. of Chicago Press, 1997). Studies with foci on women, gender, and society are Lynn Meskell, *Archaeologies of Social Life: Age, Sex, Class Et Cetera in Ancient Egypt* (Oxford and Malden, MA: Blackwell, 1999); Zahi A. Hawass, *Silent Images: Women in Pharaonic Egypt* (Cairo: American U. in Cairo Press, 2000); John Romer, *People of the Nile: Everyday Life in Ancient Egypt*

(New York: Crown, 1982); Susan Walker and Peter Higgs, *Cleopatra of Egypt: From History to Myth* (Princeton, NJ: Princeton U. Press, 2001). Regarding religion, see Dimitri Meeks and Christine Favard-Meeks, *Daily Life of the Egyptian Gods*, trans. G. M. Goshgarian (Ithaca, NY: Cornell U. Press, 1996); and Aylward M. Blackman, *Gods, Priests and Men: Studies in the Religion of Pharaonic Egypt* (New York: Columbia U. Press, 1993).

The issue of race in Egypt and antiquity is engaged by Cheikh Anta Diop, *The African Origin of Civilization: Myth or Reality*, trans. Mercer Cook (New York: L. Hill, 1974). St. Clair Drake's two-volume *Black Folk Here and There: An Essay in History and Anthropology* (Los Angeles: Center for Afro-American Studies, U. of California, 1987–90) certainly addresses identity in ancient Egypt but goes well beyond this period and place.

The question of Graeco-Roman indebtedness to early Egypt is taken up in Martin Bernal's controversial *Black Athena: The Afroasiatic Roots of Classical Civilization*, 2 vols. (London: Free Association Books, 1987–91), in the course of which race is considered. An oft-overlooked work making parallel arguments, but preceding Bernal by three decades, is George G. M. James, *Stolen Legacy* (New York: Philosophical Library, 1954). One of the responses to Bernal (and others) is Mary Lefkowitz, *Not Out of Africa: How Afrocentrism Became an Excuse to Teach Myth as History* (New York: Basic Books, 1996).

A rather comprehensive discussion of Nubian history is provided in P. L. Shinnie's massive *Ancient Nubia* (London and New York: Kegan Paul International, 1995). Nubia's rise and eventual takeover of Egypt is examined in Robert G. Morkot's *The Black Pharaohs: Egypt's Nubian Rulers* (London: Rubicon, 2000).

A bridge connecting Egyptian, Nubian, and Graeco-Roman societies via race are Frank M. Snowden, Jr.'s *Blacks in Antiquity: Ethiopians in the Greco-Roman Experience* (Cambridge, MA: Belknap Press of Harvard U. Press, 1970), and his *Before Color Prejudice: The Ancient View of Blacks* (Cambridge, MA: Harvard U. Press, 1983). Leo William Hansberry's *Africa and Africans as Seen by Classical Writers*, ed. Joseph E. Harris (Washington, DC: University Press, 1981), is also useful.

Finally, Stephen Quirke and Jeffrey Spencer, eds., allow for printed visualization of antiquity in *The British Museum Book of Ancient Egypt* (London: British Museum Press, 1992).

# CHAPTER 2

# Africans and the Bible

The Bible has affected the lives of Africans and their descendants in the Diaspora possibly more than any other document in human history. This phenomenon can be divided into at least two spheres: The first features the roles and experiences of Africans in the Bible, while the second concerns the ways in which these roles and experiences have influenced Africans living in post-Biblical times. Because the Biblical account is seen by many as prescriptive, the interpretation of African roles in the narrative is critical, as it has often determined how post-Biblical Africans were treated. In particular, the Bible has been crucial to slavery, with both benefactors and detractors of the institution taking solace in its pages.

## Egypt and Nubia in the Bible

Pharaohs of the twenty-fifth dynasty appear in the Old Testament as allies against the Assyrians, and Taharka (690–664 BCE) is mentioned by name (Isaiah 37:9; 2 Kings 19:9). Egypt and Nubia's union under this dynasty is demonstrated by the prophet Isaiah's conjoined messages to each (Isaiah 18–20). In language corresponding to Herodotus, Isaiah (18:2,7) writes this of Nubia:

> Go, swift messengers to a nation tall and smooth,
> To a people feared far and wide,

A powerful and oppressive nation
Whose land the rivers divide.

Such esteem for Nubia is consistent with the view of states along the
Nile as powerful neighbors of Israel, ever present in regional affairs. Indeed, the very formation of the Hebrew people is intimately associated
with Egypt and Nubia. Egypt in particular features large in the Old
Testament, playing successive roles as asylum, oppressor, ally, and foe.
The enslavement and subsequent divine deliverance of the Hebrews
was a source of consolation and hope for enslaved Africans and their
descendants thousands of years later. But while many identified with
the Hebrews, others celebrated the connection to Egypt.

Assuming a historical basis for Hebrew enslavement, it is unreason-
able to believe they would have avoided sexual unions with Egyptians
and Nubians for 400 years; indeed, individual stories suggest that the
interaction between Hebrews and Egyptians or Nubians may have been
significant. Even before the Hebrew community in Egypt, Egyptian
women figured prominently in the lives of the prophets. Abraham, the
father of revelatory monotheism, had a son Ishmael by the Egyptian
Hagar, and Ishmael in turn married an Egyptian woman. Upon entry into Egypt, the patriarch Joseph also married an Egyptian woman,
Asenath, who bore Manasseh and Ephraim, so that at least one of
the twelve tribes was of partial African origin. Moses himself married a Nubian woman (Numbers 12:1). These examples suggest such
women were desirable and instrumental at critical junctures, birthing
clans and nations.

Beyond the question of intermarriage is the issue of cultural influence. The Hebrews were necessarily affected by their long stay in
Egypt; after all, Joseph was embalmed. Such influence probably remained with the Hebrews for many years, as they exited Egypt with
a "mixed multitude" (Exodus 12:38). Much of the Old Testament
is concerned with eradicating that influence, along with others from
Mesopotamia. If the Exodus is afforded credibility, it gives pause that
the Hebrews, every one of them, came out of Africa after a 400-year so-
journ. The story is not unlike the human birthing process, the crossing
of the Red Sea a movement through the amniotic fluids of an African
mother.

Mention of individual Egyptians and Nubians in the Bible is relatively rare. Some are in servile positions; others are associated with

the military. They include the unnamed Nubian military courier or messenger who told King David of his son Absalom's death in battle (2 Samuel 18:19–33). Then there is Ebed-melech (or "royal slave"), a Nubian eunuch in the service of Zedekiah, king of Judah. He rescued the prophet Jeremiah from certain death by interceding for him before Zedekiah; for his intervention, Ebed-melech would be spared the coming judgment (Jeremiah 38:1–13; 39:15–18). Others with possible blood ties to Egypt or Nubia include Aaron's grandson Phinehas, possibly an Egyptian name meaning "the Nubian" (Exodus 6:25); and the prophet Zephaniah, son of "Cushi" or the Cushite (Zephaniah 1:1). Perhaps the most famous involves the Queen of Sheba, a complicated story involving a King Solomon already married to a daughter of the Egyptian pharaoh (and eventually hundreds of other women; see 2 Chronicles 8:11).

## Africans and Origins

The question of identifying Africans in the Bible is influenced by assumptions brought to the text. The exercise of "discovering" Africans in the Bible often presupposes that the document is essentially concerned with non-Africans. But what if the assumptions are different, and the Bible is presumed to be primarily concerned with "people of color," including Africans?

Independent of anthropological and archaeological records, the Bible has its own tradition of human origins. In the interpretation of that tradition over the centuries, the Garden of Eden story has rarely been situated in an African setting. A forced correlation between Biblical narrative and scientific findings, however, directs attention to East Africa and would suggest to those concerned with Biblical teachings that the earliest actors were Africans. The notion of an African Eden, however, was far from the imagination of Western slaveholding societies. Instead, a tale condemning Africans was widely accepted.

The account concerns the prophet and ark-builder Noah, and it is possibly the most dramatic example of how the interpretation of holy writ can have life-altering consequences. After the flood, the progenitors of the entire human family are listed in the "Table of Nations" (Genesis 10). According to a conventional reading, Ham became the father of "the black people," as his sons are listed as Cush, Mizraim, Put or Punt, and Canaan; that is, Nubia, Egypt, possibly Libya or lands beyond Nubia proper, and Palestine. Such a reading assumes that Noah's other two sons, Japheth and Shem, were "white" and "Asian," or at least not black.

The term *Cush* probably derives from *Qevs* and is simply a place-name, bearing no racial or ethnic connotations. The Greek terms *Ethiopia* and *Ethiopian* do not appear in the Hebrew and Chaldean Old Testament, but rather the words *Cush* and *Cushite*, suggesting Nubian features were not a concern for Old Testament writers but became one with the rise of Alexander and the ensuing period of hellenization, when translators of the Septuagint, the Old Testament in Greek, opted to substitute *Ethiopia* for *Cush*.

Although the physical features of the Cushites or Nubians were not a significant matter for early Jews, an incident that precedes the presentation of the Table of Nations would eventually be interpreted in a way that would affect issues of slavery and race for centuries to come. The incident concerns a drunken Noah whose "nakedness is uncovered" by his son Ham, a phrase with multiple possible meanings. When Noah awoke from his stupor and realized "what had been done to him," he uttered words that would have profound implications for people of African descent:

> Cursed be Canaan;
> The lowest of servants
> He shall be to his brothers.
> (Genesis 9:24–27)

The ambiguity of the passage lends itself to conflicting interpretations. Who was being cursed, Ham or his son Canaan? Did Noah's curse carry divine sanction, or was it the innocuous expletives of an angry mortal?

The interpretation of Noah's curse depends upon the perspective. Believers are divided over its meaning. To the cynical, the curse was written after the entry of the Hebrews into Palestine to justify the appropriation of land. For the eighteenth- and nineteenth-century slave-holder, it became "the Hamitic curse" and meant that African slavery had been providentially decreed. In this reading, the European slaveholder was simply fulfilling the will of God, as God's chosen instrument.

To the extent that the curse enjoys divine sanction, the likelihood that it was meant to apply to all of the descendants of Ham is mitigated by the record of the Bible itself. The only person discussed in any detail in Genesis Chapter 10, site of the Table of Nations, is one

Nimrod, son of Cush, who "became a mighty one on the earth. He was a mighty hunter before the Lord," and credited with establishing such cities as Babel and Nineveh in Assyria. If anything, Nimrod represents a tradition of imperialism and domination rather than subservience. Another example is Egypt itself, as it was the Egyptians, descendants of Ham, who were the slaveholders. Again, it was to the Nubians that the Israelites turned for help against the Assyrians out of recognition of their ascendancy. There is also the fascinating account of Moses and his Nubian bride (Numbers 12), a marriage opposed by Moses' siblings Miriam and Aaron for reasons unclear. In a stunning rebuke, Yahweh not only supports Moses but also turns Miriam's skin into a leprous, luminous white that persists for days, an unusual punishment laced with humor if not sarcasm.

Unfortunately, the import of the divine rebuke did not endure. Scholars of the revered communication would produce additional literature to accompany the scriptures and unfold their meaning. In contrast to the Jewish Talmud (a collection of laws and rabbinical wisdom and the second most holy text in Judaism), another tradition began, perhaps around the fifth century BCE, that may have characterized blackness itself as a consequence of and punishment for Ham's transgression. This tradition that can be found in the fifth-century CE literature of the Midrashim and the sixth-century CE Babylonian Talmud. However, some scholars argue that the idea of blackness as scourge actually derives from mistranslations of these texts, rather than the texts themselves.

African-born persons rarely appear in the New Testament. Jesus is said to have spent an unspecified number of his childhood years in Egypt, where in all likelihood he would have lived in the large Jewish community at Alexandria (Matthew 2:13–23). Simon of Cyrene (North Africa) is remembered for helping Jesus carry the cross (Luke 23:26; Matthew 27:32; Mark 15:21). The "Ethiopian" eunuch, who will be discussed in more detail, is prominently featured in the book of the Acts of the Apostles.

It is striking that the formation of the early Jewish state involved the literal transfer of a community from one land of Ham to another. It is therefore not possible to hold an intelligent discussion of the Old Testament without understanding the contribution of the African. It is not a question of a lone Nubian here and an odd Egyptian there; rather, the Old Testament world was awash in Africa's colors and cultures.

## The Queen of Sheba

While the Hamitic curse would be used in the future with devastating effect, another account in the Old Testament forms the basis for perhaps the most significant and certainly most hallowed tradition involving Biblical Africa, linking the continent to the African Diaspora from ancient times to the present. In arresting defiance of, and in diametric opposition to, the damnation of Canaan, the very glory of God is held to have rested upon a favored Ethiopia. The explanation of how that happened is a fascinating journey into an African reading of the Bible, and it links the continent to three separate faiths in fundamental and enduring ways.

The story begins with King Solomon, who already had ties to the Nile valley by his marriage to an Egyptian princess and possibly by way of his mother Bathsheba, whose name may signify "from the house or land of Sheba." Word of his fabled wisdom spread far and wide, eventually attracting the Queen of Sheba, who journeyed to Israel with a large retinue to hear Solomon's wisdom for herself (2 Chronicles 9:1–12; 1 Kings 10:1–13). More than favorably impressed, the Queen gave the king a large quantity of gold, spices, and precious stones. In exchange, Solomon gave unspecified gifts of his own.

According to the Ethiopian holy book *Kebra Nagast* or "Glory of Kings," completed in the early fourteenth century and drawn from the Bible, the Qur'ān, apocryphal literatures, and other sources, Solomon and the Queen, identified as Makeda in the Ethiopian manuscript, struck up a romance consummated through Solomon's guile. After nine months and a conversion to Judaism, Makeda gave birth to Menelik (literally, "son of the wise man"), who years later returned to Jerusalem where he was acknowledged by his father, crowned the king of Ethiopia, and implored to remain in Jerusalem to inherit the throne of Israel. Longing for home, Menelik instead returned to Ethiopia with a number of priests and the *Tabot* or the Ark of the Covenant (or Tabernacle of Zion). The Ark, symbol of Yahweh's presence and Israel's unique status, henceforth rests, according to this tradition, in Ethiopia, thereby transferring to the Ethiopians the honor of "God's chosen people." Likewise, the kings of Ethiopia are descendants of Solomon, each a "lion of Judah."

There are multiple layers to the story. To begin, the location of "Sheba" is in dispute: many cite Saba in Yemen as the most likely site, while some insist upon Nubia or Ethiopia. Interestingly, Jesus simply refers to the "Queen of the South" who came "from the ends of the earth" to hear Solomon's wisdom (Matthew 12:42; Luke 11:31), a characterization of space and distance in remarkable resonance with Homer's *Odyssey*, wherein the Ethiopians are described as "the most remote of men," dwelling by the streams of Ocean, "at earth's two verges, in sunset lands and lands of the rising sun." As Ethiopia did not exist during the time of Solomon, the only viable alternative to Yemen for Sheba's location is Nubia, where the queen may have been one of the Candaces. In the end, Sheba's precise location may not matter very much, as populations and cultural influences regularly crisscrossed the Red Sea in antiquity; in fact, southern Arabia was periodically dominated by powers on nearby African soil, particularly from 335–370 CE and 525–575 CE, when Ethiopia ruled portions of the southern peninsula.

Another complication is the *Kebra Nagast*'s claims of an initial association with Judaism. Ethiopia is better known as a Christian state. Founded at Aksum (Axum) in 59 CE, Ethiopia became home to Amhara-Tigrean, Galla, Afar, Somali, and Omotic populations, distinguishing it both culturally and territorially from Nubia (which lay to the north). Christianity entered Ethiopia early; tradition links missionary activity to the apostle Matthew, but Ethiopia's definitive turn to Christianity took place in the middle of the fourth century CE, when King Ezana and the royal court embraced the new religion, and in the fifth century CE, when large-scale conversions occurred. In 1135, the Aksumite rulers were overthrown by the founders of the Zagwe dynasty, whose greatest achievement was the creation of a remarkable ceremonial center at Lalibela (or Roha, named after the dynasty's most illustrious ruler), site of churches hewn from "living rock," fashioned deep in the earth. The Zagwes were in turn overthrown by the Solomonids in 1270, claiming descent from Solomon and Makeda.

The Solomonids drew upon traditions enshrined in the *Kebra Nagast* to legitimate their seizure of power, claiming the best of both worlds by trumpeting their alleged hereditary connections to Israel while simultaneously championing Christianity. Led by a literate elite who wrote in Ge'ez (or Ethiopic), Christian Ethiopia experienced an efflorescence under the Solomonids, particularly from the thirteenth through the sixteenth centuries. Although severely challenged by Ahmad Granye's sixteenth-century Muslim campaign that saw widespread destruction of churches and monasteries, only to be followed by incursions of Galla or Oromo in the sixteenth through the nineteenth centuries, Ethiopia's unique Christian legacy survived. Ethiopia would become an icon in the modern African Diaspora, a symbol of independence and fierce pride, and the focus of a new religion developed in the Caribbean.

## Beta Israel

The Solomonids were not the only ones to draw from the *Kebra Nagast* for legitimation. The Jews of Ethiopia, who refer to themselves as the *Beta Israel* ("House of Israel") and take umbrage at the term *Falasha* ("stranger, wanderer," coined by non-Jewish Ethiopians), also claim descent from Solomon and Makeda. The Beta Israel have a different account of what happened following Menelik's return to Ethiopia: With the Ark of the Covenant in tow, Menelik's entourage came to a river and separated into two companies. Those who crossed eventually became Christians, while those who paused remained Jews: a marvelous allegory at the least.

Scholars and politicians have debated whether the Beta Israel are "true" Jews for centuries. Aside from the Solomon–Makeda tradition (given little credence by many scholars), there are other, competing theories attempting to explain how Jews came to Ethiopia. In 1973, for example, Israel's Sephardic Chief Rabbi recognized the Beta Israel as true Jews, a remnant of the lost tribe of Dan (one of the ten who seemingly vanished after their capture by Assyria in 722 BCE). Other scholars cite evidence of a Jewish military garrison at Elephantine Island, near the traditional border of Egypt and Nubia, between the seventh and the fifth centuries BCE. Yet others point to the proximity of southern Arabia, in which communities of Jews have lived since the seventh century BCE, with most arriving after the destruction of Jerusalem's Second Temple in 70 CE.

Whatever their origins, the Beta Israel's subsequent history in Ethiopia is also a matter of scholarly contention; some maintain they were persecuted and harassed for most of their existence, while others argue the relationship between Jews and the Christian state was at times complementary and cooperative. The Beta Israel took refuge in the mountain fastnesses of Ethiopia and were cut off from world Jewry. There they continued to sacrifice animals, observe the Sabbath, follow other religious laws and dietary proscriptions, and circumcise on the eighth day. They lost the Hebrew language, however, speaking in Amharic (a modern language) and praying (while facing Jerusalem) in Ge'ez. Armed with the Torah but unaware of the Talmud, Ethiopian Jews managed to survive. Toward the end of the twentieth century, they participated in the general immigration of Jews to Israel (the *aliyah*) in spectacular ways: In 1984, so-called Operation Moses brought 16,000 Ethiopian Jews to Israel, followed by the airlifting of thousands more in 1991. Media images of these "black Jews" arriving in Israel was nothing less than electrifying. That there were verifiable African Jews with a venerable past raised new questions about the scope of the African Diaspora.

## The "Ethiopian" Eunuch and the Call to Christianity

In addition to the Queen of Sheba and the Beta Israel, the account of the "Ethiopian" eunuch has also fired imaginations across time and space. The New Testament records the baptism of "an Ethiopian eunuch, a court official of Candace, queen of the Ethiopians, who was in charge of all her treasure" (Acts of the Apostles 8:27–40). As Ethiopia either did not yet exist or was just coming into being, and as a series of female rulers of the Nubian state of Meroë held the title *Candace*, this encounter probably refers to a Nubian court official who, after his baptism, "went on his way rejoicing," presumably all the way to Nubia. Christianity had certainly entered Nubia by the second century (following the establishment of the Coptic church in Egypt), but Nubia did not convert en masse to Christianity (according to area tradition) until the mid-sixth century and the arrival of missionaries from Byzantium. For the next 800 years Nubia flourished as a Christian culture, its literacy based upon Old Nubian, a language written in Greek form with Meroitic vowelization. Meroë itself had ended by 350 CE, but Nubia continued on, splintering into Nobatia (or Nubia), Alwa, and Makuria. The rise of Ṣalāḥ al-Dīn and the Mamluks in Egypt in 1169 began Christian Nubia's gradual decline until 1323, when a Muslim ruler took power. Nubian Christianity survived into the sixteenth century, in retreat from a growing Islamized and Arabized Nubian population and government.

Like Egypt, Nubia, and Ethiopia, North Africa also converted to Christianity, although the region's rapid embrace of Islam in the seventh and eighth centuries raises doubts about the depth of its preceding commitment. Even so, North Africa was the site of a brilliant Christian civilization, producing the likes of Saint Augustine of Hippo (354–440), born in North Africa and likely of Berber descent. Christian scholars and leaders located throughout Egypt and North Africa played major roles in the various schisms and doctrinal disputes characterizing the troubled history of the early church. However, while North Africa and Egypt provided the setting, European languages dominated the religious discourse; Latin was used in the North African church, and Greek in the Coptic.

An African past filled with splendor and pageantry would serve to defend against the onslaught experienced by the enslaved in the Americas, who were repeatedly told that Africa held no historical significance. Though ancient and in a corner of the continent from which the vast majority of the enslaved did not hail, Egypt, Nubia, and Ethiopia were yet in Africa, and therefore they represented the dignity of the entire continent, a place of honor bestowed largely through exposure to Christianity and Judaism. By the nineteenth century, the prophesy that "Ethiopia shall soon stretch her hands out to God" (Psalm 68:31) would be interpreted by many as a call to convert masses of Africans and their descendants to Christianity, thereby shaping Africa and its Diaspora in profound ways.

## Suggestions for Further Reading

In addition to some of the relevant suggested readings for Chapter One, especially that of St. Clair Drake, works covering the general history of Ethiopia include Harold G. Marcus, *A History of Ethiopia* (Berkeley: U. of California Press, 1994); Jean Doresse, *Ethiopia*, trans. Elsa Coult (London: Elek Books and New York: Putnam, 1959); and Sergew Hable Sellassie, *Ancient and Medieval Ethiopian History to 1270* (Addis Ababa: United Printers, 1972).

Regarding the *Kebra Nagast*, the only English translation available remains, curiously, E. A. Wallis Budge's *The Queen of Sheba and Her Only Son Menyelek (Kebra Nagast)* (London and Boston: The Medici Society, Ltd., 1922). Given the date of the translation and Budge's reputation as something of a racist, a modern translation is sorely needed. Donald N. Levine's *Greater Ethiopia: The Evolution of a Multiethnic Society* (Chicago: U. of Chicago Press, 1974) provides a critical reading of both *Kebra Nagast* and the development of Ethiopian society.

An excellent work on the Beta Israel is Steven Kaplan's *The Beta Israel (Falasha) in Ethiopia: From Earliest Times to the Twentieth Century* (New York: New York U. Press, 1992), which can be joined with a study edited by Tudor Parfitt and Emanuela Trevisan, *The Beta Israel in Ethiopia and Israel* (Surrey: Curzon Press, 1999).

Concerning the Hamitic curse, see David M. Goldenberg, *The Curse of Ham: Race and Slavery in Early Judaism, Christianity and Islam* (Princeton, NJ: Princeton U. Press, 2003), for a discussion of its development as an idea, and Stephen R. Haynes, *Noah's Curse: the Biblical Justification of American Slavery* (New York: Oxford U. Press, 2002), for an indication of how the myth came to be exploited. Finally, among the most important works addressing blacks or Africans and the Bible are James Cone, *For My People: Black Theology and the Black Church* (Maryknoll, NY: Orbis Books, 1984); Charles B. Copher, *Black Biblical Studies: An Anthology of Charles B. Copher* (Chicago: Black Light Fellowship, 1993); Cain Hope Felder, *Troubling Biblical Waters: Race, Class, and Family* (Maryknoll, NY: Orbis Books, 1989) and his *Scandalize My Name: A Critical Review of Blacks in the Bible and Society* (Silver Spring, MD: Beckham House, 1995).

# CHAPTER 3

## Africans and the Islamic World

We tend to know more about Africans in the Americas than elsewhere in the Diaspora. However, as this chapter makes clear, millions of Africans entered Islamic lands, where they made important contributions to extraordinary civilizations, from the heartlands of the faith to Muslim Spain. An extended discussion of this major component of the African Diaspora is warranted, as the juxtaposition of the similarities and differences between this experience and that of Africans in the Americas yields far greater insight into the condition of displacement than does a lone hemispheric focus.

We begin with a brief consideration of Muḥammad, born circa 570 CE in the city of Mecca, an oasis important as both marketplace and site of religious shrines. Muḥammad was sensitive to the disparities between rich and poor, and his meditations resulted in a series of revelations that began when he was forty years of age; three years later, he began heralding a message centering on the oneness of God, his own role as God's messenger, the Last Day, and the need for a response of submission, gratitude, worship, and social responsibility. Encountering resistance and harassment, Muḥammad and his companions found asylum in Medina, and in 630 they accepted Mecca's peaceful surrender. By the time of his death in 632, the whole of the Arabian peninsula was united under Muḥammad's control. By 656, Islam had expanded into Syria, Iraq, Egypt, and North Africa, and by 711, Muslim armies had conquered parts of the Iberian peninsula as well.

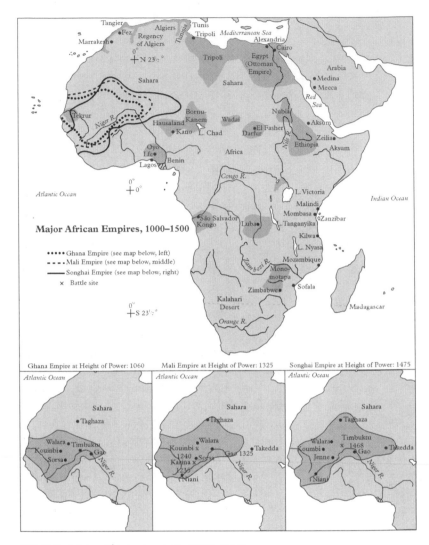

**MAP 2**. Major African empires, 1000–1500.

Islam's move into Egypt (or *Misr*) and North Africa (or *al-Maghrib al-Aqṣā*, "the far West") was accompanied by the gradual Arabization of the population (the spread of Arabs and their language and culture). As part of a larger Muslim world that was quickly becoming a mighty empire, Egypt and North Africa once more became destinations for other Africans, while simultaneously serving as sources of emigration to such places as Portugal and Spain.

## Golden Lands

Where Muslim armies spearheaded Islam's expansion into North Africa and Egypt, Muslim traders and clerics led the religion's spread into regions south of the Sahara. Regularized trade between North and subsaharan Africa became possible with the first-century CE introduction of the camel from the Nile valley to the Sahara's southern fringes near Lake Chad, after which they spread further west. By the fourth century, camel caravan patterns crisscrossed the desert.

West Africa became associated with gold early in the history of Islam; indeed, one of the earliest West African states, Ghana, became known as "the land of the gold" through the Arabic writing of geographers between the eighth and eleventh centuries. Ghana, home to the Serakole (northern Mande-speakers), was located in the *sāḥil* ("shore") between the Sahara and the savannah (flat grasslands) further south, as were Gao (on the eastern Niger buckle) and Kanem (along the northeastern side of Lake Chad); together they were introduced to the ninth-century Islamic world as *Bilād as-Sūdān*, or "land of the blacks." A brief review of developments within this region and East Africa is important, for as these lands were in direct contact with the Muslim world, they constitute the beginning of this component of the African Diaspora.

West African gold was exchanged primarily for salt (from desert mines and evaporating ponds at the mouth of the Senegal River and elsewhere). The gold was transported to North Africa, then east to Egypt and as far as India, where it served as payment for spices and silks; it was transported across the Mediterranean to pay for European goods and currency. Trade from the West African hinterland to the sahel was organized and controlled by West Africans, who over the centuries developed an extensive network operated by the *Juula* (Mande for "merchant") and Hausa traders. Once in the sahel, gold and other commodities were transported north through the Sahara by the Tuareg, Berber-speaking desert-dwellers, along with Arab merchants. The arrangement was to the immediate advantage of West Africans, who maintained secrecy of the gold's sources, but ultimately it was to their detriment, as they did not control the trade through the desert. A pattern developed early in West Africa, whereby external powers acquired long distance, multiregional trade experience. Those with such expertise eventually took command of the trade and dictated its terms, notwithstanding West Africa's appreciable influence.

Ghana, though still in existence in the twelfth century, was eclipsed in the thirteenth by Mali, populated by southern Mande-speakers fashioned into an empire by the emperor Sunjaata around 1230. As was true of Ghana, Mali was also associated with gold in the Muslim world, but unlike Ghana, Mali slowly became a part of that world through the early conversion of its rulers. The fourteenth-century travels and eyewitness accounts of Ibn Baṭṭūṭa (d. 1368) reinforced the image of Mali as a land of wealth, as did the pilgrimage to Mecca of *Mansa* Mūsā (reigned 1312–1337). Although a diminished Mali would continue through the seventeenth century, its stature in the western Sudan (from the Atlantic Ocean to the Niger buckle) was eclipsed in the fifteenth century by imperial Songhay, whose origins go back to the seventh century and Gao. By the fifteenth century, Islam had become the religion of the court and the merchant community; commercial towns such as Timbuktu and Jenne were transformed into centers of Islamic education and intellectual activity, a development begun under *Mansa* Mūsā of Mali. As was true of Ghana and Mali, Songhay was known as a major source of gold, and the disruption of the gold trade under *Sunni* 'Alī (1464–1492) was a principal factor in *Askia* Muḥammad Ture's 1492 seizure of power.

Viewed as a wealthy land, the western Sudan was increasingly incorporated into the Islamic world. North Africa, Egypt, and the western Sudan exchanged emissaries and written communication (in Arabic). Houses of wealthy merchants were often allied to leading clerical and political families through marriage. All of this resulted in the rise of an elite in the western Sudan, connected through religion, marriage, and commercial interests and accorded prestige by coreligionists in North Africa and Egypt. Muslim West Africa would therefore be differentiated from non-Muslim West Africa, for whom the Islamic world held contempt. Stated differently, the Muslim world entertained no single image of subsaharan Africa, distinguishing its various populations on the basis of Islam and related notions of civilization. The status of the land as opposed to the individual was critical; a Muslim was one who practiced the religion, but a Muslim land was one over which Muslim rule had been established. Songhay, with a majority non-Muslim population, was a Muslim land.

Part of the central Sudan (from the Niger buckle to the Lake Chad area) had a decidedly different trade relationship with North Africa.

The independent city-states of Hausaland were apparently slower to embrace Islam than their western Sudanic counterparts, but by the second half of the fifteenth century such cities as Kano and Katsina were under Muslim control and were integrated into long-distance trade. In contrast to Hausaland, the states of Kanem and Bornu near Lake Chad had an Islamic pedigree with considerable historicity. Kanem, for example, was under Muslim rulers by the tenth century, who performed the *ḥājj* (pilgrimage) as early as the eleventh, while establishing Islamic offices in Kanem's government. They eventually fled anti-Islamic forces to the southwestern edge of Lake Chad and established Bornu.

Unlike their western Sudanic counterparts, Kanem and Bornu's exports were primarily captives (captives were also exported by Mali and Songhay but were of secondary importance), which were exchanged for cloth, firearms, and other commodities. A major trade route linked Lake Chad to Tripoli by way of the Fezzan. The route was a notorious highway for captives well into the nineteenth century. Captives were supposedly non-Muslims, but there is evidence that many Muslims were taken as well. *Mai* Idrīs Alooma (reigned 1570–1602), "the learned, just, courageous and pious Commander of the Faithful," developed quite the reputation as a slave raider.

The question of African captives arises again in conjunction with the history of East Africa, specifically the Swahili coast. To be sure, maritime trade in the Indian Ocean is of significant antiquity. By the second century BCE or earlier, regular traffic linked East Africa to Arabia, India, and southwest Asia by way of prevailing monsoon winds. The *dhow*, far more efficient than the camel, sailed the Indian Ocean in one-third the time of a Saharan caravan crossing, carrying the equivalent of 1,000 camel loads. Seafaring was dominated more by Arabs and Indians than Africans, while Africans along the coast controlled access to the East African interior, analogous to the western Sudan's relations with Tuareg and Arab merchants, with sea and sand as barrier and bridge. In the case of the Swahili coast, however, the bridge is the more appropriate metaphor, as the East African littoral was more fully integrated into the trade of the Indian Ocean and Red Sea, a commercial complex both massive and lucrative. In exchange for such imports as Chinese porcelain, cowry shells, glass beads, and large quantities of cotton cloth from India and China, East Africa exported ivory, gold, mangrove poles (for housing in the Persian Gulf), and human beings.

To speak of East Africa is to discuss Swahili culture and language, which incorporates Arabic and (to a lesser extent) Malagasy words and concepts. Arabs (and apparently Persians) settling along the coast often intermarried with the local population, resulting in a fusion of genes and lifestyles. The apogee of the Swahili coastal towns lasted from the ninth through the fifteenth centuries CE; this was an age of royal courts, stone palaces, beautiful mosques, and internal plumbing in the best houses. Trade and urban growth corresponded to changes in the Islamic world, as the Muslim political center shifted from Damascus and the Umayyad caliphate (661–750) to Baghdad and the Abbasids (750–1258), thereby elevating the Persian Gulf's importance. This period in East African history came to an abrupt halt with the arrival of Vasco da Gama and the Portuguese in 1498. Seven years later, Portuguese men-of-war returned to destroy Kilwa and inaugurate a new era in the Indian Ocean.

## Pilgrims and Scholars

Many subsaharan Africans entered the Islamic world as fellow believers, usually by traveling to the Middle East and North Africa to make the pilgrimage, to study, or to teach. A number of individuals from subsaharan Africa were regarded as learned and pious. Examples include the eminent scholar Aḥmad Bābā, taken captive from Timbuktu to Marrakesh in 1594 following the Moroccan conquest of Songhay, where he was imprisoned for two years and taught classes for large numbers until his return to Timbuktu in 1608. A second example is Ṣāliḥ al-Fulānī, an obscure West African scholar from Futa Jallon (in contemporary Guinea), who headed for Cairo and finally Medina, where he studied and eventually taught from 1791 to his death in 1803–1804.

A tradition of royal pilgrimage dates back to the eleventh century in West Africa and includes the rulers of Kanem, Mali, and Songhay. However, the quintessential hajj was that of Mali's *Mansa* Mūsā in 1324. With a retinue of thousands of soldiers, slaves, and high officials, he brought such large quantities of gold to Egypt that its value temporarily depreciated. Less significant for the Muslim chroniclers of the trip, but more stunning in its implications and symbolism for our purposes, was the manner in which *Mansa* Mūsā entered Egypt. In what must have been a sight for the ages, Mūsā and his thousands encamped around the pyramids prior to entering Cairo. For three days, the glory of imperial Mali and the wonder of ancient Egypt, two of the most powerful icons of the African Diaspora, became one.

## The Enslaved

In contrast to those making the pilgrimage, other subsaharan Africans entered the Islamic world as slaves. Muslim societies made use of slaves from all over the reachable world. Europeans were just as eligible as Africans, and Slavic and Caucasian populations were the largest source of slaves for the Islamic world well into the eighteenth century, especially in the Ottoman empire. Race was therefore not a factor – at least not until the eighteenth and nineteenth centuries, when European expansion forced a closer association between blackness and slavery.

When the discussion is restricted to Africa, tentative estimates for the transsaharan, Red Sea, and Indian Ocean slave trades are in the range of 12 million individuals from 650 CE to the end of the sixteenth century, and another 4 million from the seventeenth through the nineteenth centuries. In other words, as many or more captive Africans may have been exported through these trades as were shipped across the Atlantic, although the latter took place within a much more compressed period (fifteenth through the nineteenth centuries). To be sure, these estimates are imprecise and possibly misleading. It is difficult to separate, for example, the Red Sea and Indian Ocean trades, and not all who were transported through the Indian Ocean landed in Islamic lands. Even so, the number of enslaved Africans in the Islamic world was clearly significant.

Slavery in Arabia was already an accepted practice by the time Muhammad was born; the Qur'ān assumes as much and, far from simply condoning it, attempts to improve the servile condition while promoting manumission at the same time. Islam held that freedom was the natural condition of human beings, and only certain circumstances allowed for slavery. According to a strict interpretation of Islamic law, or *sharīʿa*, only those non-Muslims who were without a protective pact (*ʿahd*) with Muslims, who rejected the offer to convert to Islam and were then captured in a war (*jihād*), could be enslaved. However, after the first century of Islam, reality diverged from theory, and most were in fact captured through raids and kidnaping and then sold to merchants. Stated another way, slavery in the Islamic world was a business.

Keeping in mind the theory–reality divide, Muslims slaveholders were to treat the enslaved with dignity and kindness. Slaves could marry with the slaveholder's consent, and they were not to be over-worked or excessively punished; those seriously injured were to be freed. They were to be provided with material support and medical attention into old age. The enslaved were property, to be bought and sold like any other chattel, yet their undeniable humanity created tensions that Islamic law attempted to resolve. Above all, slaveholders were enjoined to facilitate the conversion of the enslaved; uncircumcised males were circumcised from the outset, and they were given Arabic names. In an interesting parallel with the Americas, these names comprised a "special" category of nomenclature, names of "distinction" for the enslaved. Such appellations included Kāfār ("camphor") and 'Anbar ("ambergris") for males; and Bakhīta ("fortunate"), Mabrūka ("blessed"), and Za'farān ("saffron") for females. The majority of the enslaved were therefore converted to Islam, and some became literate in Arabic and were taught to read the Qur'ān.

However, conversion to Islam did not obligate slaveholders to free their slaves; slaveholders were only encouraged by the Qur'ān to do so. The ideal was to enter into a manumission contract (*mukātaba*), whereby the enslaved person would be allowed to make and save enough money to pay an agreed upon amount to purchase her or his freedom. As would also be true in the Americas, the acquired freedom was qualified in that the freed person remained a client of the former slaveholder and always in his debt, a condition passed down through several generations.

One of the most arresting aspects of the transsaharan, Red Sea, and Indian Ocean slave trades is that they were primarily transactions in females and children. Young girls and women were used as domestics and concubines, and often both, as the male slaveholder enjoyed the right of sexual access. The concubine is referred to in the Qur'ān as "that which your right hands possess" (*mā malakat aymānukum*). Domestic work included cooking, cleaning, and wet-nursing (tasks that would become just as familiar to many African-descended women in the Americas), and there is evidence that some were (illegally) forced into prostitution. A slaveholder on occasion married an enslaved female, but in those instances she first had to be freed. As for concubines, the Muslim world had an order of preference, beginning with white females, many of whom were obtained from the Balkans and lands in the southwest of what was formerly the Soviet Union and referred to as the *saqāliba* or Slavs (although the term would come to include non-Slavs). Next in order of preference were Ethiopian, Nubian, and other women from the Horn of Africa, called the *habashiyyāt* (or simply Habash when men were included), often found in the service of middle-class slaveholders. They enjoyed greater status and privilege than did other African women, who were allegedly the least preferred. According to Islamic law, the concubine who bore the slaveholder's children (thereafter known as an *umm walad*) could never be sold away, and she was automatically freed upon his death. In contrast to what would develop in the Americas, the children of a slaveholder and a concubine followed the status of the father and became free. An example of how this could work is found in imperial Songhay, where every one of the *askias* following *Askia al-hājj* Muhammad (d. 1529) was the son of a concubine. Yet another illustration concerns the 'Alawid ruler Mūlāy Ismāʿīl (reigned 1672–1727) of Morocco, whose mother was a black concubine.

Some concubines and female domestics were kept in large harems, where sexual exploitation was erratic and unpredictable. Women in such circumstances inhabited a world of instability, as advancing age and the failure to bear children or secure slaveholder interest could result in their sale. Central to the organization of such large harems was the eunuch or *tawāshi*, also referred to as *khādim* ("servant"), *fatā* ("young man"), and *aghā* ("chief"). The primary responsibility of the eunuch was to maintain order; his emasculation "perfected" him for such purposes, as he remained physically strong but incapable (for the most part) of posing a sexual threat. As was true of concubines, those transformed into eunuchs came from Europe and Asia and Africa, but in this instance it was the African eunuch who appears to have been preferred (at least in the Ottoman capital of Istanbul). Because they were privy to the inner workings of the household, these individuals could amass significant influence in both the household and the society (assuming a prominent family). The authority of the *Kislar Aghā*, the Ottoman sultan's head eunuch, was legendary. In apparent violation of Islamic law, such eunuchs were allowed to own other eunuchs and concubines. According to one nineteenth-century account of the chief African eunuchs of Mecca, they were even married to enslaved Ethiopians, a most curious arrangement.

The procedures by which males became eunuchs rank among the most inhumane. Young boys were commonly forced to endure the operation, which involved removal of the testes or both testes and penis.

Because the operation was abhorrent to Muslims, it was performed by Christians (and perhaps Jews) in such places as Baghirmi near Lake Chad, in Ethiopia, and in other locations. Accounts of the process veer toward the macabre, as young males were gelded and placed in the sand up to their navels to heal. Those able to urinate after some days were herded off through the Sahara; those who could not were left to die. In addition to serving in the harems, some were chosen to serve in the mosque of the Ka'ba in Mecca and in Prophet Muḥammad's mosque in Medina. Many who began the desert trek did not complete it, expiring along the way. The number of eunuchs in the Muslim world is difficult to estimate, but the claim that the sultan Mūlāy Ismā'īl personally owned over 2,000 suggests their numbers were significant. Indeed, so many more entered the mutilation process than exited; a credible estimate is that only 10 percent survived the operation, which meant that some 20,000 young males perished to achieve Mūlāy Ismā'īl's 2,000.

Africans were also used as laborers in large agricultural ventures and mining operations. They supplied the backbreaking, bloodcurdling labor for the salt mines of Taghāza in the western Sahara and the copper mines of Tegidda in what is now Niger. The model of exploiting subsaharan labor may have been provided by the Tuareg and Arabo-Berbers of the Sahara, who had a long-standing tradition of using subsaharan African slaves to herd animals and collect wood and water.

Agricultural projects in the Islamic world generally did not approach the magnitude of the American plantation until the emergence of clove cultivation in such places as Zanzibar in the nineteenth century, but African enslaved labor was used in date production in Saharan oases and in tenth-century Arabia, near Bahrain. African slave labor was also used in the cultivation of sugar in the Ahwāz province of what is now western Iraq in the ninth century, together with the large-scale use of East African slave labor in nearby southern Iraq and Kuwait, in what was called the Sawād. There, captives from the interior of East Africa, the Zanj, were expended to drain vast marshlands. The conditions under which the Zanj labored were so stultifying, so deplorable, that they produced one of the most spectacular slave revolts in the history of both the African Diaspora and the world as a whole. Unifying under the charismatic leadership of 'Alī b. Muḥammad, son of an Iraqi father and a mother from Sind (the lower Indus valley), the Zanj waged insurrection for fifteen years, from 868 to 883, capturing the city of Basra and marching on Baghdad itself, center of the Muslim world. With their defeat, the Zanj were ruthlessly exterminated, the experiment using their labor in southern Iraq abandoned. In fact, some scholars speculate that the Zanj left such a bitter taste in the mouths of the Abbasids that it influenced the brutish depiction of blacks in *The Thousand and One Nights*.

One of the more visible uses of enslaved African labor was in the military, one of the few institutions allowing for any degree of upward mobility for persons of African descent throughout the history of the entire Diaspora. Slave armies were in a number of places in the Islamic world by the ninth century. The concept was to create a military that, as a result of its very foreignness and alienation, owed its total allegiance to the ruler. Those destined for such armies were usually acquired through purchase rather than war, and they included Turks, Slavs, Berbers, and other Africans. In fact, most military slaves were non-African and were often organized into separate units based on ethnic origin and background. Specific terms were used to identify armies as both servile and ethnically distinct: the *Mamlūks*, a servile army that eventually seized power in Egypt and Syria from 1250 to 1517, were mostly from the Black Sea region; the Janissaries (or *kuls*), who took control of the Ottoman empire in the seventeenth and eighteenth centuries, hailed from the Slavic and Albanian populations of the Balkans. The term *ʿabīd*, however, was apparently used exclusively for subsaharan African slave armies.

The ʿabīd army was developed in Egypt under the Turkish governor Aḥmad Ṭūlūn (d. 884), who garrisoned them separately from the Mamlūk division. This particular ʿabīd army was probably Nubian. The immediate successors to the Ṭūlūnids also maintained servile black troops, as did the Fāṭimids, who began in North Africa (in 909) before moving their capital to Cairo in 969, maintaining large numbers of black servile soldiers in both places. In Egypt these soldiers grew powerful, and skirmishes between them and nonblack units increased in number and violence. A final conflict, the "Battle of the Blacks" or the "Battle of the Slaves," took place in 1169, when Ṣalāḥ al-Dīn led his nonblack forces against some 50,000 black soldiers and drove them out of Cairo into southern Egypt. All-black units would not be used again in Egypt until the nineteenth century under Muḥammad ʿAlī.

Black slave soldiers were also used in North Africa by the ninth-century Aghlabid dynasty and thereafter under successive regimes. Further west, in what is now Morocco, the Almoravid leader Yūsuf

b. Tāshīn (d. 1106) was surrounded by a bodyguard of 2,000 black
soldiers, and the successors to the Almoravids, the Almohads, also
used black soldiers. The ultimate in the use of servile black soldiers
took place under Mūlāy Ismāʿīl (reigned 1672–1727), son of the black
concubine, who along with his 2,000 black eunuchs was reported to
have maintained 150,000 black troops, having ordered the seizure of all
black males throughout the kingdom. The troops were provided black
females and were forced to swear personal allegiance to Mūlāy Ismāʾīl
upon the *hadīth* (traditions of Muḥammad) collected by al-Bukhārī,
and they were therefore known as *ʿabīd al-Bukhārī*. This *ʿabīd* army
grew enormously powerful, determining the succession to the throne
for thirty years after the death of Mūlāy Ismāʿīl, choosing from among
his 500 sons. In 1737 the *ʿabīd* army was brought under control by
Mūlāy Muḥammad III using an Arab force. Black soldiers continue
to serve in the Moroccan army to the present day, only no longer as
slaves.

## Iberia

Mention of the Almoravids and Almohads redirects our attention to
Iberia (Spain and Portugal), site of a remarkable Muslim civilization
from 711 to 1492. When Muslim forces crossed Gilbraltar into Spain
in 711, it was a combined army of Berbers, subsaharan Africans,
and Arabs. The invading Muslim armies renamed the peninsula al-
Andalus (an apparent corruption of the term *Vandal*, from the former
occupiers). By 720, the Muslims laid claim to territory south of the
Pyrenees and parts of southern France, and in 732 they encroached
further into France, where they were engaged outside of Tours and
defeated at the Battle of Poitiers by Charles Martel. Celebrated in Europe as a major victory over Islam, the event known as the "Highway
of the Martyrs" (*Balāṭ al-Shuhadāʾ*) by the Muslims was, from their
perspective, little more than an insignificant border raid. The "land
of the Franks," as France and much of western Europe were known,
was culturally unremarkable, economically unimportant, and of little
interest to Muslims.

Those portions of Iberia under Muslim control answered to the
Umayyads of Damascus until 750, when the Abbasid caliphate arose
and shifted the center of the Muslim world to Baghdad. A member of
the Umayyad family fled to Iberia where he restructured the Umayyad
caliphate, rupturing the dream of a single Muslim empire. Muslims

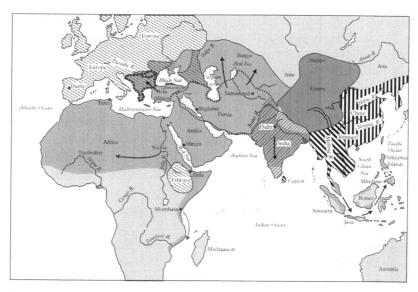

**MAP 3**. Spread of Islam to 1500.

would conquer Sicily between 827 and 902 and move into parts of southern Italy, but the eleventh century saw the return of Sicily to Christian control, as well as the slow erosion of Muslim power elsewhere in Italy and Iberia.

Al-Andalus was a Muslim state controlled by Arabs in command of Berbers and subsaharan Africans. However, conflict between Berbers and Arabs stemmed from an almost uninterrupted history of invasion and occupation of North African territory, beginning with the Carthaginians and followed by the Romans, the Vandals, the Byzantines, and lastly the Arabs. Berbers resisted Arab domination militarily, but they also resisted by embracing an aberrant form of Islam, Kharijism, which advocated democratic and egalitarian principles. The strategy of adopting altered expressions of an oppressor's religion, thereby transforming it into a tool of liberation, would also be used in the New World. Berbers further resisted by creating politically autonomous space, establishing a number of Kharijite states in North Africa after 750; Kharijite communities remain in the mountains and remote areas of Algeria and Tunisia. In this way, they were not unlike the maroons of the Americas.

Yet another path of resistance was direct confrontation, a road leading back to ancient Ghana. The West African savannah was crucial to the rise of the Berber Almoravid movement in the eleventh century.

Berbers in southern Morocco noted Ghana's spectacular growth and trade, and they concluded that it was the key to both the transsaharan trade and al-Andalus. Like the leaders of Egypt's eighteenth dynasty, who secured their control over Nubian resources before launching campaigns into Palestine and Syria, the Almoravids began their activities by first focusing on West Africa. Their bid for power became part of a religious reform movement, and by the mid-eleventh century the Almoravids seized control of the southern and northern termini of the transsaharan trade. Financing their operation with West African gold, the Almoravids also used West African soldiers, slave and free. By century's end, the Almoravids succeeded in bringing not only all of Morocco and western Algeria under their control, but also al-Andalus as well, founding Marrakesh as their capital. For the first time in history, a single Berber power controlled much of North Africa and Iberia, and Africans would rule the "kingdom of the two shores" for nearly 300 years.

The Almoravids were succeeded by the Almohads (1146–1269), who also used West African soldiers. Like Mūlāy Ismāʿīl of the seventeenth century, al-Manṣūr (reigned 1184–1199) was a leader who was possibly of West African ancestry. Another was Abū al-Ḥasan (reigned 1331–1351) of the later Marinid dynasty. Earning a reputation for cruelty, Abū al-Ḥasan exchanged embassies with *Mansa* Mūsā prior to the latter's death, and he was a great patron of the arts. The examples of Abū al-Ḥasan, al-Manṣūr, and Mūlāy Ismāʿīl demonstrate the difficulties in distinguishing between Berbers and subsaharan Africans, as extensive, centuries-long interaction between these regions necessarily meant a significant sharing of genes; an ostensibly Berber-looking individual may have in fact had considerable subsaharan ancestral ties. Europeans could and did distinguish between African groups, but their tendency to label all as Moors (literally, "blacks"), suggesting all Africans were part of a continuum of related characteristics, is not without warrant. Whatever the nature of their congenital relations, Africans of varying backgrounds in Iberia tended to participate in cultures knitted together by Islam. In this way, it may be better to read the designation *Moor* as a cultural rather than racial or ethnic qualifier.

Africans were present in al-Andalus throughout the 800-year period of Muslim domination, contributing to an intense period of intellectual and cultural production. It was during the Muslim domination of Iberia that the sciences and technology and the arts, including astronomy, medicine, alchemy, chemistry, physics, mathematics, literature, and philosophy, received a tremendous boost. Indeed, the knowledge of the ancients, including Greek philosophy, had been lost to Europe for hundreds of years, as Latin and Greek had nearly disappeared. Muslim, Jewish, and Christian scholars uncovered and translated the mostly Greek texts into Arabic, by which Europe reconnected with its past. The works of Plato, Aristotle, Ptolemy, Euclid, and the physicians Hippocrates and Galen were among the many reintroduced to Europe during this period. Prominent scholars of the period include Ibn Sīnā (or Avicenna) and Ibn Rushd (also known as Averroës), who was born in Córdoba under Almoravid rule in 1126 and went on to translate and comment on the works of Aristotle as well as establish a reputation as a scientist, mathematician, philosopher, and poet. Made possible by the support of Almohad ruler al-Manṣūr, Ibn Rushd's work, some thirty-eight volumes of it, became popular largely through Spanish Jewish scholars, a circle that included Mūsā Ibn Maymun (or Maimonides). Students from all over Europe, including France, Germany, England, and Italy, came to study in al-Andalus, often becoming literate in Arabic. The intellectual productivity of Muslim Iberia, as well as other parts of the Muslim world, was an important foundation for the Renaissance of western Europe.

In addition to their contribution to various branches of knowledge, Muslims introduced styles of architecture resulting in stunning blends of structure and landscape, of which al-Hambra is a prime example. Cities they founded include Córdoba, Seville, Toledo, and Granada, each known for a particular quality. Córdoba was a city of libraries; Seville was associated with music. Muslim cities were well planned, featuring aqueducts, gardens, public baths, and fountains to embellish mosques, hospitals, and other buildings public and private. Supplying the urban centers were fields given enhanced fertility through revamped irrigation systems and the introduction of such crops as cereals and beans. However, the Muslim geographic imagination was by no means confined to the Iberian city and countryside; rather, Muslim scholars refined geography by more accurately measuring distances (although they remained hampered by ancient models), and they introduced to the Western world seafaring tools and techniques such as the astrolabe, the lateen sail, and the method of tacking. Some of these innovations were modified from their use in the Indian Ocean, and in any event they proved critical to the development of European seafaring and subsequent commercial and imperial expansion.

## India

While there are numerous scholarly works on al-Andalus or Moorish Spain, what is known about the subsaharan African contribution
to this brilliant civilization is far from satisfactory. Research on the
African presence in India is similarly in its infancy. Matters are complicated by an ancient, pre-Islamic society in which the four major
castes (Brahman, Kshatriya, Vaishya, and Shudra) are hierarchically
arranged in a manner corresponding with color (*varna*). Thus, the
lowest, servile caste, the Shudra, is characterized in the ancient Vedic
literature as "black" and "dark complexioned," but as there are many
dark-skinned populations throughout the world, attempting to locate
Shudra origins in Africa may be pointless.

Given the historicity and expanse of Indian Ocean trade, Africans
necessarily voyaged to the Indian subcontinent prior to the rise of
Islam. However, it is with that religion's movement into the subcontinent that the African presence becomes better documented. India
initially experienced Islamic incursions as early as 711, and in the late
tenth century Muslim forays from what is now Afghanistan and Iran
resulted in considerable plundering. Islam reached its political zenith
in the subcontinent under the Delhi Sultanate (1206–1526) and the
Mughals (1526–1739).

Free Africans (as well as non-Africans) operated in Muslim-ruled
India as merchants, seafarers, clerics, bodyguards, and even bureau-
crats. Regarding slavery, African women and men assumed familiar roles as concubines and servile soldiers; in 1459, for example,
some 8,000 served in Bengal's army. Called "Habshis" (from the
word *habashiyyāt*) and "Siddis" (from the title *sayyid*, afforded cap-
tains of vessels), Africans settled in a variety of locales. Enclaves of
Siddis can presently be found in such places as Gujarat (western India),
Habshiguda in Hyderabad (central India), and Janjira Island (south
of Bombay); the names *Habshiguda* and *Janjira* reflect an African
ancestry.

During the time of the Mughals, there were a number of African
Muslim rulers in the subcontinent. At least several Habshi rulers were
in the breakaway province of Bengal (eastern India), including Mālik
Andil (or Saiffuddīn Firuz, 1487–1490) and Nāṣiruddīn Maḥmūd II
(1490–1491). There were also several rulers in the Deccan break-
way province of Ahmadnagar who were of African descent, including

Chand Bibi (d. 1600), a princess who led Ahmadnagar resistance against the Mughals. Perhaps the most famous of all was Mālik Ambar (d. 1626), who supported Chand Bibi's struggle against the Mughals until her assassination. Mālik Ambar, possibly Ethiopian born, was brought to India as a slave and eventually served as a highly educated military commander. Noted for his religious tolerance and patronage of the arts and learning, he ruled for twenty years and earned the admiration of Indians and Europeans alike.

## The Image of the African in the Islamic World

The Muslim view of the African was an evolutionary process, informed by changing circumstances over time. Whatever the initial attitude toward the African, the trade in slaves via the Sahara, Red Sea, and Indian Ocean had some impact, but the fact that enslaved Europeans and Asians were also imported into the Islamic world, and in greater numbers until the eighteenth century, suggests that the slave trade alone was not solely responsible for a less than complimentary view of the African. Other factors, essentially cultural, must have played a role.

There is no trace of racism in the Qur'ān. Rather, there is the assertion that difference is of divine decree:

> And among His signs is the creation of the heavens and the earth, and the diversity of your languages and colors. In that surely are signs for those who know.
>
> (sūra or chapter 30, *al-Rūm*, verse 23)

This nonevaluative acknowledgment of what is now called racial diversity is indicative of the early Muslim period in the Arabian peninsula. There, color was both insignificant and variable, depending upon who was being compared. While Bedouins were usually described as brown or olive, Arabs at times characterized themselves as black vis-à-vis red Persians, but in comparison with black Africans these same Arabs became red or even white. Furthermore, the concept of red took on metaphoric meaning with Islam's early expansion, as the hated red Persians were now the subjects of the Arabs, and redness took on a pejorative connotation. In this way, Greeks, Spaniards, and other Mediterranean populations also became red.

It is not surprising that the Qur'ān is devoid of racial bias, or that Arabs depicted themselves as black and brown. Seventh-century Arabia was surrounded by far more powerful Sassanian (Persian), Byzantine, and Ethiopian empires, who fought each other for influence in the peninsula. The dominant peninsular power was Yemen in the southwest (called *Arabia Felix* by the Romans), which was distinct from the rest of the peninsula because of its urban-sustaining agriculture and because of extensive ties with Ethiopia. The latter had both invaded and conquered southern Arabia in the fourth century, taking control of the spice and silk trade between the Mediterranean and the Indian Ocean that passed through Arabia. With Sassanian help, the Yemenis pushed the Ethiopians out around 375, but the Ethiopians returned triumphantly in 512. The subsequent defeat of Ethiopian garrisons led to another Ethiopian expedition around 525. A few years later, divine intervention, according to the Qur'ān (sūra 105, *al-Fīl*, or "the Elephant"), turned back an Ethiopian assault on Mecca.

Ethiopian incursions are but one example of interaction between the Horn of Africa and Arabia that has existed for millennia; related languages and cultures are another. Such interconnectedness suggests that Ethiopians and Nubians made contributions to the Yemeni and Arab gene pool, along with other populations from the Horn. It is therefore no surprise that one of the greatest poets of pre-Islamic Arabia was 'Antara (or 'Antar), son of an enslaved Ethiopian or Nubian mother and an Arab father. Born in the pre-Islamic *jahilīyya* period ("time of barbarism"), 'Antara followed his mother's status and was a slave, but he earned his freedom through military prowess. His background is similar to that of another figure of the early Islamic period, Khufāf b. Nadba, son of an Arab father and enslaved black mother who rose to become head of his (Arab) group or "tribe." On the other hand, many Arabs had black skin but apparently were not descended from Africans; such was true of 'Ubāda b. al-Ṣāmit, an Arab of noble birth and a leader of the Arab conquest of Egypt.

The impression that blackness was no barrier is bolstered by the example of Muḥammad himself, who, facing mounting opposition to his message, sent seventy of his followers to seek asylum with the Ethiopian ruler in 615, presaging the official *hijra* or "flight" to Medina in 622. Muḥammad's action revealed his esteem for the piety of the Ethiopians, a sentiment consistent with Homer's much earlier characterization of the "Ethiopians." There were also a number of persons of Nubian or Ethiopian descent among the Companions of the Prophet, perhaps the most famous having been Islam's first muezzin (who calls the faithful to prayers), Bilāl b. Rabāḥ, born into slavery in Mecca and an early convert to Islam. Purchased and manumitted by Abū Bakr (Islam's first caliph or successor to Muhammad as well as his father-in-law), Bilāl became the Prophet's personal attendant. In addition to Bilāl, notables of known African descent include the caliph ʿUmar (634–644), the grandson of an Ethiopian or Nubian woman, and the conqueror of Egypt; and ʿAmr b. al-ʿĀṣ, similarly descended from an Ethiopian or Nubian female ancestor. The Prophet himself may have been of partial African descent, as his grandfather and paternal uncle Abū Ṭālib were both reputed to be "black." Therefore, significant Ethiopian or Nubian influences were circulating at the very core of Islam's foundation. Given Ethiopia's ascendancy, if anyone felt inferior in the seventh century, it would have been the Arabs.

And yet, there is something unsettling about these relations. One wonders if the potential for bias was not already present in pre-Islamic and early Islamic Arabia, for, despite the prominence of all of these men of Ethiopian or Nubian descent, it is striking that so many of them descend from enslaved mothers. Perhaps free Nubian or Ethiopian-born males were much rarer in Arab society than enslaved Nubian or Ethiopian women, so that the most common African figure in Arab society was a female slave. If so, Arab society may have begun associating Africans with slavery before the rise of Islam. ʿAntara reflects an Arab acceptance of difference, but his own background suggests that Africans within the Arab world largely entered by way of the servile estate.

The expansion of Arab armies in the seventh and eighth centuries was probably the period during which Arab views of Africans began to change. Arabs were already suffering from ethnocentricity, as Islam had been revealed to an Arab and the revelation forever sealed in his language. It was not even clear that Islam was meant for non-Arabs. With the world now divided into believers and infidels, the rise of the transsaharan, Red Sea, and Indian Ocean slave trades did not bode well for Africans, especially those with whom Arabs had little experience. Their high regard for the Ethiopian and Nubian continued, but they were distinguished from other Africans such as the Nūba, Bujja (Beja), Zanj, and the Sūdān (from West Africa). Lack of familiarity played some role, but since most Africans entered Islamic lands as young females, the Arab view of Africans was also informed by the perception of African women. Whatever the answer, Muslim societies became increasingly accustomed to seeing Africans as enslaved menials. The struggle over the meaning of blackness in early Islamic society can be seen in the poetry of "the crows of the Arabs" (*aghribat al-ʿArab*), men who lived during the pre-Islamic and early Islamic periods and who were dark-skinned but not necessarily of African ancestry. These poets alternately bemoaned and defended their blackness. One Suḥaym (d. 660), whose name means "little black man," wrote this:

> If my color were pink, women would love me
> But the Lord has marred me with blackness.
>
> Though I am a slave my soul is nobly free
> Though I am black of color my character is white.

A century later, one of the most popular of these poets, Abū Dulāma (d. ca. 776), was a court jester for the Abbasids in Baghdad; he wrote the following in derision of his mother and family:

> We are alike in color; our faces are black and
> ugly, our names are shameful.

One hundred years later, one of the best-known composers of prose in classical Arabic literature, Jāḥiẓ (d. 869), also alleged to be of partial African ancestry, wrote (among other things) that the Zanj "are the least intelligent and the least discerning of mankind."

Some of this literature comes out of the Persian Gulf, where one of the consequences of the Zanj revolt may have been an anti-Zanj backlash of sentiment. Some scholars see the revolt as the principal cause of antiblack expressions, but the revolt did not begin until 868, well after many of these black poets were already dead. Yet another argument is that Persian Zoroastrianism and Manichaeism, with their emphasis on conflict between darkness and light, associated darkness with dark skin and light with white skin and influenced Muslim thinking. While this is all speculative, one source makes clear the view of the African in the Persian Gulf. *The Thousand and One Nights*, an apparent compilation of stories developed by Persian, Indian, and Chinese travelers and merchants, is associated with the early days of Baghdad's Abbasid caliphate. Black folk are mentioned frequently in the book, principally as slaves or servants of some kind. Enslaved black men are also featured at the book's beginning, engaged in sexual escapades with King Shahzāmān's wife and twenty other female members of his household. Some of the most pervasive stereotypes of black folk known in the

Western world were therefore already taking shape in ninth-century Iraq and elsewhere in the Islamic world.

Those Muslims arriving at a negative assessment of the African did not do so on their own, but in dialogue with other traditions and preceding opinions. One influence was Galen (fl. 122–155), whose work on anatomy remained the seminal text in medicine for both Christians and Muslims through the medieval period. Galen was the official physician for gladiators at the Pergamum circus, and there presumably came into contact with blacks. In an interesting and fateful conjunction, it was the famous al-Mas'udī (d. 956) who introduced Galen to the Muslim world by quoting the Greek physician's observations of black men. Galen, al-Mas'udī stated,

> mentions ten specific attributes of the black man, which are found in him and no other; frizzy hair, thin eyebrows, broad nostrils, thick lips, pointed teeth, smelly skin, black eyes, furrowed hands and feet, a long penis and great merriment. Galen says that merriment dominates the black man because of his defective brain, whence also the weakness of his intelligence.

Besides Galen, other sources were interpretations of Christian and Jewish texts condemning black skin as the curse of Ham.

Not all Muslims adopted unfavorable views of blacks. There were those who respected Africans, citing their roles as Companions of the Prophet as well as their virtues. The "defenders of the blacks" included such leading intellectuals as Jamāl al-Dīn Abū'l-Faraj b. al-Jawzī (d. 1208), who wrote *The Lightening of the Darkness on the Merits of the Blacks and the Ethiopians*; and the Egyptian scholar Jalāl al-Dīn al-Suyūṭī (d. 1505), who wrote *The Raising of the Status of the Ethiopians*. Individuals such as al-Suyūṭī had substantial experience with subsaharan Africans and knew a number of their scholars and political leaders personally. One must therefore be careful not to paint the entire Muslim world with the same broad stroke.

Furthermore, it is not clear that prior to the sixteenth century the Muslim view of Europeans was any better than their assessment of Africans. The idea that geography and climate determined group characteristics was popularized by the tenth-century Persian physician Ibn Sīnā. Because of western Europe's cold climate and cultural unattractiveness, Muslims by and large held little respect for it, enslaving many from southeastern Europe. Arab and Persian Muslims who may have

felt contempt for Africans also felt superior to Europeans, as the following quote from an Arab living in eleventh-century al-Andalus reflects:

> For those who live furthest to the north . . . the excessive distance from
> the sun in relation to the zenith line makes the air cold and the at-
> mosphere thick. Their temperaments are therefore frigid, their humors
> [dispositions] raw, their bellies gross, their color pale, their hair long and
> lank. Thus, they lack keenness of understanding and clarity of intelli-
> gence, and are overcome by ignorance and dullness, lack of discernment,
> and stupidity. Such are the Slavs, the Bulgars, and their neighbors.

In view of the symmetry in opinions toward select Africans and Europeans, the divergence in the Muslim view between the two groups
may well have come after the sixteenth century, when the trade in
Europeans began to diminish as its counterpart in Africans continued. By the eighteenth century, there was a fast association between
subsaharan Africans and slavery in the central Islamic lands, whereas
the enslavement of Europeans had largely become a thing of the past,
confined to memory and books.

## Slavery's Aftermath

What became of all these African slaves in the Islamic world? The answer is by no means obvious, as descent traced through the free male
line obscures if not erases African maternal ancestry. A look at contemporary Arab populations in North Africa, Palestine, the Arabian
peninsula, and even the Saudi royal family reveals discernible African
features, but studies are insufficient to make conclusive statements. In
Morocco the fate of subsaharan blacks is clearer, as the descendants of
slaves, the *haraṭīn* (called *bella* further east), continue in servile subjec-
tion to Arabic- and Berber-speaking masters to the present day. The
free descendants of the *haraṭīn* also continued in subordination and
second-class citizenship through the nineteenth and into the twentieth
centuries, heavily dependent upon patron families. Like their American cosufferers, large numbers of the *haraṭīn* found themselves sharecropping in southern Morocco, along the fringes of the Sahara, effectively barred from any meaningful social mobility and virtually shut
out of systems of education. Nevertheless, also like their American
counterparts, the dispossessed of Morocco have experienced changes
for the better with the twentieth century's progression. One famous

community of blacks in Morocco are the *gnawa*, noted for their distinct musical traditions. In Morocco, Tunisia, and Algeria, the descendants of subsaharan Africans (and North Africans, for that matter) practice Islam along with *bori*, a cosmology concerned with the spirit world's interaction with the corporeal. Bori is a mixture of spirits – infants, nature gods, spirits of deceased Muslim leaders, Muslim *jinn* (spirits), and so forth – who cause illness and who are appeased through offerings, sacrifice, and dance possession. West African communities practicing bori, such as the Songhay, Bambara, and Hausa, were distinguished in North Africa at least through the mid-twentieth century. The practice of bori within dominant Muslim societies parallels a similar persistence of subsaharan African religions in the Christian-controlled Americas, and it is a testimony to the tenacity of African culture even under duress.

In India and Pakistan, the descendants of the Habshis and Siddis no longer speak African languages, but their worship and music and dance are suffused with African content, influencing adherents of both Hinduism and Islam. Hindu Siddis in India, for example, use only Siddi priests for guidance in life, who have expertise in engaging Siddi spirits; in Pakistan, the "Sheedis" venerate the Shi'ite leader Imam Husain (martyred at Karbala in 680) in a way that transforms the latter into an active force. In addition to those of clear African descent are the vast millions of Dalits, with whom the former may have intermingled, along with the Shudra caste. Dalits, formerly referred to as "untouchables," were considered ritually polluting and outside of the caste system, even below the Shudras. The Shudras, Dalits, and Siddis have all experienced severe discrimination, their darker skins not unrelated to their suffering.

Perhaps the greater mystery concerns the old Ottoman empire. Approximately 362,000 Africans were imported into its heartland during the nineteenth century alone. The slave trade was abolished there in 1857, at which point all freed persons were required to serve as domestics in designated households (presumably to preserve slaveholder interests). Perhaps the disproportionate use of eunuchs, combined with the high ratio of females to males, explains the apparent disappearance of blacks there. It should be noted, however, that diffused settlements of "Negroes" existed along the western slope of the Caucasus mountains, in what is now Abkhazia and Georgia, until recent times. They may have been descendants of the enslaved brought to the Black Sea region by the Ottomans; alternatively, they may be related to the ancient people of "Colchis," as the area was called by the Greeks, where, records Herodotus, the inhabitants were "black-skinned with wooly hair."

## Suggestions for Further Reading

On the early or classical period of Islam's history, one may begin with Albert Habib Hourani, *A History of the Arab Peoples* (Cambridge, MA: Belknap of Harvard U. Press, 1991). More challenging is the first volume of Marshall G. S. Hodgson's three-volume *The Venture of Islam: Conscience and History in a World Civilization* (Chicago: U. of Chicago Press, 1974) and Fred Donner's *The Early Islamic Conquests* (Princeton, NJ: Princeton U. Press, 1981). For Muhammad, see W. Montgomery Watt's classics, *Muhammad at Mecca* (Oxford: Clarendon U. Press, 1953) and *Muhammad at Medina* (Oxford: Clarendon U. Press, 1956). An accessible reading of the sayings and traditions of the Prophet is Alfred Guillaume, *The Life of the Prophet: A Translation of Ishaq's Rasul Allah* (Oxford: Oxford U. Press, 1967).

The scholarship regarding Islam in early West and East Africa is voluminous, as is obviously true of the literature on Islam in general. One could begin with Mervyn Hiskett's *The Development of Islam in West Africa*, although it is more concerned with what becomes Nigeria. Nehemia Levtzion's *Islam in West Africa: Religion, Society and Politics to 1800* (Brookfield, VT: Variorum, 1994) and his *Ancient Ghana and Mali* (London: Methuen, 1973) are also useful. There are excellent articles in Nehemia Levtzion and Humphrey J. Fisher, eds., *Rural and Urban Islam in West Africa* (Boulder, CO: Rienner, 1986). More challenging but thorough are the contributions to the first volume of J. F. A. Ajayi and Michael Crowder, eds., *History of West Africa* (London: Longman, 1985), 3rd ed. Though dated, two enjoyable classics remain Félix Dubois, *Timbuctoo the Mysterious*, trans. Diana White (New York: Longmans, Green and Co., 1896) and E. W. Bovill, *The Golden Trade of the Moors* (London: Oxford U. Press, 1968). For African urban areas, see Graham Connah, *African Civilizations. Precolonial Cities and States in Tropical Africa: An Archaeological Perspective* (Cambridge: Cambridge U. Press, 1987). For East Africa specifically, see J. F. Safari, *The Making of Islam in East Africa* (Dar es Salaam: Benedictine Publications Ndanda-Peramiho, 1994). Biancamaria Scarcia Amoretti's *Islam in East Africa, New Sources: Archives, Manuscripts and Written*

*Historical Sources, Oral History, Archaeology* (Rome: Herder, 2001) is a collection of data from a 1999 conference, and it is helpful. For more focused studies, consider Randle L. Pouwells, *Horn and Crescent: Cultural Change and Traditional Islam on the East African Coast, 800–1900* (Cambridge: Cambridge U. Press, 1987) and Frederick Cooper, *Plantation Slavery on the East Coast of Africa* (New Haven, CT: Yale U. Press, 1977).

Mention of Cooper's work provides a segue into the topic of slavery. Ralph Austen's *African Economic History: Internal Development and External Dependency* (London: J. Curry; Portsmouth, NH: Heinemann, 1987) contains an important discussion of the volume and organization of the various external slave trades, while Paul E. Lovejoy's *Transformations in Slavery: A History of Slavery in Africa* (Cambridge and New York: Cambridge U. Press, 1983) and Patrick Manning's *Slavery and African Life: Occidental, Oriental, and African Slave Trades* (Cambridge: Cambridge U. Press, 1990) combine these insights with discussions of domestic slavery and arguments about the implications of slave trading for Africa. Moving to the actual sites of enslavement, John O. Hunwick's "African Slaves in the Mediterranean World: A Neglected Aspect of the African Diaspora," in Joseph E. Harris, ed., *Global Dimensions of the African Diaspora* (Washington, DC: Howard U. Press, 1993), is an excellent overview. R. Brunschvig's "Abd," in *The Encyclopedia of Islam* (Leiden: E. J. Brill, 1960), new ed., addresses the equation of African slaves with this term. Bernard Lewis's *Race and Color in Islam* (New York: Octagon Books, 1971) and his *Race and Slavery in the Middle East: An Historical Enquiry* (New York and Oxford: Oxford U. Press, 1990) are probably the most thorough discussions of the African presence in the Islamic world, although they are somewhat controversial in that translations from Arabic to English tend to favor the more pejorative of possible meanings. Compare with Murray Gordon, *Slavery in the Arab World* (New York: New Amsterdam, 1989), who emphasizes the sexual component of slavery. Important studies in various sites of the Islamic world include John Ralph Willis, ed., *Slaves and Slavery in Muslim Africa* (London, England, and Totowa, NJ: 1985), 2 vols.; Y. Hakan Erdem, *Slavery in the Ottoman Empire and Its Demise, 1800–1909* (New York: St. Martin's Press, 1996); Alexandre Popovi'c, *The Revolt of African Slaves in Iraq in the 3rd/9th Century*, trans. Léon King (Princeton, NJ: Markus Weiner, 1999); and Ehud R. Toledano, *Slavery and Abolition in the Ottoman Middle East* (Seattle: U. of Washington Press, 1998). Graham W. Irwin's *Africans Abroad* (New

York: Columbia U. Press, 1977) provides translations of important documents. Information and accounts of the movement and experiences of slaves in Africa and the Middle East can be found in Martin Klein, *Slavery and Colonial Rule in French West Africa* (Cambridge: Cambridge U. Press, 1998); Paul Lovejoy and Jan Hogendorn, *Slow Death for Slavery: The Course of Abolition in Northern Nigeria, 1897–1936* (Cambridge: Cambridge U. Press, 1993); and John O. Hunwick and Eve Trout Powell, eds., *The African Diaspora in the Mediterranean Lands of Islam* (Princeton, NJ: Markus Weiner, 2002).

Concerning more contemporary subsaharan communities in North Africa and their cultures, see Mohammed Ennaji, *Serving the Master: Slavery and Society in Nineteenth-Century Morocco*, trans. Seth Graebner (New York: St. Martin's Press, 1998); Émile Dermenghem, *Le culte des saints dans l'islam maghrébin* (Paris: Éditions Gallimard, 1954); Vincent Crapanzano, *The Hamadsha: A Study in Moroccan Ethnopsychiatry* (Berkeley: U. of California Press, 1973); A. J. N. Tremearne, *The Ban of the Bori: Demons and Demon-Dancing in West and North Africa* (London: Heath, Cranton, and Ouseley, 1914); and Janice Boddy, *Wombs and Alien Spirits: Women, Men, and the Zār Cult in Northern Sudan* (Madison: U. of Wisconsin Press, 1989).

Context for the question of Africans in India is provided by K. N. Chaudhuri, *Asia before Europe: Economy and Civilisation of the Indian Ocean from the Rise of Islam to 1750* (Cambridge: Cambridge U. Press, 1990). Joseph E. Harris was one of the first to pursue this topic in *The African Presence in Asia; Consequences of the East Asian Slave Trade* (Evanston: Northwestern U. Press, 1971). Fitzroy A. Baptiste's "The African Presence in India," in *Africa Quarterly* 38 (no. 2, 1998: 92–126), is a fine analysis, linking the discussion to Trinidad. V. T. Rajshekhar raises vexing issues in *Dalit: The Black Untouchables of India* (Atlanta, GA: Clarity Press, 1995), while Vijay Prashad argues for coalitions that are based on racial categories in "Afro-Dalits of the Earth, Unite!," in *African Studies Review* 43 (no. 1, 2000: 189–201). The most recent literature is to be found in Edward Alpers and Amy Catlin-Jairazbhoy, eds., *Sidis and Scholars: Essays on African Indians* (New Delhi: Rainbow; Trenton, NJ: Africa World Press, 2003).

Concerning Moorish Spain, one should begin with Jamil M. Abun-Nasr, *A History of the Maghrib in the Islamic Period* (Cambridge: Cambridge U. Press, 1987). For the adventurous with interest in North Africa, look at Ibn Khaldun's *The Muqadimmah*, trans. Franz Rosenthal (New York: Pantheon Books, 1958) and his *Histoire des Berbères et des dynasties musulmanes de L'Afrique septentrionale,* trans. (Paris: P. Geuthner, 1925–56). Other references include L. P. Harvey, *Islamic Spain, 1250–1500* (Chicago: U. of Chicago Press, 1990); D. Fairchild Ruggles, *Gardens, Landscape, and Vision in the Palaces of Islamic Spain* (University Park: Pennsylvania State U. Press, 2000); Ivan Van Sertima, *Golden Age of the Moor* (New Brunswick, NJ: Transaction, 1992); Mark D. Meyerson and Edward D. English, eds., *Christians, Muslims and Jews in Medieval and Early Modern Spain: Interaction and Cultural Change* (Notre Dame, IN: U. of Notre Dame Press, 1999); Thomas F. Glick, *From Muslim Fortress to Christian Castle: Social and Cultural Change in Medieval Spain* (Manchester, England: Manchester U. Press; New York: St. Martin's Press, 1995); and Hugh Kennedy, *Muslim Spain and Portugal: A Political History of al-Andalus* (London and New York: Longman, 1996). Bernard Lewis's *The Muslim Discovery of Europe* (New York: W. W. Norton, 1982) and Maribel Fierro, *Judíos y musulmanes en al-Andalus y el Magreb: contactos intelectuales* (Madrid: Casa de Velázquez, 2002), provide a discussion of Europe's intellectual engagement with Muslims in Iberia and elsewhere.

# II

## "New" World Realities

# CHAPTER 4

# Transatlantic Moment

European engagement with the Muslim world contributed to a cultural awakening and commercial expansion resulting in profound political transformations. An energetic Europe burst upon the world scene in the fifteenth century, ushering in a new era. Labor exploitation was key to the expansion, and critical to such labor was the capture and enslavement of Africans. African captives in the Muslim world were important and numerically significant, but the transatlantic trade was exceptional for its high volume and compact duration, with the overwhelming majority of Africans transported in the eighteenth and nineteenth centuries. The consequences for Africa and its exported daughters and sons were catastrophic.

Like the inner workings of a clock, the interconnectedness of several global developments gave rise to the transatlantic slave trade. Christian–Muslim conflict, international commerce, sugar, and New World incursions were foremost in creating circumstances whereby the African emerged as principal source of servile labor, laying the foundations of the modern world.

## Reconquista

Muslim forces in al-Andalus, never in control of the entire Iberian peninsula, were continually threatened by Christian enemies during their nearly 800-year rule. The latter stages of the struggle for Iberia, referred to as the "reconquest" by the Christians, unfolded at the same time as an equally momentous contest between Christian and Muslim powers raging near the Black Sea. There, Muslims fought for control of the old Byzantine or eastern Roman empire (referred to by the Muslims as *Rūm*). In both Iberia and the Black Sea region, Muslims and Christians sold their captives into slavery.

The means by which captives were marketed underscores the period's expansive commercial activity. Maritime innovations allowed the Italian city-states of Pisa, Genoa, and Venice to participate in an eastern Mediterranean trade principally involving silk, spices, and sugar; but they also trafficked in war captives. The Genoese, for example, sold Christian captives to Muslims, and Muslim captives to Christians, by the thousands, while the Venetians purchased captives from the Black Sea. Many, mostly women, were brought to Italy, where they performed agricultural and domestic tasks left undone by an Italian population reeling from the Black Death. The newly enslaved joined the ranks of the similarly exploited in Crete and Cyprus, but especially in Sicily, southern Italy, Majorca, and southern Spain, where slavery was of a considerable vintage. The enslaved in Sicily were mostly Muslim and, like Venice and other Italian sites, female.

If the fourteenth century saw increased reliance upon captive labor in the Mediterranean, the fourteenth and fifteenth witnessed changes in the source of that labor. The reconquest of Portugal in 1267 signaled the beginning of the end of territorial disputes between Muslims and Christians. Muslim power in Spain also began to gradually decline as a result of battles and treaties. Iberia as a source of servile labor dried up, forcing Europe to turn elsewhere. By the end of the fourteenth century, the demand for slaves was largely met by captives from the Black Sea. But the struggle for Byzantium ended in 1453 with the Muslim conquest of Constantinople (henceforth Istanbul) and the consolidation of lands in Anatolia (Asia Minor) and adjoining the Black Sea. Captives were thereafter funneled to Muslim markets. Some forty years later, the combined forces of Castile and Aragon defeated the last Muslim bastion in Iberia, Granada, bringing the reconquest to an end in 1492.

With these reservoirs of servile labor tapped out, the northern Mediterranean was in need of workers, a demand occasioned by, among other projects, the cultivation of sugarcane. Spreading from southeast Asia to India in antiquity, sugarcane was introduced to Persians and Arabs during Islam's early years. They transferred its production to Syria and Egypt, and later to North Africa, southern Spain,

Sicily, Cyprus, and Crete. European crusaders first came into contact with sugar in the Holy Lands, and they developed their own sugar plantations in Cyprus, Crete, and Sicily by the early thirteenth century. Europe gradually acquired a taste for sugar (although expensive until the nineteenth century and frequently used for medicinal purposes), having known only honey as a sweetener. Italian merchants spearheaded its production by supplying the capital and technology for its expansion into southern Iberia and (eventually) Madeira and the Canary Islands off the West African coast.

While the Italians provided the financing, the Portuguese supplied the labor. How the Portuguese secured the labor, however, is very much connected to Indian Ocean commerce. Both the Italians and the Portuguese had long been interested in accessing its lucrative trade directly, as opposed to going through the Red Sea and Arabian peninsula. This long-range goal of eliminating the Muslim middleman, together with such short-term objectives as securing outlets for West African gold, led the Portuguese and Italians to explore the West African coast during the first half of the fifteenth century. By 1475, the Portuguese had crossed the equator, and by 1487 they had rounded the Cape of Good Hope. By then, the Portuguese were exporting as much as 700 kilograms of West African gold in a peak year, and averaged 410 kilograms per year in the first twenty years of the sixteenth century, accounting for nearly one-fourth of all West African annual gold production. Vasco da Gama's 1497–1498 voyage signaled Portugal's entrance into the Indian Ocean; by 1520 the Portuguese were an Indian Ocean power.

Busy with gold and empire, the Portugese also tapped into West African labor. The Guanches, the indigenous population of the Canaries, were taken by the Portuguese and enslaved in both Madeira and the Mediterranean in the early fifteenth century. Lisbon began importing as many as 1,000 West Africans annually from 1441 to 1530; from there they were dispersed to southern Spain, Portugal, and elsewhere in the Mediterranean. However, it was Madeira that emerged as the most important Portuguese possession, with its cultivation of sugarcane, initially with Guanche and then West African mainland labor (the Guanches were eventually extinguished as a group by European diseases). By the 1490s, Madeira was a wealthy Portuguese colony, exporting sugar throughout Europe and the Mediterranean. In 1495, the planters of Madeira began operations in the West African islands of São Tomé and Principe, operations so successful that the Old World slave trade remained numerically dominant until the middle of the sixteenth century.

The use of black slaves to cultivate sugarcane therefore did not begin in the Americas, but in the Mediterranean and on West African coastal islands. Columbus's 1492 voyage to the "Indies" (to avoid circumnavigating Africa) set into motion a process that, among other things, transferred a system of slavery from the Old World to the New. The gradual exploitation of African labor was consequently not the result of some far-reaching European design to demean and debilitate Africans and Africa – at least not by the fifteenth century. In a real sense, Africa was a casualty of geography as much as greed.

## Scope of the Trade

The trickle of African captives in the second half of the fifteenth century turned into a veritable flood by the seventeenth century. Columbus made his "discoveries," and in 1501 Pedro Cabral returned to Portugal with claims to Brazil. The movement of the Portuguese and Spanish into the New World saw the rise of mining and agricultural industries and an increased reliance on captive African labor that was due, most importantly, to epidemiology. In sum, Europeans introduced an entirely new disease environment into the Americas, from which indigenous peoples had no immunity. The latter were subjected to smallpox, measles, influenza, diphtheria, whooping cough, chicken pox, typhoid, trichinosis, and enslavement, and the results were catastrophic: In central Mexico alone, an estimated pre-Columbian population of 25 million fell to 1.5 million by 1650, after which it slowly recovered; in Hispaniola, native Arawak numbers plummeted from approximately 7 million to less than 500 by the 1540s. In total, an indigenous population as high as 100 million (or less than 20 million, depending on the estimate) was decimated by as much as 90 percent by the late eighteenth century, a process referred to as the Great Dying.

Africans, in contrast to the indigenous population, shared with Europeans a certain proportion of the Old World disease environment. African mortality rates in the Americas were alarmingly high as a result of other factors, as were those for Europeans in places like seventeenth-century Virginia, but neither was quite as devastating as those visited upon the indigenous. The Great Dying, European familiarity with African enslaved labor, and the cost-effectiveness of transporting Africans to the Americas explains their enslavement in the Americas, one of the most extensive mass movements in history, a displacement to beat all displacements.

Within ten years of Columbus' 1492 voyage, enslaved Africans were in the New World, along with sugarcane and experienced planters from Portugal and the Canaries. Hispaniola (current day Haiti and the Dominican Republic), Cuba, and other Spanish-claimed territories were early destinations, and by the 1520s, Africans were replacing the indigenous Taíno in servile capacities, including gold and silver mining. From 1521 to 1594, from 75,000 to 90,000 Africans were brought to Spanish-held territories, with over half going to Mexico. Approximately 110,525 Africans entered Mexico and Peru between 1521 and 1639; by the time of formal emancipation in 1827, some 200,000 Africans had labored in Mexico alone. By 1560, Africans outnumbered Europeans in Cuba and Hispaniola, and by 1570 they equaled the number of Europeans in Mexico City and Vera Cruz.

Not all Africans entering the New World in the sixteenth century were enslaved. Free Africans took part in the military conquest alongside white conquistadores. Africans and their descendants had long resided in various Spanish towns, where they often experienced a freedom qualified by substantial financial hardship. The opportunity to sail for the New World was welcomed by individuals like Juan González de Léon, who among other things served as an interpreter of the Taíno language, and Juan Garrido, who came to Seville in 1496 and thereafter enlisted for service in the Americas. Garrido fought against the Taíno in Hispaniola, and both men participated in Ponce de Léon's conquest of Puerto Rico beginning in 1508. From Puerto Rico, Ponce de Léon raided the Caribs for captives in Santa Cruz, Guadaloupe, and Dominica, with the assistance of both men. The two even accompanied Juan Ponce de Léon to Florida in 1513 and 1521, mining for gold for a time.

Though there were black explorers and conquerors (dubious distinctions to say the least), slavery in sixteenth-century Spanish-claimed lands was far more significant, and even more so in Portuguese-held Brazil. Sugarcane was planted as early as the 1520s in the northeastern region of Pernambuco, and with the arrival of planters from Madeira and São Tomé, the industry grew slowly. Portuguese involvement in Kongo and Angola saw a dramatic increase in the importation of African captives, and by 1600 Brazil had outstripped Madeira as the world's leading sugar producer. Brazil was the port of call for the vast majority of captive Africans for the whole of the seventeenth century, accounting for almost 42 percent of the total.

The early African presence in the Americas was but the beginning of woes. The export figure remains a matter of debate, with some arguing for estimates that trend toward 100 million (including losses in Africa). The scholarly consensus, however, is that approximately 11.9 million Africans were exported from Africa, out which 9.6 to 10.8 million arrived alive, translating into a loss during the Middle Passage of about 10 to 20 percent. Some 64.9 percent of the total were males, and 27.9 percent children. The transatlantic slave trade spanned 400 years, from the fifteenth through the nineteenth centuries. The apex of the trade, between 1700 and 1810, saw approximately 6.5 million Africans shipped out of the continent. Some 60 percent of all Africans imported into the Americas made the fateful voyage between 1721 and 1820, while 80 percent were transported between 1701 and 1850. In comparison with the trade in Africans through the Sahara, Red Sea, and Indian Ocean, the bulk of the Atlantic trade took less than one-tenth of the time.

Many European nations were involved in the slave trade. Britain, France, Sweden, Denmark, and Holland all joined Spain and Portugal at different points in time, as did Brazil and the United States. From the fifteenth century through the middle of the seventeenth, Spain and Portugal controlled the trade; Spain transported relatively few captives under its own flag, relying instead upon foreign firms to supply its territories under a licensing system called the *asiento*. From the mid-seventeenth century, a number of European entities entered the slaving business in addition to those previously mentioned, including the Brandenburgers, Genoese, and Courlanders. Throughout the eighteenth century and into the first decade of the nineteenth, the height of the trade, British and French involvement accounted for at least 50 percent of the trade.

Of all the voyages for which there is data between 1662 and 1867, nearly 90 percent of captive Africans wound up in Brazil and the Caribbean; indeed, Brazil alone imported 40 percent of the total trade. That part of the Caribbean in which the English and French languages became dominant yet transformed through African inflections, syntaxes, and vocabularies, was not far behind Brazil, receiving 37 percent of the trade in more or less equal proportions. Spanish-claimed islands accounted for 10 percent of the Africans, after which North America took in 7 percent or less.

## African Provenance

Nearly 85 percent of those exported through the Atlantic came from one of only four regions: West Central Africa (36.5 percent), the Bight of Benin (20 percent), the Bight of Biafra (16.6 percent), and the Gold Coast (11 percent). The busiest ports in these regions were Cabinda and Luanda (West Central Africa), Cape Castle and Anomabu (Gold Coast), Bonny and Calabar (Bight of Biafra), and Whydah (Bight of Benin). Slavers (slave ships) often took on their full complement of captives in single regions of supply, and Africans emanating from the same regions tended to be transported to the same New World destinations. Captives from West Central Africa comprised the majority of those who came to Saint Domingue (present day Haiti) and South America, accounting for an astounding 73 percent of the Africans imported into Brazil. The Bight of Benin, in turn, contributed dis proportionately to Bahia (northeastern Brazil) and the francophone Caribbean outside of Saint Domingue; six out of every ten from the Bight of Benin went to Bahia, while two out of every ten arrived in francophone areas. The Bight of Biafra constituted the major source for the British Leeward Islands and Jamaica, although the Gold Coast supplied 27 percent of those who landed in Jamaica and was clearly the leading supplier to Barbados, the Guyanas, and Surinam. Sierra Leone (a region that includes the Windward Coast in this discussion) provided 6.53 percent of the total export figure, followed by Southeast Africa and Senegambia at 5.14 percent and 4.3 percent, respectively. Transshipments between New World destinations could be substantial.

A review of these regions reveals considerable complexity not only with respect to language and culture, but also as it concerns forms of government, agriculture, regional and transregional commerce, and technologies relating to each of these categories. Stated differently, while there were many similarities, there were appreciable differences of every kind among the captives.

West Central Africa was a vast region dominated by the states and populations of Kongo and Angola. Life conformed to the four ecological zones (river, swamp, forest, and savannah) of the Congo River basin, the people further linked by closely related Bantu languages. Statecraft in the region ranged from kingdoms to villages, with Kongo, Ndongo, Kasanje, and Loango representing states of substantial size and elaboration. Agriculture, the material basis for these societies,

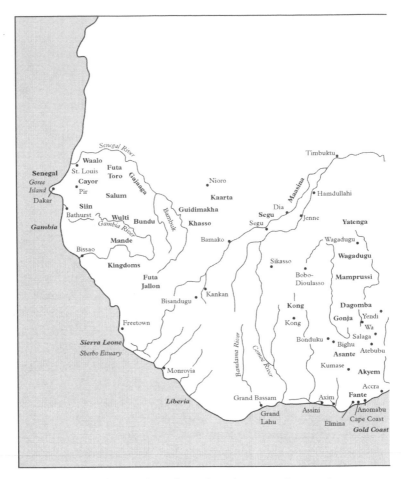

**MAP 4.** West Africa in the eighteenth and nineteenth centuries.

was usually performed by women (except land clearing), whereas men hunted and tended fruit and palm trees.

Communities throughout West Central Africa believed in a supreme deity, often referred to as Nzambi a Mpungu, and related spiritual entities. Since the fifteenth century, a tradition of Christianity was established in the region, the result of Portuguese commercial activities. The social history of seventeenth- and eighteenth-century Kongo arguably revolved around the exchange between Christianity and Kongolese religion, giving rise to an Africanized Christianity best symbolized by the life of Dona Beatrice Kimpa Vita (1682–1706), leader of a

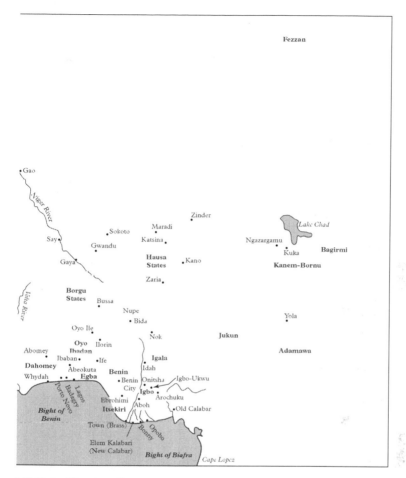

**MAP 4.** (*Continued*)

religious movement that sought to reconstruct a Kongo reeling from war. A prophet–priest or *kitomi*, her claim to be the incarnation of St. Anthony, combined with her teachings that Jesus, Mary, and the prophets were all Kongolese, are examples of the way Christianity was reconfigured to accommodate West Central African values. Dona Beatrice Kimpa Vita was burned at the stake for heresy.

In West Central Africa, spirits of the dead who had led good lives were believed to live in *mpemba*, a subterranean realm separated from the living by a large body of water, or *kalunga*. The deceased changed color within ten months of their demise, becoming white. It is therefore

**FIGURE 1.** Cape Coast Castle, Gold Coast, 1948.

no surprise that Europeans were initially viewed as departed spirits, having crossed the kalunga of the Atlantic.

The Bight of Benin, the second leading source of captives, was the land of the Fon, Ewe, and Yoruba groups. The Ewe (concentrated in present-day Togo and southeastern Ghana) were organized into more than 100 autonomous states, whereas the Fon of Dahomey (contemporary Benin) absorbed Weme, Allada, and Whydah to form a single centralized power in the eighteenth century. The Yoruba of what is now southwestern Nigeria also witnessed expansionist polities, but they were more centered on their respective towns and thereby much more urban than others. There are many exceptional features of Fon–Ewe–Yoruba cultures, not the least of which are the bronzes and sculptures of Benin and Ife. However, the gods of the Fon–Ewe (*vodun* or *loas*) and the Yoruba (*orishas*) are so numerous and unique that they further distinguish the region. The Yoruba orishas include Olodumare (high god), Oshun (goddess of fresh water and sensuality), Ogun (warrior god of iron), Eshu-Elegba (or Ellegua, trickster god of the crossroads), Shango (god of thunder and lightning), and Yemanja (mother of all orishas and goddess of the oceans); and they correspond in some instances to the Fon–Ewe *loas* of Mawu-Lisa (high god), Aziri (a riverain goddess), Gu (god of iron and warfare), and Legba (god of the crossroads; keeper of the gate). Mawu-Lisa, for example, is a composite of female and male characteristics, representing the Fon–Ewe ideal.

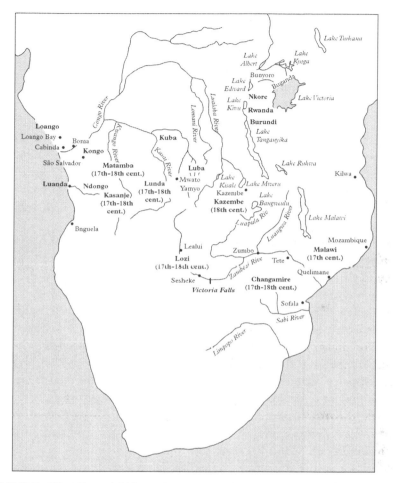

**MAP 5.** West Central Africa, 1600–1800.

These beliefs would become central to practices in such places as Haiti, Brazil, and Louisiana.

In contrast to the Yoruba, most of the Igbo, Ibibio, Igala, Efik, Ijo, Ogoni, and other groups of the Bight of Biafra (southeastern Nigeria) were organized into villages. The Igbo, Ibibio, and Ijo were the largest, and the Igbo in particular were marked by dense populations and agrarian economies. For the most part, theirs were independent "village democracies," in which important decisions were made by a male peasantry individually distinguished by varying statuses of achievement. Men conducted long-distance commerce, but women controlled local trade, keeping any money they earned in communities that were mostly patrilineal (tracing descent and inheritance through the male line). Women also regularly fought to defend their villages. Above all else, though, women were revered as mothers, wives, and keepers of the soil. Regarding the latter, they enjoyed a special connection to Ala (or Ana), the earth mother. Ala and the land (*ala*) were highly esteemed and inextricably interwoven, forming the basis of Igbo law. Ala was functionally the most important deity in Igbo society, although she was not the high, creator god. That honor was held by Chineke or Chukwu, who, like the Fon–Ewe's Mawu-Lisa, was a blend of male and female components (*chi* and *eke*), and from whom sprang powerful spiritual forces known as the *alusi* or *agbara* as well as the personal guardian spirit or chi of each individual. The ancestral dead, the *ndichie*, added to the realm of the disembodied.

According to Igbo beliefs, the individual in consultation with his or her chi undertook a plan of action that resulted in high individual achievement, guided by a philosophy and value system stressing success and known as *ikenga*. The individual drive of the Igbo, together with their regard for the earth and belief in destiny, would clearly influence the direction of African-derived cultures in the Americas.

Regarding the Gold Coast, its southern half was dominated by Akan and Ga speakers, the former in turn divided into Twi and Baule speakers. As was true of the Igbo, women were prominent in Akan societies, as is evident in the belief that their ancestresses came from the sky or earth to found the first Akan towns in the forests. Matrilineal for the most part, Akan clans each claimed descent from a common mother. Each clan had a male and a female head, and women played critical roles as advisors and heads of the matriclans. Similar to the Igbo, the Akan espoused belief in the earth mother, Asase Yaa, who, together with the high god Onyame (or Onyankopon), created the world. In keeping with most African theologies, the Akan high gods were remote, but the next order of deity, the *abosom* (who numbered in the hundreds), were accessible.

Akan societies contributed to the wide variety of political contexts out of which captives were taken. In this case, Akan speakers were either a part of the expansionist Asante empire (established around 1680) or they lived in its shadow. Asante was a vast realm ruled by the *Asantehene* (king) and a bureaucracy intent on maximizing trade with both the African hinterland and with Europeans on the coast. Gold, in addition to captives, was a key export; gold dust was the standard currency of Asante. One of the most militarily powerful and structurally complex states in all of Africa, Asante's political union was symbolized by the *Sika Dwa*, the Golden Stool.

Sierra Leone was a region whose interior was dominated by the large Muslim theocracy of Futa Jallon, and by a series of independent, small-scale villages along the coast composed of multiple groups. A discussion of the coast underscores the rural existence of a majority who were farmers, fishers, and hunters. Although many groups were patrilineal, women tended to wield extraordinary influence through their roles as expert agriculturalists and leaders of "secret societies." Concerning the former, women cultivated rice, cotton, and indigo, skills that would be coveted in North America. Secret societies, in turn, were instrumental in intervillage diplomacy and commerce, and they were critical to the maintenance of social order. The Sande or Bundu society of women was one of the better known organizations, but women also played leading roles in such male societies as the Poro. What therefore emerges from the Sierra Leonian region are gender relations that may have been more egalitarian than elsewhere.

While located in Sierra Leone's hinterland, Futa Jallon was also vitally connected to the Senegambian region. We have already discussed Islam in Africa, so it is sufficient to observe that from the seventeenth through the nineteenth centuries, militant or reformist Islamic states were founded in Senegambia (and indeed throughout West Africa), and Futa Jallon was a key participant in this development. Muslims captured non-Muslims in wars and were themselves captured, and captives from both sides wound up in the Americas. Muslims were exported through Senegambia, Sierra Leone, and the Bight of Benin, the latter mostly the result of conflict between Muslim Hausa-Fulani (related groups in contemporary northern Nigeria) and Yoruba combatants (some of whom were Muslims themselves). Muslims were also exported from the Gold Coast, but to a lesser extent. A number of Malagasy and Swahili captives from the coast of Southeast Africa were probably Muslim, but many would have been from the interior and therefore non-Muslim.

## Belly of the Whale

The transatlantic transport of all of these various Africans to the Americas qualifies as the quintessential moment of transfiguration, the height of human alienation and disorientation. It is a phenomenon unlike any other, with millions forcibly removed from family and friends and deposited in lands foreign and hostile. It cannot be compared with the millions of Europeans who voluntarily crossed the Atlantic, a journey which for all of their troubles was their collective choice. Words will never convey the agony, despair, and bewilderment of these innocents, the depth of their suffering, the pain of their separation. The transatlantic voyage, also called the Middle Passage, was an unspeakable horror.

The movement across the Atlantic actually began on African soil, where those captured in the hinterland were brought to coastal holding stages, or barracoons. Between initial capture and the barracoon, anything was possible, including escape. Alternatively, they could have been taken north to the transsaharan trade, or retained in Africa as slaves, where eventual export to the Americas (or the Mediterranean) was a continual possibility. Welcome to the realm of uncertainty and fear, gateway to the land of the macabre.

Reference to captives points to the debate over the capture itself. Do scholars who maximize African involvement in the capture and sale of other Africans do so for the purpose of minimizing Western culpability? Are those who are appalled by the very suggestion of African participation in the slave trade motivated by the same logic, only in reverse? The truth of the matter may be more nuanced than straightforward. There can be no doubt that European and American demand for slave labor drove the entire enterprise. It is also the case that Europeans entered Africa and hunted humans like prey, especially in the case of the Portuguese in Angola and Mozambique. But it is equally undeniable that, as was true of the transsaharan trade, there were African groups and governments involved in the capture of other Africans, together with instances of cooperation between European and African traffickers. At Bonny in the Bight of Biafra and points along the Gold Coast, for example, Europeans used "boating," or the sailing of small vessels upriver to purchase captives from villages along the banks, a practice also found along the Windward Coast. While other African states and groups resisted the slave trades and may have been successful in defending some, they clearly could not save nearly 12 million others.

Notions of African unity, and even "race" for that matter, were alien to Africa until relatively recently. As has been discussed, Africa was inhabited by people of differing cultures, religions, and political agendas, and these differences were exacerbated (or created) to feed the slave

FIGURE 2. Slave coffle, western Sudan, 1879–1881. From Joseph Simon GalliÉni, *Mission d'exploration du Haut-Niger: Voyage au Soudan Francais* (Paris, 1885), p. 525. Library of Congress, Prints and Photographs Division, LC-USZ62-32008.

trade. Raids, kidnaping, and warfare produced most captives, while individuals found guilty of crimes, or sold into bondage to pay debts, were also taken. Indeed, with the acceleration of the slave trade came a corresponding surge in the number of persons convicted of crimes. Can African participation in the slave trades be divorced from the engines of European and American demand? Culpability was shared, but was it symmetrical, and does the answer matter?

Captured Africans, in their forced march from the hinterland to the sea, could cover substantial distances, anywhere from 100 to 700 kilometers, depending upon place and time. They could take four months or longer to reach the coast. Loss of life during the trek is conservatively estimated to have averaged 10 to 15 percent, and in Angola it reached an obscene 40 percent. Captives who reached the shore could remain there for months, as a result of poor health and the need to convalesce, or to wait for the next slaver. Ports with established traffic attracted larger numbers of slavers with greater frequency and differed, along with other barracoons, in type and size. Some barracoons were simply pens exposed to the elements, sometimes adjacent to European factories (trading posts). Others ranged from weather-protected dwellings to fortified castles. Still others, according to Mungo Park's late-eighteenth-century observation along the Gambia, were compounds attached to nearby communities, for "if no immediate opportunity offers them to advantage, they are distributed among the neighbouring villages until a slave ship arrives, or until they can be sold to black traders who sometime purchase on speculation." Park described their circumstances, stating that "the poor wretches are kept constantly fettered, two and two of them being chained together, and employed in the labours of the field; and I am sorry to add, are very scantily fed, as well as harshly treated."

The Gambian experience paralleled that of the Angolan. The latter involved coffles averaging 100 captives from the interior. They were fed the cheapest food, often rotten, which they were forced to carry. Bound and brutalized, they were taken to Luanda, where conditions remained deplorable, and there branded three times: on the right breast with a royal coat of arms, on the left breast or arm to indicate individual ownership, and on the chest with a small cross, as captives were baptized before embarking for Brazil. They then waited for weeks if not months, chained and exposed, with little to eat and little to wear, eating, sleeping, and eliminating in the closest of spaces. As many as 12,000 captives arrived annually in Luanda for export; between 6,000 and 7,000 survived for eventual shipment. The "putrid miasmas" of human filth and disease and death filled the air, circulating throughout the city.

The boarding of captives did not necessarily mean that the voyage was underway. There were often further delays of weeks if not months, as the slaver sailed from barracoon to barracoon until a full complement was achieved. A Middle Passage of only two or three month's duration was not the experience of many; rather, the total amount of time from the initial capture to embarkation could last the better part of a year.

The *James* departed England on April 5, 1675 and did not arrive in Barbados until May 21, 1676. Having reached Assini (on the Gold Coast) on August 30, the *James* exchanged commodities for both gold and captives at several points along the coast until January 11, 1676, when the vessel arrived at the English factory near Wyemba. There the slaver boarded captives each day for about a week, most of whom were described as "very thin ordinary slaves," indicative of the preceding ordeal onshore. The *James* made yet another stop at Anomabu and did not set sail for Barbados until March 8, 1676.

Similarly, the Dutch slaver *St. Jan* began loading captives at Ardra in the Bight of Benin, also called Slave Coast, on March 4, 1659. The ship continued east, picking up additional captives and supplies in the Bight of Biafra. By the time the *St. Jan* left the Biafran area for the Cameroon River on May 22, it had boarded 219 Africans. From that time to August 17, the vessel journeyed along the coast in search of food as far as Cape Lopez (just south of the equator). The search for provisions was a major preoccupation for slavers, and the captain of the *James* complained that his search for food was a "great trouble." His concern was echoed by the captain of the *Arthur* operating in the Biafran Bight in February of 1678: "This day we sentt our Boat att Donus to see whatt might be done there, wee finding negroes to be Brought on Board of us fast enough but wee nott free to deale in many fearing lest wee should take in negroes and have noe provitions for them." It was Barbot's calculation at the beginning of the eighteenth century that a "ship that takes in five hundred slaves, must provide above a hundred thousand yams; which is very difficult, because it is hard to stow them, by reason they take up so much room."

Once purchased by European slavetraders, captives were often branded with the company's coat of arms. These became their only coats, as they were usually stripped of all clothing. In 1699, Bosman recorded that "they came aboard stark naked as well women as men; in which condition they are obliged to continue, if the master of the Ship is not so charitable (which he commonly is) as to bestow something on them to cover their nakedness." Some 128 years after Bosman, Mayer noted in 1827 that two days before captives were loaded onto the slaver, the heads of both males and females were shaved. And then:

> On the appointed day, the *barracoon* or slave-pen is made joyous by the abundant 'feed' which signalizes the negro's last hours in his native country. The feast over, they are taken alongside the vessel in canoes; and as they touch the deck, they are entirely stripped, so that women as well as men go out of Africa as they came into it – *naked*. This precaution, it will be understood, is indispensable; for perfect nudity, during the whole voyage, is the only means of securing cleanliness and health.
>
> Brantz Mayer, *Captain Canot, or, Twenty Years of an African Slaver* (New York: Appleton, 1854), p. 102.

While slavetraders may have been primarily concerned with hygiene, they were not oblivious to the psychological implications of denuding. Contrary to popular ignorance, most Africans did not go about butt naked, swinging through trees, but in fact placed great value on textiles, the primary commodity for which captives were traded to Europeans in the first place. The humiliation of prolonged nakedness before captors, the opposite sex, and children seared into the psyche an overwhelming sense of vulnerability.

Captives did not suffer silently. To the contrary, they often rebelled. To prevent mutiny and escape, male slaves were chained together at the wrists and ankles in groups of two as soon as they were boarded. Women and girls were physically separated from the males and usually unfettered, an arrangement that became standard procedure by the last quarter of the eighteenth century. The segregation of the sexes was maintained throughout the voyage except under certain circumstances on deck. Europeans had learned to prepare for rebellion as early as 1651, when captain Bartholomew Haward was told that "there is put aboard your Pinck *Supply* 30 paire of shackles and boults for such of your negers as are rebellious and we pray you be veary carefull to keepe them undr and let them have their food in due season that they ryse not against you, as they have done in other ships."

The separation of male and female captives also facilitated the long, sordid history of the rape of African women and girls by European men, a humiliation that began before they were ever sold to New World planters (who promptly went out and did the same). In point of fact, crews were given sexual access to captive females as a matter of policy. Even a small number of females violated infrequently was sufficient to establish the assailability of the captive population.

In addition to fetters, captives were often kept below deck, in the hold of the slaver, until the African shoreline was no longer in sight. This was done to discourage revolt, for the African maintaining visual contact with her homeland was sorely tempted to return. The *Hannibal*'s Captain Phillips poignantly records the African response: "The negroes are so wilful and loth to leave their own country, that they have often leap'd out of the canoes, boat and ship, into the sea, and kept under water till they were drowned to avoid being taken up and saved by our own boats, which pursued them; they having a more dreadful apprehension of Barbadoes than we have of hell."

That the African viewed the New World as hell is related to her fear that Europeans were cannibals. Barbot records that it "has been

**FIGURE 3.** The Africans of the slave bark *Wildfire*, brought into Key West on April 30, 1860. From *Harper's Weekly* (June 2, 1860), vol. 4, p. 344. Library of Congress, Prints and Photographs Division, LC-USZ62-41678.

observ'd before, that some slaves fancy they are carry'd to be eaten, which make them desperate; and others are so on account of their captivity: so that if care be not taken, they will mutiny and destroy the ship's crew in hopes to get away." Olaudah Equiano, upon seeing whites for the first time, became "persuaded that I had got into a world of bad spirits, and that they were going to kill me. . . . When I recovered a little, I found some black people around me. . . . I asked them if we were not to be eaten by these white men with horrible looks, red faces, and long hair." Equiano's apprehensions were consistent with those in West Central Africa (Equiano was an Igbo from what is now southeastern Nigeria), where Europeans were seen as spirits, their advent a portent of death. Such was the fear of the New World, so overwhelming was the sense of separation from family and land, that many chose to starve themselves; refusing to eat was an option so pervasive that crews often had to use force. Those who resisted were given a "cat," or flogging. In the face of their past capture, present suffering, and less-than-bleak future, many chose suicide by other means. Those who could went over the side; those who could not often went insane.

But many did not go insane or over the side, and because the slave trade was, in the final analysis, a business transaction, the African had to be maintained in some fashion. Captives were therefore usually fed twice a day aboard the slavers. Their diet included horse beans, rice, yams, limes, lemons, ground Indian corn, and palm oil. Meat was extremely rare, though fish caught along the voyage was occasionally provided. Water was obviously highly valued and rationed.

Medical practitioners called surgeons were often included among the crew to attend the medical needs of the captives. Of dubious ability and questionable reputation, these surgeons were further restricted by few resources. They monitored the health of the captives on a regular basis, segregating those with serious illnesses and treating them with such physics as wine or sago, a starchlike substance. The surgeons examined captives on African coastal shores to determine their fitness, and they prepared them for market once the New World was reached.

The consequences of the surgeons' limitations and the cramped, filthy conditions aboard the slavers was nothing short of ruinous. Diseases assailing the captives included dysentery (the "flux" or the "bloody flux"), measles, scurvy, and "fever." Ophthalmia, a condition leading to blindness (possibly related to river blindness), was widespread. Yaws was as prevalent and potentially fatal. Intestinal worms added to the collective misery. Aside from the bloody flux, contracted from food and water contamination, smallpox was of greatest concern; whole ships were quarantined upon reaching New World destinations until the pox had run its course and was no longer contagious.

Spacing also contributed to captive misery, and "tight packing" occurred frequently aboard slavers. Scholars disagree over its precise frequency and over its impact on the health of the captive population, but there can be little doubt that tight packing contributed to suffering, and suffering is definitely a health issue.

In addition to those who did not survive the Middle Passage, many perished in Africa itself. Depending upon the specific region in question, from 10 to 40 percent of those captured in the interior died en route to the sea, at which point at least another 10 percent expired while awaiting export along the coast, during the barracoon phase. When mortality rates from points of capture through the Middle Passage are combined, rates that do not take into consideration those initially killed in slaving raids and wars, from 30 to 70 percent of those captured for eventual export to the Americas never arrived. Mutinies and shipwrecks added to the hosts of the dead. Slave ships, in the Dutchman Bosman's words, were "always foul and stinking." The "stench of a slave ship could be scented for miles," the slave deck "so covered with blood and mucous that it resembled a slaughter-house." The surgeon Isaac Wilson was convinced that two-thirds of the 155 who perished aboard the *Elizabeth* (out of 602) died from "melancholy," observing that once the captives were taken aboard, "a gloomy pensiveness seemed to overcast their countenances and continued in a great many." The sounds emanating from slavers usually included a "howling melancholy noise." To combat this mother of all blues, captives were brought on deck and forced to dance and sing, and sometimes had to be beaten to get them to comply. An early form of minstrelsy, this feigned animation in the midst of such sorrow demonstrates the deep and complicated history of black performance, its relationship to coercion both disturbing and instructive.

From the belly of the whale, the sons and daughters of Africa were dispersed all over the New World, occupying every conceivable place, performing every imaginable task. The terror of the passage would be forever seared into the memory of the dispersed, a memory passed on to descendants. But for all of the horror of the transatlantic slave trade, it did not completely rupture ties to the homeland. Africa would remain a central consideration in the hearts and minds of many, the dream of reconnection, of reversing sail, one of the Diaspora's central challenges.

## Suggestions for Further Reading

The best place to begin examining the volume of the transatlantic slave trade is the database compiled by David Eltis, Stephen D. Behrendt,

David Richardson, and Herbert Klein entitled *The Trans-Atlantic Slave Trade: A Database on CD-ROM* (Cambridge: Cambridge U. Press, 1999), which contains records for over 27,000 voyages, the most comprehensive response to Philip D. Curtin's groundbreaking *The Atlantic Slave Trade: A Census* (Madison: U. of Wisconsin Press, 1969). Works mentioned in the preceding chapter's suggested reading section, such as those of Patrick Manning and Paul E. Lovejoy, are applicable here as well. The literature on the transatlantic slave trade, exploring the economic, political, and social implications for all or segments of those involved, is in fact vast; one would want to include, however, Joseph E. Inikori's *Forced Migration: The Impact of the Export Slave Trade on African Societies* (New York: Africana, 1982); Joseph E. Inikori and Stanley L. Engerman, *The Atlantic Slave Trade: Effects on Economies, Societies, and Peoples in Africa, the Americas, and Europe* (Durham, NC: Duke U. Press, 1992); and Joseph C. Miller, *Way of Death: Merchant Capitalism and the Angolan Slave Trade, 1730–1830* (Madison: U. of Wisconsin Press, 1988).

John K. Thornton, *Africa and Africans in the Making of the Atlantic World, 1400–1800* (Cambridge: Cambridge U. Press, 1998), 2nd ed., and David Brion Davis, *Slavery and Human Progress* (New York: Oxford U. Press, 1984), have excellent chapters on the emergence of the trade in the Mediterranean and Iberia. The work of A. J. R. Russell-Wood, especially *A World on the Move: The Portuguese in Africa, Asia, and the Americas, 1415–1808* (Manchester: Carcanet Press; New York: St. Martin's Press, 1992), provides keen insight into Iberian developments as they relate to the slave trade. Ruth Pike's *Aristocrats and Traders: Sevillian Society in the Sixteenth Century* (Ithaca, NY and London: Cornell U. Press, 1972) is also pertinent, while Eric R. Wolf's *Europe and the People Without History* (Berkeley: U. of California Press, 1982) remains a pathclearing contribution.

For the Middle Passage, see Olaudah Equiano, *The African: The Interesting Narrative of the Life of Olaudah Equiano* (London: Black Classics, 1998) for a firsthand account. Elizabeth Donnan's *Documents Illustrative of the History of the Slave Trade to America* (Washington, DC: Carnegie Institute, 1930–35) has information on this and other aspects of the slave trade. For interpretative analyses, see Herbert S. Klein, *The Middle Passage: Comparative Studies in the Atlantic Slave Trade* (Princeton, NJ: Princeton U. Press, 1978).

A discussion of the Middle Passage as well as the origins and cultures of transported Africans can be found in Michael A. Gomez,

*Exchanging Our Country Marks: The Transformation of African Identities in the Colonial and Antebellum South* (Chapel Hill: U. of North Carolina Press, 1998). An interesting and at times technical study of the impact of Old World migrations into the New is located in Guy A. Settipane, ed., *Columbus and the New World: Medical Implications* (Providence, RI: Oceanside, 1995). Finally, treatment of these and other issues is contained in Joseph E. Harris, *The African Diaspora*, eds. Alusine Jalloh and Stephen E. Maizlish (College Station: Texas A & M U. Press, 1996).

# CHAPTER 5

# Enslavement

Africans experienced a most painful introduction to the New World. The forced march to the sea and the subsequent horrific sea voyage represent the birth of not only the modern African Diaspora but also modernity itself. Europe's rise and expansion were undergirded by slavery; its economic prosperity was fundamentally related to the exploitation of Africans (an argument championed by Trinidadian scholar Eric Williams). The vast wealth, considerable privilege, and seemingly limitless opportunities associated with American elites were all achieved on the backs of impoverished Africans and subjugated Native Americans. To be sure, a peasantry and working class from all points of the globe would eventually find themselves in the Americas, where they would also make contributions under exploitative conditions. Even so, it was enslaved African labor that paved the way for all to come.

Focus on the introduction of Africans as enslaved workers does not reject the possibility of a pre-Columbian African presence. Artifacts, archaeological remains, linguistic evidence, Native American traditions, and European explorer accounts render plausible the idea that Africans crossed the Atlantic at some unspecified point prior to Columbus. Indeed, there are references in West African sources to transatlantic voyages under imperial Mali in the fourteenth century, so the effort was probably made. It would not appear, however, that these earlier Africans achieved a regular correspondence with Native Americans, a steady commerce that for subsequent Africans was eventually established at their very considerable expense.

**MAP 6.** Latin America, 1828.

## Aspects of American Enslavement

A consideration of slavery can begin with Brazil. This vast, Portuguese-claimed territory has a diverse economic history with fluctuating agricultural periods. Northeastern Brazil was the destination of the vast majority of Africans from the second half of the sixteenth century through the whole of the seventeenth, with the captaincies (provinces) of Bahia and Pernambuco receiving the lion's share of a work force

**FIGURE 4.** Slave market, Pernambuco, Brazil, 1820s. From Maria Graham, *Journal of a Voyage to Brazil* (London, 1824), opposite p. 107. Library of Congress, Prints and Photographs Division, LC-USZ62-97202.

cultivating sugarcane. From the late seventeenth century through the mid-eighteenth, gold and diamond mining redirected as many as two-thirds of all Africans to the captaincies of Minas Gerais, Mato Grosso, and Goiás. However, with the collapse of the mining boom by the 1770s, the majority returned to Bahia and Pernambuco to produce sugarcane and tobacco. Cotton became significant early in the nineteenth century, but from the 1820s coffee was king, resulting in the growth of African slavery in central and southern Brazil, particularly Rio de Janeiro, Minas Gerais, and São Paulo.

The various agricultural regimes, fluctuating demographics, differing climates, and changing rates of captive importation meant that slavery in Brazil was multifaceted and complex. However, three aspects of Brazilian slavery stand out: First, the number of Africans imported into Brazil was enormous; second, Africans brought to Brazil were overwhelmingly male, in ratios of nearly 3:1; and third, the percentage of children brought into central and southern Brazil was astonishing, accounting for nearly 40 percent of enslaved persons.

Concerning the English-speaking Caribbean, the British arrived in Jamaica in 1655, having established a presence in St. Kitts (St. Christopher) in 1624, Barbados in 1627, Nevis in 1628, and Montserrat and

Antigua in the 1630s. Limited arable land in St. Kitts, Nevis, Montserrat, and Antigua meant that these islands could not compete with Barbados, the wealthiest and most densely populated of English colonies in the seventeenth century. Originally covered by thick tropical growth with neither mountains or rivers, Barbados had a high percentage of cultivable land, and it was cleared for sugarcane within the first forty years of foreign occupation. However, the exactions of sugarcane, combined with territorial limitations, eventually exhausted the soil.

Jamaica was also relatively abundant in arable flat land. The Spanish maintained a minimal presence for 150 years before 1655 and the English incursion. English-speaking Jamaica was "founded in blood," seized from the Spanish by a motley crew of unruly soldiers. For the remainder of the seventeenth century, it was the principal site for buccaneering operations against the Spanish. The end of the century, however, saw a transition from pirating and small-scale farming to large-scale plantation agriculture, in concert with a dramatic rise in the number of black slaves, soaring from 514 in 1661 to 9,504 in 1673. Between 1671 and 1679 another 11,816 Africans arrived, and by 1713 the enslaved population had reached 55,000, larger than that of Barbados. The year 1817 saw the largest number of slaves in Jamaica,

MAP 7. Caribbean map.

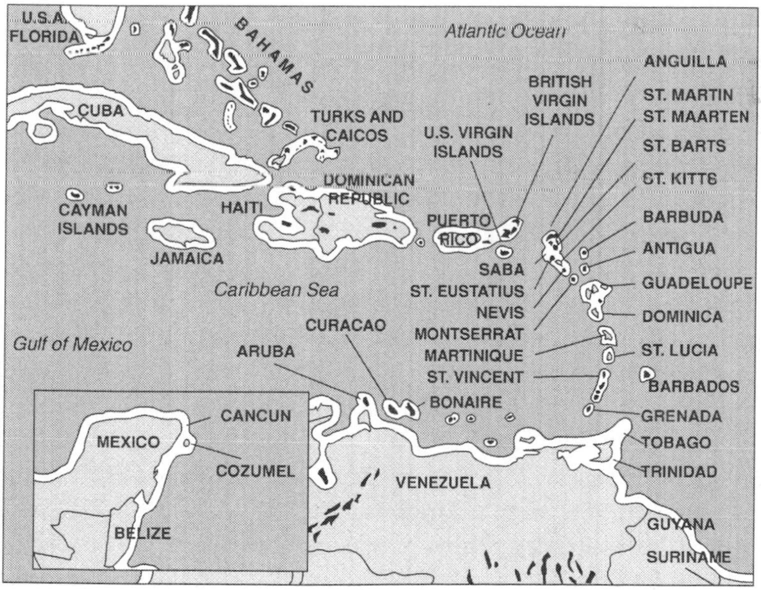

some 345,252, but by that time many persons of African descent were
no longer slaves. The island developed a reputation as the preserve of
Akan speakers from the Gold Coast, but in fact more were imported
from the Bight of Biafra. These two regions account for the origins of
some 62 percent of all Africans arriving in Jamaica, and they enjoyed
considerable cultural and social influence.

In addition to amassing the largest group of slaves in the British
Caribbean, Jamaica also had one of the most diversified economies
of the region. By 1832, slightly less than one-half of all the enslaved
worked on sugar plantations; 14 percent worked on coffee plantations,
13 percent worked in "livestock pens," 7 percent inhabited minor sta-
ple plantations, 8 percent lived in towns, and 6 percent performed
general labor. Owing to environmental needs, sugarcane plantations
were concentrated along the island's northern coast but could also be
found elsewhere.

European occupation of Trinidad began in July of 1498, and for
the next 300 years the island languished under Spanish domination
and neglect. This changed with the *cédula* (decree) of 1783, by which
migration and slavery's expansion were encouraged through the offer of land. Any purported Roman Catholic from a nation friendly
to Spain could swear an oath and receive free land; additional land
was provided for every slave imported. The cédula's terms essentially
excluded all but the French, a group that included wealthy planters,
the Irish (Northern), and others of various backgrounds, who would
later be joined by those fleeing the French Revolution. By 1784, the
island was effectively a French colony, with the French outnumber-
ing the Spanish 20:1. Immigrants arrived that year from Grenada,
Martinique, Guadeloupe, St. Lucia, and Cayenne, speaking French
and Creole languages (mixed African and European tongues). Their
numbers would be augmented by Royalist planters fleeing the Haitian
Revolution (1791–1804).

In contrast to Jamaica, Barbados, and other Caribbean islands, the
arrival of substantial numbers of enslaved Africans in Trinidad was relatively late. The absence of both gold and significant Spanish interest in
agriculture meant that Trinidad's pre-1783 population was never more
than a few thousand; for example, in 1777, there were 200 enslaved
blacks, 870 free "mulattoes," and 340 whites in Trinidad. However,
by 1789, the population had increased to 18,918, including 2,200 indigenous people, 10,100 enslaved persons, 4,467 free "coloreds," and
2,151 whites. The African distribution in Trinidad reveals that nearly

63 percent arrived from the Bight of Biafra, followed by 18.2 percent from West Central Africa, 10.4 percent from the Gold Coast, and 4.5 percent from the Bight of Benin.

The British seized Trinidad in 1797, by which time the island had over 150 sugar estates. Sugarcane had become the island's most important crop; by 1832, 90 percent of the total value of Trinidad's exports was provided by sugar and its by-products, requiring some 70 percent of the enslaved labor. The impact of the 1783 cédula was the swift peopling of the island and the emergence of a bustling export economy.

While the sugar industry was important in Trinidad, cocoa, coffee, and cotton were also grown. Cocoa production had continued from the Spanish period, expanding even more rapidly during sugar's spectacular rise. Cocoa, however, was a smallholder's specialty, principally cultivated by the free colored and black populations and therefore not as dependent on slave labor. In 1810, at least 20 percent of Trinidad's population was free and colored, owning 37.3 percent of all estates and 31.5 percent of all the slaves. The large percentage of free persons growing cocoa explains its expansion, but the fact that they were overwhelmingly smallholders partially accounts for cocoa's mere 6.2 percent of the total value of exports in 1832, together with the observation that demand for cocoa only became very significant in the 1860s, when the taste of the drink *chocolat* was improved by the addition of the powderized extract.

Slavery in the Caribbean was distinguished from its North American counterpart by the presence of large plantations and the widespread absence of plantation owners. By convention, a North American plantation was an enterprise of 20 or more slaves, whereas Caribbean plantations had at least 100 slaves and often considerably more than that. Absentee ownership of Caribbean plantations increased toward the end of legal slavery in the British West Indies, and it underscores the relatively small number of whites in the islands. In Jamaica, for example, the black population already constituted 90 percent of the total by 1734.

Captive males were imported into the anglophone Caribbean at twice the rate of their female cosufferers, although early in the histories of Jamaica and Trinidad the proportions were more or less the same. Taking the anglophone Caribbean as a whole, we can see that life and labor were extremely arduous. Early in the history of the Caribbean, the relatively low costs of procuring captives from Africa made it less expensive to simply replace enslaved workers with new recruits rather than promote stable families and strategies of reproduction in the islands. Imbalanced sex ratios and appalling working conditions resulted in a life expectancy of less than ten years upon disembarkation. In Barbados, for example, the importation of some 85,000 captives between 1708 and 1735 raised the enslaved population from 42,000 to only 46,000.

As was true throughout the Americas, newly arriving Africans, referred to as "fresh" or "saltwater" blacks, often underwent a painful period of adjustment known as "seasoning," lasting up to three years. It was during this time that captives became enslaved, whereas prior to disembarkation anything was possible, including mutiny. Seasoning involved acclimating to a new environment, new companions, strange languages and food, and new living arrangements. Above all, seasoning involved adjusting to life and work under conditions cruel and lethal. As a result of brutal treatment, the shock of the New World, disease, and the longing for home, between 25 and 33 percent of the newly arrived did not survive seasoning.

Slavery required force, coercion, or it could not operate. The whip was therefore everywhere employed, supplemented by an assortment of tortures and punishments in the Caribbean chamber of horrors. The unimaginable included burning body parts with varying degrees of heat, chopping off limbs, placing the slave in stocks, and implementing solitary confinement. Women, many pregnant, were whipped on their bare behinds, after which salt and pepper were often poured into the wounds along with melted wax – a reflection of slavery's sadistic nature.

Throughout the English-claimed Caribbean, women worked in many of the same capacities as men, particularly on large plantations. During harvest between October and March, they worked eighteen hours or more a day in the sugarcane fields and in the sugar mills; by the early nineteenth century, three-quarters of the enslaved throughout the Caribbean were working on sugarcane plantations. These plantations required greater female participation in the fields than did coffee plantations because of the disproportionate use of males in processing the cane, and it was the sugarcane plantation, generally an unhealthy place, that had the highest rates of slave mortality, morbidity, and infant mortality rates (followed by coffee plantations, and then cocoa and cotton plantations). In addition to working as hard as men, women and girls were susceptible to sexual exploitation in ways and at rates that did not apply to men (the subject of males as victims of sexual assault has received little scholarly attention, with the exception of lynching and its attendant castration ritual). Absentee owners had to rely on managers and overseers, both white and black, who viewed sexual access as their right. Many enslaved children resulted from these unions; the question of how these interactions should be understood is a matter of debate. The rewards of voluntary cooperation could have included an easier life, but avoidance of violation may not have always been possible, especially when enslaved women (and their families) risked serious reprisal for refusing advances. The element of coercion was therefore present in every case, even in romanticized unions of "consent." Enmity between black and white women was a by-product, the latter often as harsh in their treatment of slaves as white men.

The official value of the Caribbean's slave-produced exports to England was fourteen times that of exports from North American colonies north of the Chesapeake before 1765, at which time their value dropped to ten times as great. Indeed, the value of exports to Britain from the anglophone Caribbean led that of commodities from Asia, Africa, Latin America, and the whole of North America from 1713 to 1822, while the same anglophone Caribbean was the principal importer of British goods in comparison with Africa, Asia, and Latin America. Clearly, the British-held Caribbean was of enormous value and importance to Britain, premised on the backs of African labor.

In 1697, Hispaniola was formally divided into Spanish-held Santo Domingo and French-controlled Saint Domingue (later Haiti, which reunited with Santo Domingo from 1822 until 1844, when the latter declared its independence as the Dominican Republic). As important as the British Caribbean was to Britain, the French-held territory of Saint Domingue was, by 1789, the wealthiest of all West Indian colonies. The French national economy benefited from slavery in Saint Domingue as much as did the rich planters, but events on the island, particularly the revolution of 1791–1804, were arguably of even greater significance to the African-descended throughout the Americas, and these were certainly influential in France's decision to cede vast territories to the United States in the Louisiana Purchase of 1803.

*Engagés*, or white indentured servants of peasant and working class backgrounds from France, were originally called upon to provide labor in Saint Domingue. Under three-year contracts, the engagés were eventually working alongside small numbers of Africans. The move to indigo production by 1685 was a definitive turn in Saint Domingue's history, as the importation of Africans increased significantly. With the introduction of sugarcane twenty years later, Africans became the overwhelming source of labor, with the engagés acting as the overseers and tradesmen. Between 1680 and 1776, nearly 700,000 Africans were brought to Saint Domingue, producing a population of nearly half a million by 1789. Of that figure, some two-thirds were African born, significant in light of the Haitian Revolution. West Central Africans, following the earlier arrival of small groups from Senegal through Sierra Leone in the sixteenth century, would eventually account for nearly 48 percent of the total number imported, followed by 27 percent from the Bight of Benin.

As was true of places like Jamaica, Saint Domingue's plantations were characterized by increasing absentee ownership, with some owners never having seen the island. Absentee interests were represented by agents or managers, *procureurs*, who acquired a kind of power of attorney and enjoyed all of the advantages of the absentee owner. Both absentee and in-country owners were known as *grands blancs*, as were French merchants and colonial officers in the cities. Other whites were *petits blancs*, many descendent from seventeenth-century engagés, while others were such townspeople as barristers, shopkeepers, carpenters, criminals, and debtors. The petits blancs were sometimes called *faux blancs* and even *nègres-blancs* by blacks, an indication of low esteem. But is this "white trash" characterization convincing as an expression of derision, or does it ultimately rest upon the disparagement of blacks?

The concept of race, the notion that human beings can be clearly differentiated into basic, hierarchically arranged categories based upon certain combinations of shared physical characteristics, developed in tandem with slavery. The concept emphasizes difference rather than commonality, and as a tool of power and privilege it has few rivals. The specifics of race would vary throughout the Americas, but the essence of the idea was consistent: Whites and blacks, as categories of contrasting mythical purity, also represent the concentration of power, wealth, and beauty in the former case and the absence of such in the latter. Native peoples, Asians, and persons of "mixed" heritage were located along the continuum between the black–white polarities; in some societies, mixed groups achieved a stable intermediary status, where in others they shared economic and social disabilities similar to those of blacks. White elites used race to their personal advantage; poor whites accepted race because it ennobled them, granting them a status that could never be challenged by darker people, with whom they refused to see any similarity of circumstance. On the other hand, some of African descent also came to embrace the concept of race, as they suffered as a group and saw benefit in collective resistance. However, as will be discussed concerning Brazil in the nineteenth and twentieth centuries, race could not only be kaleidoscopic in variation among those born in the Americas, but even the African born did not always accept associations based upon skin color, preferring a cultural and linguistic-based identity instead.

Race was also complex in Saint Domingue. In addition to whites and the enslaved were the *affranchis*, or free blacks, and *gens de couleur* ("persons of color" or mixed ancestry). The affranchis, mostly women, numbered about 27,500 in 1789, equaling the number of whites and owning about 25 percent of the enslaved. Some 15 percent of this group lived in urban areas, including Cap Français and Port-au-Prince, and accounted for 11 percent of the total urban population. Two-thirds of the affranchis were gens de couleur, largely the consequence of liaisons between white slaveholders or their managers and enslaved females, a system of concubinage in which ties between slaveholder or manager and enslaved often carried the understanding that children from such unions would be free. As a result, there developed a sizeable free colored population by the beginning of the eighteenth century, and by 1789 their numbers were greater than their counterparts in the whole of the British- and remaining French-claimed Caribbean combined. Affranchis took advantage of the rapid rise in coffee cultivation, and by the middle of the eighteenth century they were planters in their own right. A few even joined the exclusive grands blancs club of sugarcane planters, but most were excluded by their inability to inherit or own money (or its equivalent in land) beyond a specified amount, thus explaining their concentration in coffee cultivation as well as various trades and commerce.

Because the affranchis were dominated by gens de couleur, they constituted a third racial category and were used as a buffer group between whites and the enslaved masses. Striving to be accepted by whites, the affranchis adopted their tastes and habits, and because many were slaveholders, they identified with powerful, white property interests. However, although at least 300 planters were married to women of color by 1763, there was no reciprocation of policy in kind.

Affranchis could not hold public office, vote, practice law or medicine, or participate in certain trades. By the 1770s, they could not take the names of their former owners, they could not enter France for any reason, and they were subject to sumptuary laws. However, they were required to render militia duty to protect the colony, serving in their own units commanded by white officers. Affranchis exclusively comprised the *maréchaussée*, whose chief function was to hunt down runaway slaves, a role played by poor whites in the United States (where they were called patrollers, or "patty-rollers" by blacks). By making the maréchaussée exclusively colored, the whites in power drove a deep wedge between them and the vast majority of Africans and their descendants. However, by refusing to grant them full rights and privileges, whites denied the affranchis access to full freedom. They therefore became a subject caste, with serious implications for the future of Saint Domingue.

By 1789, Saint Domingue was the site of more than 3,000 indigo plantations, 2,500 coffee plantations, nearly 800 cotton plantations, and 50 cocoa plantations. Such was the island's coffee production that it became the world's leader after 1770. But it was Saint Domingue's dominance in sugar production that distinguished it. By the time of the Haitian Revolution in 1791, Saint Domingue's sugarcane industry was operating at peak capacity, with almost 500,000 enslaved laborers on nearly 800 plantations producing 79,000 metric tons of sugar, compared with the 60,900 metric tons of Jamaica's 250,000 enslaved population. France reexported rather than consumed most of the 1791 sugar crop from its colonies, thereby supplying 65 percent of the world's market in sugar, 50 percent of which came from Saint Domingue. In contrast, Britain consumed most of its Caribbean-produced sugar and only reexported 13 percent to the world market between 1788 and 1792. The divergence between France and Britain is partially explained by wine and rum; the French were far more interested in the former, whereas Saint Domingue sugar was used in the rum production of various colonies as a result of its higher sucrose content and lower production costs.

The riches of Saint Domingue were built on the backs of black suffering. The context for that suffering was a shortened life span, when in the eighteenth century half of all newly arriving Africans lived another three to eight years. As for those born into slavery in Saint Domingue, the so-called creoles, they could expect a working life of fifteen years. As was true of the early British strategy in the Caribbean, the French determined it more cost-effective to simply replace worn-out, useless, or dead slaves with new arrivals.

By the 1780s, the male-to-female ratio in Saint Domingue stood at 120:100, down from the high of 180:100 in 1730. Both women and men were organized into work groups or *ateliers*, and both sexes performed heavy labor in the fields that included tilling, weeding, clearing trees and brush and stones, digging trenches and canals, and planting and picking. Work days averaged eighteen hours, with some slaves working twenty-four-hour shifts. For those on sugarcane plantations, the grinding season between January and July followed the harvest and was just as arduous, whereas coffee plantation workers labored under a seasonal system that was different yet taxing. Field hands were the backbone of the labor regime, but enslaved workers were also boilermen, furnacemen, carpenters, masons, coopers, wheelwrights, and stockmen. Males dominated such jobs, while women and girls performed most agricultural tasks; in the 1770s and 1780s, some 60 percent of the field hands were female. Females were also dominant as washerwomen, house servants, and seamstresses, tasks that would inordinately feature women of African descent throughout the twentieth century in various parts of the Americas. Most cooks were males, while valets and coachmen were always so. Creoles rather than the African-born filled most domestic jobs; whites were more comfortable with those who could speak their language and who were, in many instances, of partial European descent.

Like their counterparts in the British-claimed Caribbean, the enslaved in Saint Domingue maintained their own provision grounds, small plots of land upon which they cultivated crops for personal consumption. The enslaved had to squeeze in time to attend their gardens, usually on Sundays, holidays, and around noon during the week, when they had a two-hour respite. Surpluses from their provision grounds were sold in nearby towns on Sundays and holidays, an activity dominated by women. Women-controlled markets may have resulted from restrictions placed upon men by slaveholders, but such markets were probably a continuation of West African practices, where women were often in charge of local markets. As West African organizational continuities, the provision grounds and market days of the Caribbean are often cited as features further distinguishing the experiences of blacks there from their cosufferers in North America.

Provision grounds and markets notwithstanding, the enslaved of Saint Domingue were, generally speaking, perpetually hungry and consistently malnourished. This should not have been the case, since the institution under the French (like slavery in the Islamic world) was regulated, at least in theory, by a body of rules known as the *Code Noir*, first promulgated in 1685. The idea was to minimize the brutality of the slave regime as a whole and the slaveholder in particular by requiring certain minimum standards of treatment. The hours worked by the enslaved, the amount of food they received, and the types of punishment permissible were all covered by the Code Noir. As was true in the Islamic world, however, there was often a chasm between theory and reality. The enslaved were overworked and underfed.

They were also severely abused, and in ways as savage and shocking as could be found anywhere in the New World. In addition to the tortures mentioned as part of the British Caribbean experience, slaveholders in Saint Domingue added such measures as hurling humans into blazing ovens; cramming their orifices with gunpowder and igniting the powder, transforming their bodies into human fireballs; mutilating their body parts (especially the genitalia, male and female); burying victims alive after forcing them to dig their own graves; burying individuals up to the neck, allowing for the slow dismantling of sugar-covered heads by insects and animals; and so on. Could anything concocted in the Western imagination regarding African "savagery" be any more perverse?

Given Saint Domingue's prominence in the production of sugar, the Haitian Revolution instigated a "dramatic transformation" of the world sugar market, occasioning an upsurge in sugarcane production elsewhere. Jamaica and the British isles were the initial beneficiaries of Saint Domingue's demise, with Jamaican sugar production doubling between 1792 and 1805. Jamaica's production continued to be substantial if not quite so prodigious, but it would be replaced as the leading sugar producer by Cuba in the 1820s. Brazil would compete, but its market share was hampered by outdated technology and inadequate transport. Cuba continued to dominate world sugar production in the second half of the nineteenth century, but it suffered a decline in sugar prices from the rise of the French beet sugar industry between 1827 and 1847.

Regarding slavery in Spanish-held territories, Hispaniola was probably the first site to which enslaved Africans were brought early in the sixteenth century, and *ladinos*, or Africans with some command of either Spanish or Portuguese, were the first to be imported. But as early as 1503, Nicolás de Ovando, Hispaniola's first royal governor, petitioned Spain to stop sending ladinos to Hispaniola because they were suspected of inciting revolt. Instead, de Ovando requested the importation of *bozales*, or "raw," unacculturated Africans directly from West Africa. The governor did not appreciate, however, that ladinos and bozales were coming out of the same region, Senegambia, and that the former's familiarity with European culture was mitigated by their shared cultural ties with the latter, with Islam as an important factor. The revolts therefore continued, and it was not until 1513 that the Spanish began to import Africans from West Central Africa. By 1514, there were some 1,000 ladinos and bozales in Hispaniola, along with 689 Europeans.

Nicolás de Ovando may have also been responsible for introducing Africans in Puerto Rico in 1509, when he brought them from Santo Domingo. By the following year, an unspecified number of Africans were on the island along with 200 Europeans. The 1516 appeal of Dominican friar Bartolomé de Las Casas to prohibit the enslavement of Native Americans and enslave Africans and Europeans instead reinvigorated the African trade. Charles I restarted the shipment of Africans in 1517, an important decision for Puerto Rico, whose *boricua* or native population was in decline, as was its gold supply. Colonists, faced with the choice of either abandoning the island or developing an alternative source of income, chose the latter and planted sugarcane. The first *ingenio* (sugar mill and surrounding lands) was established on the grasslands of San Germán (contemporary Añasco) in 1523. In addition to Hispaniola and Puerto Rico, there was also a Senegambian presence in early-sixteenth-century Costa Rica and Panama.

By 1529, Africans had arrived in Venezuela in small numbers. Initially a "poverty-stricken outpost" of Spanish imperialism, Venezuela by the eighteenth century had become a leading source of cacao. The slave trade, insignificant before the eighteenth century, accelerated between 1730 and 1780, providing labor for the production of cacao, sugar, indigo, and hides. Pearl divers of African descent were also used in Venezuela (and Colombia). The end of the "cacao boom" around the turn of the century led to the eventual cessation of the slave trade in 1810, by which time there were some 60,000 enslaved persons in Venezuela. As for Colombia and Peru, Africans destined for Lima, Santo Domingo, and Puerto Rico in the late fifteenth to early sixteenth centuries arrived initially in Cartagena. Those headed for Peru voyaged another nine to ten days to Portobelo, where they made a difficult two-day crossing through the isthmus. Africans began arriving in Peru as early as 1529 to work the silver mines (high up in the Andes), and by the middle of the century the African population in Lima was near 3,000. In 1640 there were probably 20,000 Africans in Lima, one-half of the city's population and two-thirds of the Africans in the whole of Peru.

The Peruvian economy in general and agriculture in particular benefitted from the increased African numbers. Olives, plantains, oranges, sugarcane, wheat, and barley were all cultivated by Africans, who also produced sugar and wine. They tended the cart-pulling oxen and mules, and they fulfilled various roles in trade and shipping along the Pacific coast. They were prominent as masons, carpenters, shipwrights, bricklayers, blacksmiths, and tailors, and they were employed as *jornaleros*, or day wage workers hiring out their labor. Africans were also domestics in the urban areas, especially Lima, where they were on conspicuous display. In 1791, there were 40,000 enslaved and 41,398 free blacks and persons of mixed ancestry in Peru; by the time of abolition in 1854, there were about 17,000 slaves in Peru. The 1876 census estimated the black population at 44,224.

Briefly concerning the Rio de la Plata (the estuary formed from the combination of the Uruguay and Parana Rivers), early-nineteenth-century Montevideo (Uruguay) was the port through which southeastern slave trafficking was required to pass before going on to Buenos Aires (Argentina), Paraguay, and Bolivia. Some remained in Uruguay, and from 1770 to 1810 about 2,691 Africans were imported. From 1742 to 1806, perhaps half of the slaves entering the Rio de la Plata came from Brazil, with the other half hailing directly from Africa.

We end the discussion of Spanish slavery with Cuba. Except for Havana, there were no large concentrations of Africans in Cuba prior to the eighteenth century. The slave trade was irregular, and slaves who arrived were used for diverse tasks. The island's planter class would be encouraged, however, by England's transformation of Barbados into a sugar colony, the English seizure of Jamaica in the mid-seventeenth century for the same purpose, and the corresponding establishment of the French in Saint Domingue. The cultivation of sugarcane was unevenly developed until the 1740s, when the Spanish Crown lifted all taxes on Cuban sugar entering Spain at a time when the world market was paying more for sugar. From 1750 to 1761 the number of ingenios (sugar mills and surrounding lands) increased from sixty-two to ninety-six, a portent of things to come.

The period between 1763 to 1838 brought dramatic change to Cuba. In 1763 the English occupied Havana for ten months, effectively ending the asiento system. This intervention, together with Cuban planter initiative, opened up the island to greater numbers of Africans. From 1763 to 1792, some 70,000 entered the island, followed by some 325,000 between 1790 and 1820. The second dramatic increase was in response to several developments. First, the Haitian Revolution created a tremendous void in the production of sugar and coffee, sparking a sharp rise in the price of sugar in Europe. Second, some planters fleeing Saint Domingue resettled in the eastern parts of Cuba, bringing the enslaved with them (their ranks would be joined by planters from Louisiana after the 1803 Purchase). These developments, coupled with technological improvements, led to skyrocketing sugar production in Cuba, with the number of ingenios tripling from 529 in 1792 to 1,531 by 1861. A concomitant rise in coffee production also drew heavily upon enslaved labor, with their numbers swelled by a slave trade officially abolished in 1820 but proceeding unabated through the 1860s. By 1838, Cuba had been transformed from a land of few towns, scattered ranching (*potreros*), and tobacco farms (*vegas*) to a huge sugarcane and coffee complex. By 1862, when there were more people of African than European descent in Cuba, the island held 368,550 enslaved persons, 60 percent of whom were male, working on sugarcane and coffee plantations as well as small-scale farms (*sitios*), ranches, and in tobacco fields.

Taking the slave trade to Cuba as a whole, we see that approximately 28 percent and 23 percent of the captives came from West Central Africa and the Bight of Biafra, respectively, followed by the Bight of Benin (19 percent), southeast Africa (12 percent), and Senegambia (2 percent). Over 80 percent of all Africans imported during the nineteenth century wound up on a plantation as opposed to a town (where they were domestics, tradespersons, or jornaleros). By the late 1860s, nearly 50 percent of all the enslaved worked on ingenios under white overseers (*administradores*) and their assistants (*contramayorales*), some of whom were black. Whites also occupied "skilled" positions on these plantations, while semiskilled jobs were performed by Asian indentured servants, so-called Chinese coolies, nearly 125,000 of whom entered Cuba between 1853 and 1874 and labored under slave-like conditions.

Like other Caribbean societies, Cuba also developed a free mixed race or *pardo* category of individuals; their tally was 33,886 in 1791, a figure that nearly tripled fifty years later to 88,054, when the number of the enslaved of mixed ancestry is estimated to have been 10,974. Altogether, those of mixed ancestry represented almost 10 percent of the total 1841 population of 1,007,624. The free pardo group, together with free blacks (or *morenos*), were concentrated in the towns and eastern provinces.

Like the French Code Noir, the Spanish had the *Siete Partidas*, a series of regulations originally developed in the thirteenth century that included slave codes. The Siete Partidas served as the basis for slave laws developed in 1680 and revised in 1789, 1812, and 1842, but in many if not most cases the slave codes constituted an exercise in semantics, as either they were not implemented or, in the case of the 1789 revision, not even read in Spanish-held territories.

As was true in the British and French Caribbean, slaves in early Cuba were worked to death and replaced with new recruits from Africa. The *zafra* (crop time) and *tiempo muerte* (dead season) of the agricultural cycle were both regulated by whips, stocks, and shackles. Females, outnumbered by males on the plantations 2:1, were required to return to work forty-five days after giving birth, having labored alongside males into their ninth month of pregnancy. As expected, infant mortality soared. A key indicator of the deplorable plight of those of African descent comes from a decline in their population, from 596,396 in 1860 to 528,798 in 1887, a shift from 43.7 to 32.5 percent of the total population. The decline suggests their inability to maintain their numbers absent a slave trade abolished in the 1860s, a picture inconsistent with the claim that Cuban slavery was more benign than its counterpart in North America.

And North America was no picnic. The proverbial twenty Africans who landed in Jamestown in 1619 are usually cited as the first to step foot in North America, but as early as 1526 a contingent of African captives was brought to South Carolina by the Spanish. Further, the Jamestown Twenty were indentured servants, not slaves. It was only in the second half of the seventeenth century that the fast association between African ancestry and slavery was legislatively achieved. By 1756 the African population had increased markedly, numbering some 120,156 and nearly matching the white population of 173,316. Slavery spread quickly, with Virginia, South Carolina, Maryland, Georgia, and Louisiana serving as its foundational colonies in the South, where the enslaved initially cultivated rice and indigo with women-developed

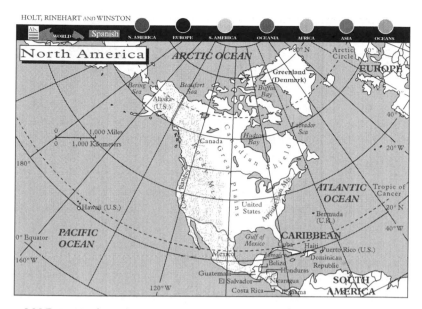

**MAP 8.** North America.

skills and techniques brought from Africa and introduced to whites. However, captive Africans were also as far north as New England, though not as numerous. Colonial New England primarily invested in slavery as a commercial enterprise; a number of slavetraders were there, and the slave trade was a major economic engine for New England until 1776. Slavetraders exchanged fish and rum for Africans, molasses and sugar, and while some Africans remained in New England to help build its ports, many were shipped elsewhere, including the Caribbean. Conversely, captives originally enslaved in the Caribbean were often shipped to New England in small parcels. By 1776, Massachusetts had the largest number of blacks with 5,249, but Rhode Island boasted the heaviest concentration, with 3,761 blacks to 54,435 whites. The Mid-Atlantic colonies of New York, New Jersey, and Pennsylvania were also slaveholding, but after the war with England the percentages of the enslaved fell; by 1790 only 28 percent of some 50,000 blacks, half of whom were in the state of New York, were enslaved. Slavery was dying out in New England even more rapidly, so that only 3,700 out of 13,000 blacks were enslaved by 1790. While rural for the most part, the total North American black population of 750,000 in 1790 also featured an urban component, principally in New York City, where there were 3,252 (of whom 2,184 were enslaved), and in

Philadelphia, where only 210 out of 1,630 were in formal bondage. In contrast to New York City, all 761 black Bostonians were free.

Toward the end of the eighteenth century, the South shifted from indigo, rice, and tobacco production to cotton, made possible by the cotton gin and the introduction of the upland, short-staple variety of the plant. The area under cultivation increased dramatically, and with it the demand for servile labor. In contrast to the early pattern elsewhere in the Americas (with the exception of Barbados), North American planters elected to create conditions in which the enslaved could sustain their numbers. The strategy worked, because by 1860 an importation of no more than 750,000 had produced a population of slightly less than 4.5 million people, more than 10 percent of whom were not formally enslaved.

Approximately 48 percent of Africans arriving in what would become the United States originated in West Central Africa and Senegambia (27 percent and 21 percent, respectively). Next came the Bight of Biafra (19 percent), Sierra Leone (17 percent, including the Windward Coast), the Gold Coast (12 percent), and the Bight of Benin (3 percent). Those from the Bight of Biafra were numerically dominant in Virginia, whereas West Central Africans were the majority in South Carolina and significant in Georgia. Senegambians were numerically superior in Maryland and Louisiana, followed (in Louisiana) by those from the Bight of Benin and West Central Africa. Senegambians were substantially represented everywhere, as were those from Sierra Leone (except in Louisiana). Of those imported, males constituted 68.7 percent and prepubescent children 19.6 percent.

The legal importation of captive Africans ended in 1808, but a clandestine trade directly from Africa, together with transhipments from the Caribbean (especially Cuba), continued until the outbreak of the Civil War. The domestic slave trade became very important, facilitating the westward expansion of white settlers and their enslaved workers by 1815. Planters relocated from the seaboard states to Alabama, Mississippi, and Louisiana, and then on to Texas. Manifest Destiny came at a high price, paid largely by Africans, Native Americans, and (later) Asians.

Although there were 8 million white Southerners in 1860, only 384,884 were slaveholders. This would suggest that the vast majority of whites had no relationship to slavery, had no vested interest in it, but just the opposite was true. Particularly after 1830, the vast majority of whites supported slavery, and the regional economy was entirely dependent upon it. The large white population was in stark contrast with the demographic picture in the Caribbean, as was the fact that some 88 percent of slaveholders in 1860 held less than twenty of the enslaved, with the vast majority of slaveholders living on their plantations. While blacks may not have been concentrated on large, Caribbean-style plantations, over 50 percent lived on holdings of twenty-five slaves or more, and some 25 percent lived on properties with fifty or more. They furthermore tended to be "clustered" on farms and plantations along rivers, in the Tidewater of Virginia, in the Georgia–South Carolina Low Country, and on the Gulf Coast, representing veritable "black belts" of people and soil. Within such concentrations, individuals from different holdings maintained a regular commerce, so that the physical configuration and frequency of interaction allowed the enslaved to somewhat approximate the intimacy of the larger Caribbean setting. Clustering not only characterized the South, but also New England as well, helping to explain significant African influences in its culture.

Unlike Spain with its Siete Partidas and Saint Dominque with its Code Noir, neither the British Caribbean nor North America developed a single system of laws governing slavery. What emerged instead was a hodgepodge of rules and regulations developed in each of the slaveholding states and colonies, in North America collectively known as the Slave Codes, which were in many ways complementary. As opposed to the French and Spanish notions of providing protections for the enslaved, the Slave Codes were more concerned with protecting the rights of the slaveholder. The enslaved were considered to be chattel, property to be bought and sold like cows and horses. As property, the enslaved could not participate in legal proceedings (unless those deliberations involved other blacks), make a contract, defend themselves against whites, buy or sell, and so on. Punishments included the infamous whip. But of course, all of this assumes an application of the law, such as it was, to cases involving slaves, when in fact whites often were a law unto themselves, treating black folk as they saw fit.

In 1850, there were 3.2 million enslaved persons in the United States, of whom 1.8 million worked on cotton plantations; others performed a variety of tasks, including raising cane in places like Louisiana. The calculation in general was that one slave was needed for every three acres of cotton. During harvest, adults were expected to pick 150 pounds of cotton per day, sunup to sundown. Given the emphasis on the cash crop, little time was available for subsistence farming. In contrast to parts of the Caribbean, some of the larger plantations featured a central kitchen where food was prepared for all, and even when there was no central facility, many received regular rations of meal and salt pork, supplemented at times with peas, rice, syrup, sweet potatoes, and fruit. It is possible for one to venture some interpretive comparisons between this North American distribution system and the provision grounds of the Caribbean, and one could assert that the different arrangements engendered docility and passivity in the recipients of the former while encouraging independence and entrepreneurship in the participants of the latter. A difficulty with such an analysis is the "collapsing" of history, or the failure to consider intervening periods of time that also affected later developments. The postemancipation period in the United States, for example, saw freedpersons more self-reliant than ever. Furthermore, many slaves in North America maintained gardens and livestock and regularly hunted and fished. North American slave gardens did not approach the scope of the Caribbean provision ground, but too much can be made of the differences.

In addition to cultivating cash crops, the enslaved in North America were carpenters, coopers, wheelwrights, painters, seamstresses, tailors, shoemakers, masons, and the like, and they were hired out by slaveholders to earn additional income. The hiring out process, more vigorous during the "lay-by" period between harvest and new planting, was similar to the Spanish *jornal* system, although the latter appears to have afforded more autonomy. In urban areas there were other uses for slaves, such as working on the docks as porters. While most of the enslaved in the various towns were used in domestic capacities and as common laborers, others built southern railways; some found themselves in the iron and lead mines of Kentucky or in textile mills from Florida through Mississippi.

The issue of nonagricultural, vocational skills raises the question of literacy among the enslaved. Through the nineteenth century, many people, white, black, and red, could not read or write in the American South (or anywhere else, for that matter). Given that the overall rate of literacy was low, it comes as no surprise that the Slave Codes often included laws against educating the enslaved; the ability to read and write could be used against slaveholder interests. Despite these concerns and the overall abysmal level of literacy among slaves, there are numerous instances of their learning to read and write. In fact, slaveholders themselves sometimes taught those they claimed to own; Frederick Douglass, for example, was taught by his mistress. But beyond the realm of the exceptional experience, and contrary to expectation, there were even a few schools in the South established for the education of black children, or in which a few black children were enrolled along with white children.

Literacy among the enslaved did not exclusively depend on receiving an education in American schools or at the feet of a slaveholder. Many slaves, perhaps thousands, entered North America already literate, some having learned Portuguese or Spanish or French, and others Arabic. Recent research has shown that the number of Muslims entering North America from West Africa was much higher than formerly believed. Individuals such as Umar b. Said (d. 1864), who wound up in North Carolina, and Bilali, who lived on the Georgia sea island of Sapelo during the early nineteenth century, were just two of a number of individuals who left written documents and represent the many literate in Arabic.

Differing skills and varying sorts of responsibilities meant that, while most were enslaved, not all experienced the institution in the same way. While too much can be made of the divide between so-called field and house negroes, as there are many instances of cooperation and collaboration between the two categories, they nevertheless represented different levels of material comfort, exposure to abuse, and even status, however relative. In the same way, the enslaved who were hired out in urban areas, or who enjoyed skills beyond the agricultural, had the potential to pass through enslavement in a fashion less brutalizing than the average field hand. Such distinctions provided one of the bases for eventual class distinctions within the African-derived community. Another basis was color differentiation, but this factor had to be teamed with some vocational distinction to make a difference. Stated another way, there were plenty of lighter-complexioned persons who remained field hands and who made common cause with their darker-hued brethren, but those who were selected to learn other trades, or who were put to work as domestics, were disproportionately lighter-skinned persons.

Those who acquired additional skills were in instances able to save money and purchase their freedom. Likewise, those whose fathers were white (the 1850 census states there were 246,000 mixed race persons out of 3.2 million enslaved) were in better position to acquire their freedom, although this was far from guaranteed. As a result, the acquisition of freedom was another basis for eventual class divisions within the black community and was related to vocational training. In 1790 there were 59,000 free blacks in the United States, with 27,000 in the North and 32,000 in the South. By 1860 there were 488,000 free blacks, 44 percent of whom lived in the South. Of course, the concept of a "free" black in a slaveholding society has many limitations, and there were any number of laws issued for the purpose of inhibiting such freedom, in the North as well as the South. Nevertheless, in spite of heavy repression, those of African descent were able to register modest gains. In 1860, black folk owned over 60,000 acres of land in Virginia, with urban properties worth $463,000; in Charleston, 359 blacks paid taxes on properties valued at more than $778,000. In Maryland they paid taxes on properties exceeding $1 million in value. New Orleans represented the pinnacle, as blacks in 1860 owned properties worth more than $15 million.

One of the more interesting anomalies of North American slavery was the black slaveholder. He or she was usually someone who purchased his or her spouse, or some other relative, to deliver the person from slavery. However, there were blacks who were clearly slaveholders in the grandest sense, such as Cyrian Ricard of Louisiana, a slaveholder of ninety-one persons. It can be observed in his personal, written communications with neighboring white planters that he fancied himself a peer. As such, Monsieur Ricard joins the company of many in places like Trinidad, Saint Domingue, and Brazil, who also saw no contradiction in the observation that they, as descendants of Africans, claimed to own others of similar descent. In the long annals of history, Europeans have held other Europeans in bondage, as have Asians and Africans. That the Ricards of North America appear an oddity underscores the degree to which slavery in the New World was racialized. But the example of Ricard, as unsavory as it seems, cannot be interpreted to mean that anyone in America could have become a slaveholder (assuming the desirability of such a goal). Does the example of Cyrian Ricard have any implications for contemporary society, where success stories of African Americans are often employed as an argument against the existence of systemic barriers over which so many of African descent have yet to vault?

Although scholarly debate continues, the essence of the thesis raised by Eric Williams concerning the relationship between slavery, the transatlantic slave trade, and the economic development of Europe and North America remains viable. While scholars may bicker over the profitability of the slave trade, there can be little doubt that participation in it provided a boost to such port cities as Lisbon, Nantes, Liverpool, and Bristol, stimulating a commercial expansion that resulted in the rise of such related industries as shipbuilding, port expansion, the establishment of businesses to service the ports, and so on. These secondary and tertiary economic benefits were important and are not unlike the central role played by slavery and the slave trade in the economy of the United States. The tentacles of both the trade and the institution were far-reaching, touching if not enveloping the lives of many. Even leading universities such as Brown, Harvard, and Yale were the beneficiaries of the nefarious enterprise. Brown University was founded in part by slavetraders John and Nicolas Brown, while the founder of Harvard Law School endowed the school with money from slavetrading in Antigua. As for Yale University, its first professorship was endowed by one of the most notorious slavetraders of his day, Philip Livingston, and the school's first scholarships came from the profits of slaveholder George Berkeley's New England plantation. We could go on.

By 1840, the American South was cultivating some 60 percent of the world's cotton, representing more than 50 percent of the value of all exports from the United States. This means that goods and capital imported to develop the United States were largely paid for by slaves. Ports such as Charleston and New Orleans were not only paid for with cotton grown by slaves but also were literally dug out of the earth by the enslaved, as was true of a significant proportion of the country's colonial and antebellum infrastructure. New York City, for example, was a major and direct beneficiary of enslaved labor, as cotton was distributed and exported from there in exchange for fees and services connected to insurance, interest, commissions, shipping and handling charges, and so on. Thus, it is not at all surprising that Wall Street, site and symbol of the world's leading financial markets, was originally the site of a slave market. The argument can even be extended, as 70 percent of the cotton grown in the American South was used by Britain's textile industry, and it was by means of textile exports that Britain financed its empire. The statement, "We built this country," commonly heard in African American casual conversation, is no groundless assertion; indeed, not to take anything away from the millions of European and Asian immigrants who also labored in the United States, the statement is more accurate than not. In fact, it leads to the following query: Just who were the founding fathers, and what about the founding mothers?

A bloody apocalypse would bring the institution of slavery to an end in the United States. But neither did that war, nor myriad emancipatory actions throughout the Americas, simply materialize out of thin air. Rather, all such actions developed out of a context of long and bitter struggle waged by people of African descent, a struggle to which the next chapter turns.

## Suggestions for Further Reading

The literature on slavery in the Americas is massive, examining general trends and specific regions and locales; the treatment, cultures, and societies of the enslaved; the lives of slaveholders; relations with other societal components, the economies affected, the role of ideologies; and so on. One could begin with Eric Williams, *Capitalism and Slavery* (Chapel Hill: U. of North Carolina, 1944), for a discussion of its impact on capitalist development, and contrast it with David Eltis, *The Rise of African Slavery in the Americas* (Cambridge and New York: Cambridge U. Press, 2000). David Brion Davis's *The Problem of Slavery in Western Culture* (Ithaca, NY: Cornell U. Press, 1996) and *The Problem of Slavery in the Age of Revolution, 1770–1823* (Ithaca, NY: Cornell U. Press, 1975) remain valuable contributions, although they are not so much concerned with the slave experience as with the implications of slavery for Western society.

As for Caribbean slavery, Carolyn E. Fick's *The Making of Haiti: The Saint Domingue Revolution From Below* (Knoxville: U. of Tennessee Press, 1990) is a wonderful introduction to Haitian slavery and is a response to the pioneering contribution of C. L. R. James, *The Black Jacobins; Toussaint Louverture and the San Domingo Revolution* (New York: Dial Press, 1938). Both of these works inform the next chapter of this book. Another highly useful compilation is Verene Shepherd and Hilary McD. Beckles, *Caribbean Slavery in the Atlantic World: A Student Reader* (Kingston, Jamaica: Ian Randle; Oxford: James Currey; Princeton, NJ: Markus Weiner, 2000). Others include Orlando Patterson, *The Sociology of Slavery: An Analysis of the Origins, Development and Structure of Negro Slave Society in Jamaica* (London: MacGibbon and Kee, 1967); Richard S. Dunn, *Sugar and Slaves: The Rise of the Planter Class in the English West Indies, 1624–1713* (Chapel Hill: U. of North Carolina Press, 1972); B. W. Higman, *Slave Populations of the British Caribbean, 1807–1834* (Baltimore, MD: Johns Hopkins U. Press, 1984); James Millette, *Society and Politics in Colonial Trinidad* (Curepe, Trinidad: Omega, 1970); Gabriel Debien, *Les esclaves aux Antilles françaises, XVIIe–XVIIIe siècles* (Basse Terre: Société d'histoire de la Guadeloupe, 1974); Sidney Mintz, *Sweetness and Power: The Place of Sugar in Modern History* (New York: Viking, 1985); Carl Campbell, *Cedulants and Capitulants: The Politics of the Coloured Opposition in the Slave Society of Trinidad, 1783–1838* (Port of Spain Trinidad: Paria Pub. Co. 1992); and Bridget Brereton, *A History of Modern Trinidad, 1783–1962* (Port of Spain, Trinidad: Heinemann, 1981). For the cocoa industry in Trinidad, see Kathleen E. Phillips Lewis, "British Imperial Policy and Colonial Economic Development: The Cocoa Industry in Trinidad, 1838–1939" (PhD dissertation, University of Manitoba, Winnipeg, Canada, 1994).

Works focusing on women and gender in the Caribbean include Verene Shepherd, Bridget Brereton, and Barbara Bailey, eds., *Engendering History: Caribbean Women in Historical Perspective* (Kingston, Jamaica: Ian Randle and London: James Currey, 1995); and Hilary McD. Beckles, *Natural Rebels: A Social History of Enslaved Women in Barbados* (London: Zed, 1989). Darlene Clark Hine and David Barry Gaspar, eds., in *More Than Chattel: Black Women and Slavery in the Americas* (Bloomington: Indiana U. Press, 1996), expand the scope of the discussion.

For Latin America and Brazil, see Gonzalo Aguirre Beltrán, *La población negra de México: estudio ethnohistórico* (Mexcio, DF: Fondo de Cultura Economica, 1972), 2nd ed.; Frederick P. Bowser, *The African Slave in Colonial Peru, 1524–1650* (Stanford, CA: Stanford U. Press, 1974); Colin Palmer, *Slaves of the White God: Blacks in Mexico, 1570–1650* (Cambridge, MA: Harvard U. Press, 1976); Leslie B. Rout, Jr., *The African Experience in Spanish America: 1502 to the Present Day* (Cambridge: Cambridge U. Press, 1976); Franklin W. Knight, *Slave Society in Cuba During the Nineteenth Century* (Madison: U. of Wisconsin Press, 1970) and *The African Dimension in Latin American Societies* (New York: Macmillan, 1974); Rolando Mellafe, *La introducción de la esclavitude negra en Chile: tráfico y rutas* (Santiago, Chile: Editorial Universitaria, 1984); Laird W. Bergard, Fe Iglesias García, and María del Carmen Barcia, *The Cuban Slave Market, 1790–1880* (Cambridge: Cambridge U. Press, 1995); Stuart Schwartz, *Sugar Plantations in the Formation of Brazilian Society: Bahia, 1550–1835* (Cambridge and New York: Cambridge U. Press, 1985); Mary C. Karasch, *Slave Life in Rio de Janeiro, 1808–1850* (Princeton, NJ: Princeton U. Press, 1987); and Katia M. de Queirós Mattoso, *To Be a Slave in Brazil, 1550–1888*, trans. Arthur Goldhammer (New Brunswick, NJ: Rutgers U. Press, 1986).

For what becomes the United States, there are myriad studies. For the experience of slaves, John Hope Franklin and Alfred A. Moss, Jr., *From Slavery to Freedom: A History of African Americans* (New York: McGraw Hill, 1994), 7th ed., is a helpful place to start. Among the more beneficial monographs are John W. Blassingame, *The Slave Community: Plantation Life in the Antebellum South* (New York: Oxford U. Press, 1972); Ira Berlin, *Many Thousands Gone: The First Two Centuries of Slavery in North America* (Cambridge, MA: Belknap of Harvard U. Press, 1998), or his more accessible *Generations of Captivity: A History of African-American Slaves* (Cambridge and London: Belknap of Harvard U. Press, 2003); Eugene D. Genovese, *Roll, Jordan, Roll: The World the Slaves Made* (New York: Pantheon Books, 1971); Kenneth M. Stampp, *The Peculiar Institution: Slavery in the Ante-Bellum South* (New York: Knopf, 1956); Kathleen M. Brown, *Good Wives, Nasty Wenches, and Anxious Patriarchs: Gender, Race, and Power in Colonial Virginia* (Chapel Hill: U. of North Carolina Press, 1996); Brenda E. Stevenson, *Life in Black and White: Family and Community in the Slave South* (New York: Oxford U. Press, 1996); Nathan I. Huggins, *Black Odyssey: The Afro-American Ordeal in Slavery* (New York: Pantheon, 1977); and David R. Roediger, *The Wages of Whiteness: Race and the Making of the American Working Class* (London and New York: Verso, 1991). A classic remains Winthrop D. Jordan, *White Over Black: American Attitudes Toward the Negro, 1550–1812* (Chapel Hill: U. of North Carolina Press, 1968).

# CHAPTER 6

## Asserting the Right to Be

The achievement of freedom throughout the Americas, however qualified, was very much a consequence of the myriad struggles of those of African descent. Their efforts would be supported by well-meaning whites and some indigenous groups. The American War of Independence and the French Revolution would contribute concepts and language to the struggle, but the enslaved did not need theoretical principles, developed to facilitate a breakaway republic in North America or to resolve class conflict in Europe, to know much more definitively than any enunciation of Enlightenment rationality could ever approximate, the depth of their anguish and yearning for deliverance.

The fight against slavery would assume any number of shapes and was waged in a thousand theaters of war, both literal and figurative. Activities from large-scale revolt to marronage to absconding to work slowdowns to poisoning were employed throughout the period of legal enslavement. However, as the antislavery struggle progressed, it became clear that the African was not only combating a nefarious system of inequitable labor extraction but was also up against a force arguably even more insidious: the conviction that African ancestry was an immutable mark of inferiority. Slavery was to leave an indelible imprint upon the attitudes and opinions of all who lived in the Americas, particularly those of European ancestry, who by and large came to view Africans and their descendants as intellectually and morally deficient. Various ideas would come along to buttress this view, including social Darwinism and the rise of pseudoscientific racism in the nineteenth century, by which time African inferiority was held as a certainty. Given the rise of racism, the destruction of slavery did not end the woes of African-descended people. Freedom was not the absence of slavery, and in any event it did not automatically follow abolition. Even whites who supported abolition did not necessarily subscribe to its full implications – that black folk should enjoy a complete, broadly defined freedom with rights and privileges identical to that of whites. White opposition to black enslavement did not mean white acceptance of black equality; the phenomenon of racism would prove to be an even more intractable foe than the planter class.

What this meant for the African-descended is that the fight against slavery, while extremely crucial, was at the end of the day only one component of a more complex combat, a lone (though major) battle in a larger campaign for freedom. Forces of oppression assumed temporal, ever-shifting guises, and the vanquishing of one target, such as slavery, often led to discouragement and bewilderment as racism, seemingly defeated, simply morphed into a subsequent form, such as North American segregation. In view of the changing face of oppression, freedom came to mean different things to different people of African descent. We must keep in mind the variable, relative nature of freedom if we are to understand the African's fight for freedom, beginning with the struggle against slavery.

## Armed Revolt and Autonomous Space

It did not take long for Africans to revolt. Rebellion began at the initial point of capture within Africa itself, continuing down to the barracoons, and it often erupted into mutiny aboard the slavers. Once in the New World, Africans were again quick to seize upon any opportunity to reverse their circumstances. As early as 1503, Hispaniola's governor Nicolás de Ovando complained that African ladinos were colluding with the Taíno population and fleeing to the mountains to establish maroon or runaway communities. Two decades later in 1522, some twenty slaves abandoned an ingenio (a sugar mill and adjacent lands) owned by the governor of the island, Admiral Diego Columbus, son of the famed explorer and himself a substantial slaveholder. The insurrectionists mobilized an equal number of coconspirators on neighboring establishments and, machetes in hand, literally dismembered plantation personnel and livestock, leaving burned houses and crops in their wake. A mixed force of Europeans and Taíno effectively ended the revolt; when the dust settled, at least fifteen people were dead, at least nine of whom were Europeans. Diego Columbus reflected that if the uprising had not been quelled quickly, many more "Christian" lives would have been lost. Thus began the first collective insurrection of Africans in the Americas, a movement largely composed of Senegambians, some of whom were probably Muslims. Senegambians would continue to lead revolts in Hispaniola through the middle of the sixteenth century, after which they disappear from the record.

Hispaniola was not the only New World site of rebellion in the early sixteenth century. Revolts broke out everywhere: Puerto Rico in 1527; Santa Martha, Colombia in 1529; the Panamanian town of Acla in 1530; Panama City in 1531; Mexico City in 1537; the Venezuelan towns of Coro in 1532 and Buría in 1555; and San Pedro, Honduras in 1548. White colonists in Panama had complained about maroon communities prior to 1556, but by that year the maroon threat fully surfaced. Ballano, an African-born leader of royal descent, led one of these communities, a mixture of ladinos and unacculturated bozales. He was lured into attending peace talks at a banquet site and, in anticipation of Haitian leader Toussaint L'Ouverture's experience with Napoleon, was immediately captured and eventually taken to Spain; unlike Toussaint, Ballano was given a royal pension, living out his life in Seville.

In 1553, the enslaved rose up in Peru and fought the Spaniards for more than a year. They again took up arms in Santiago de Chile in 1647, when an earthquake provided the occasion for some 400 slaves to rebel under a leader known as the "King of Guinea." Venezuela experienced a series of slave uprisings, such as the 1732 revolt at Puerto Cabello and Capaya; the 1747 revolt led by Miguel Luengo (Loango) in Yare; the uprisings in Caucagua and Capaya in 1794; the rebellion of Maracaibo in 1799; and the insurrection in Sierras de Coro in 1795, probably the most significant of all, led by José Leonardo Chirinos.

Maroon formation was a central feature of Cuban slavery as well. Those fleeing the institution took refuge in the mountains, where they formed *palenques*, or *cumbes*. Life in the palenques was supported by a combination of agriculture and trade. Manioc and sweet potatoes were grown, while cattle were confiscated from neighboring estates. Honey and virgin wax were sold to outsiders in exchange for weapons, gunpowder, tools, sugar, and clothing. Transactions often required third parties, such as slaves on nearby plantations, who went to town and made the purchases.

The palenques were a constant source of concern, as they inspired rebellion and defiance among the enslaved. The government tried to eradicate the palenques between 1848 and 1853, but it was only partially successful because there were literally hundreds of palenques throughout Cuba. The more permanent, better defended ones were located in the eastern mountains, including Bumba, Maluala, Moa or El Frijol, and Tiguabos, all of which lasted until the first War of Independence in 1868, when palenque members joined the Cuban Liberation Army in large numbers. The 1868 decree of the victors recognized the right of the palenques to continue to exist; some eventually faded from existence, while others became towns or rural neighborhoods when joined by Cubans of all backgrounds. One of the most famous palenque leaders was Ventura Sánchez, whose nineteenth-century community was near Santiago de Cuba.

One pattern of resistance is therefore clear: If the enslaved could flee to an inaccessible place beyond the reach of authorities, they could live in manner more of their choosing; it was not Africa, but barring repatriation, it was as close as they were going to get. Success depended upon a number of factors, including the reception of the native population. If the enslaved could reach an understanding with them, whereby they would not be returned to white authorities, they had a chance of surviving. The understanding sometimes involved forming settlements close to but independent of indigenous communities, and at other times it meant becoming an integral part of those communities, including intermarriage.

Creating a maroon society was one thing; keeping it free of colonial control or interference was another. The former was an act of resistance and affirmation of human dignity, while the latter too often saw those values compromised. The preservation of autonomy sometimes meant yielding to the pressures of slaveholding interests to return runaway slaves in exchange for continuing noninterference. A difficult dilemma, it epitomizes a series of predicaments confronted by slaves seeking freedom. Indeed, the choices facing the enslaved were severely proscribed, and the adoption of any usually carried some element of excruciating sacrifice. Freedom was never free.

Perhaps the greatest example of the maroon community was Palmares. Established as early as 1605 and lasting until around 1695 in Pernambuco, northeastern Brazil, Palmares ("palm forests") was much more than a community of runaways. It is more accurate to think of this "black republic" as an independent state, and as such it was the first created by nonnative peoples in the New World. In the parlance of the Brazilian context, Palmares was one of ten major *quilombos* or *mocambos* (terms derived from African languages) in colonial Brazil, and of the ten, it was by far the most significant; two others, one in Minas Gerais and the other in Mato Grosso, lasted from 1712 to 1719 and from 1770 to 1795, respectively, while the other seven were wiped out within a few years of their founding. Some of these quilombos were in fact combined settlements of Africans and the indigenous population, and at least two were led by African women. In contrast, Palmares practically spanned the entire seventeenth century, with a peak population of at least 5,000 and possibly as high as 30,000. Palmares was such a threat to Portuguese interests that it endured successive military attacks from the Portuguese between 1672 and 1694 at a rate of one every fifteen months, assaults costly in lives and money.

Palmares was in reality a composite of ten federated political units or *palmars*, each of which owed ultimate allegiance to the sovereign, the *Ganga-Zumba* ("great lord"), the greatest of whom was Zumbi. Although Palmares was initially founded by African-born runaways, distinctions between those from Africa and those born in Brazil, the *crioulos*, became less significant over time; indeed, given the lengthy history of Palmares, a point was reached whereby many of its citizens knew nothing of Africa or slavery firsthand, having been born in the quilombo. Friction between the Portuguese and Palmares intensified as individuals increasingly fled the surrounding *engenhos* (sugar mills and adjacent lands) for the quilombo. The final destruction of Palmares came after a siege of forty-four days, after which the Palmares ruler was captured and decapitated, his head publicly displayed to dispel belief in his immortality.

In addition to those mentioned, Brazil was inundated with smaller quilombos throughout much of its slave history. Quilombos were found in the lands surrounding Bahia in northeast Brazil, of which Salvador was the principal port and city. A major source of sugarcane production between 1570 and 1680, Bahia registered the existence of a quilombo as early as 1575. By the turn of the seventeenth century, there were reports of maroons living in the mountains, who intermarried with the local population. The tradition of the maroon in Bahia continued through the nineteenth century, when it met with Portuguese opposition and the resulting destruction of such quilombos as the Buraco de Tatú, just outside Salvador.

The maroons of Jamaica have also attracted considerable interest. With the instability of the transition to British rule in 1655, some 1,500 of the enslaved struck out on their own, forming three distinct groups. Much has been written about two of these groups: One group settled in the mountains under the leadership of Juan Lubola, and the other gathered at Los Vermejales (or the Vermahalis), in a plateau in the interior of the island. The maroons under Lubola sided with the remaining Spanish settlers against the British until 1658, when the Spanish were defeated. Lubola promptly entered an alliance with the British that recognized the legitimacy of his 150-person community, but it also called for him to fight with the British against other maroons; the policy of forming impermanent alliances made sense, but its defects would soon be revealed. Lubola was killed in a raid on the maroons of Los Vermejales, who managed to retreat to the northeast part of the island. Los Vermejales was eventually joined in the last quarter of the seventeenth century by some 200 runaways, mostly Africans from the Gold Coast (so-called Coromantee or Kromanti, after the Gold Coast port) and Malagasy captives from a shipwreck. Together in the hills of eastern Jamaica, they established communities informed by African cultures and folkways. They became known as the Windward group, with Nanny Town as their center, named after a woman skilled in war and *obeah* (the practice of manipulating spiritual forces to inflict harm). In the meantime, another group of Gold Coast rebels settled in the mountainous areas in the island's center, and they became known as the Leeward group.

Around 1720 the First Maroon War broke out between the maroons and the British, who, moving into the northeast coast to establish new plantations, suffered continuous assault and harassment. Cudjoe, an adept in guerrilla warfare, led the Leeward group, while the Windward sector, initially under Nanny's control, was marshaled by Cuffee following Nanny's planter-instigated murder in 1733. The Maroon War dragged on, with Nanny Town changing hands several times, and in 1735 the Windward group splintered into two. One of the two factions, some 300 women, men, and children, walked more than 100 miles to join Cudjoe and the Leewards. In a defining decision that revealed the complex and contradictory nature of the Leeward leader as well as the dilemma of maroon life, Cudjoe essentially rejected the Windward refugees, accommodating them for several months until they could return to the northeast. Cudjoe, for all of his bravery and skill, was reluctant to unduly anger the British; the defense of his freedom included avoiding unnecessary confrontation.

Unfortunately for the maroon community and the enslaved, Cudjoe's war weariness, or perhaps his treachery, became apparent in March of 1739 when he agreed to a treaty with the British. Its terms recognized his community as free and owners of the land adjoining to their towns, some 1,500 acres. The treaty further allowed the maroons to hunt within three miles of a white-held establishment, to pursue their own form of justice with the exception of administering capital punishment, and to sell their produce in local markets. For such liberties, however, Cudjoe sold the store. He agreed to create roads linking his settlements to coastal plantations to promote "friendly correspondence"; he agreed to allow two white men to live among the maroons for purposes of monitoring them; but most egregious of all, he agreed to fight Britain's external enemies, to kill and destroy all in rebellion to British authority, and to return all runaway slaves to their slaveholders for compensation. Prior to the signing of the treaty, Cudjoe reportedly fell to his knees and kissed the feet of the British officer, begging forgiveness.

Certain of Cudjoe's generals could not accept this turn of events, but their attempts to organize a response were discovered; Cudjoe himself put two of them to death. Others in opposition to the treaty tried to develop strategies throughout the island, especially in Spanish Town, but authorities responded with brutal repression. The end of the First Maroon War in 1739 saw the Windwards, their numbers depleted and facing eminent war with the Leewards, sign a treaty similar to that of Cudjoe. However, the spirit of rebellion would resurface some twenty years later, directly inspired by the early maroon example.

In Antigua, maroons preceded the rapid, late-seventeenth-century advance of sugarcane. By 1678 there were about 4,500 residents on the island, more or less equally divided between Africans and Europeans, but already there were significant problems with runaways, especially in the southwest, in the Shekerly Hills of St. Mary's Parish. Records show that the maroons were a hodgepodge of African groups, including Akan, Igbo, "Angolans," and Malagasy. These strongholds threatened British planters, but the latter had time on their side, with the eventual deforestation of the island as the principal reason for the termination of the maroon threat.

In the islands controlled by the French, maroons were divided into *petit* and *grand marronage*. The former involved small groups who abandoned the plantation for several days, only to return. Grand marronage could also involve small numbers, but it was characterized by the fairly permanent nature of the stay and therefore of greater concern. One of the first to come to the attention of the French was a group of about 400 to 500 in Martinique who, under the leadership of Francisque Faboulé in 1665, stirred such trouble that the authorities negotiated a short-lived agreement with them. Faboulé was granted his freedom and 1,000 pounds of tobacco, while his followers were given immunity from punishment. Faboulé would form another group of runaways, but he was eventually captured and sent to the galleys.

Guadeloupe also had its share of maroons; one group was an amalgam of Africans and the indigenous population led by Gabriel as early as 1707. Gabriel viewed his community as autonomous, and he preferred to be called "Monsieur le Gouverneur." Though they raided for livestock, the maroons in Guadeloupe were even more notorious for taking enslaved women, a reflection of imbalanced sex ratios. By 1726 some 600 maroons were living in four distinct communities in Guadeloupe.

In Saint Domingue, maroons were famous for frequent raids on nearby plantations that netted livestock while leaving fields ablaze, suggesting an interest not only in survival but also in the destruction of slavery altogether. The French responded with a vigorous campaign, and although leaders of the various maroons were captured and punished, the communities themselves continued under new leaders. In the area around le Cap, for example, leaders such as Noël wrecked havoc until his capture in 1775, only to be replaced by Télémaque Conga and Isaac and Pyrrhus Candide, who pursued the triple objectives of livestock confiscation, female abduction, and field torching. The most famous of all Saint Domingue's maroon societies was le Maniel. Established at some point before the end of the seventeenth century, le Maniel successfully defended against repeated attacks throughout the eighteenth century and witnessed the dawn of Haiti. Le Maniel owed much of its success to its location on the border with the Spanish-held eastern part of the island, from which it received support against the French. Indeed, together with the southern mountainous area, the Spanish-held section of the island was the preferred destination of most maroons, where some 3,000 were estimated to have settled by 1751.

In general, the maroon communities of Saint Domingue were overwhelmingly male, with women accounting for no more than 20 percent of the population. Most were born in West Central Africa and had labored in the fields. Although removed from the plantation, the maroons stayed in touch with those who remained, receiving provisions and news of slaveholder activities and intentions. The maroons also kept lines of communication open with free blacks who gave some assistance, a reminder that interaction within Saint Domingue society could be fluid.

François Makandal is probably the most famous of the maroon leaders. His background is rather curious, as he was supposedly born in an Islamic society in West Africa, raised as a Muslim, and literate in Arabic. Captured at the age of twelve and shipped to Saint Domingue, his grounding in Islam may have been incomplete, for by the time we encounter him on the island, Makandal is a fully emerged voodoo priest. Voodoo, *vodu,* and *vodun* derive from Dahomean words for "gods"; the religion as practiced in Haiti, Martinique, Louisiana, and Mississippi represents both a transformation and amalgamation of various religions from West and West Central Africa, specifically Fon–Ewe–Yoruba influences from the former and Bakongo elements from the latter. As a result of either an amputated hand from sugar mill machinery or a dispute with a slaveholder over a black woman, Makandal set off on an independent course. An eloquent man with extensive knowledge of both medicinal and injurious properties of plants and herbs, he developed a following of undetermined size. In concert with those who systematically pillaged estates, but unlike others content to live in isolation, Makandal developed a conspiracy to destroy slavery as an institution, and he recruited from the plantations. The blow for freedom was to begin with a general poisoning of the water in the town of le Cap, highlighting poisoning as a weapon of choice among the enslaved in Saint Domingue. As would be true in many conspiracies, carelessness led to his arrest in early 1758, before the revolt could begin, and after a brief but sensational escape, he was recaptured and burned at the stake. Makandal's career was an indication, however, of epic events to come forty years later. The revolution that would ultimately arrive saw the forces of marronage combine with those on the plantation to effect sweeping change.

In various places throughout the Caribbean, Africans and Native Americans engaged in a complex set of relations. Not unlike the dilemma facing the Jamaican maroons, the Arawak and Carib confronted the issue of runaways in their efforts to defend their freedoms from European colonial powers. The Arawak and Carib were formidable forces in the eastern and southern Caribbean, and unlike their indigenous counterparts in the larger islands (or Greater

Antilles), they used their considerable naval capabilities to both defend themselves and counterattack Spanish positions in the sixteenth and seventeenth-centuries. Runaways often reached their territories, where they either merged or formed associated but independent communities. Some merged communities reportedly began with seventeenth-century shipwrecks, such as the "Black Caribs" of St. Vincent, whose descendants were later taken to Belize, Guatemala, and Honduras, where they form the Garifuna nation (or Garinagu, as they prefer to name themselves); and the "Zambos Mosquitos" of Nicaragua's Mosquito Coast. Reasons for not forming single communities included either party's desire to preserve its cultural integrity. But the African was also aware that the Carib and Arawak had their own version of slavery, and sometimes reenslaved runaways for their own purposes or returned runaways to Europeans. Runaways were especially vulnerable following peace treaties between native groups and Europeans, a provision of which invariably called for the return of the absconded. For example, runaways were returned to the French in the mid-seventeenth century as part of a treaty, but apparently not fast enough, as token Carib compliance caused the French to oust them from Martinique in 1658. The Black Caribs of St. Vincent stopped returning runaways to the English after 1680, having come to regard runaways as societal members. Runaways from the neighboring islands of Guadeloupe, Barbados, and Martinique reached such numbers, however, that the threatened and overextended St. Vincent Caribs relented and agreed to return the later arrivals.

The territory that would become the United States also had maroon communities; at least fifty existed in the swamps, forests, and mountains of Florida, Louisiana, Mississippi, Alabama, Georgia, Virginia, and the Carolinas between 1672 and 1864. Often ephemeral and numerically smaller than their counterparts elsewhere in the Americas, these maroons were frequently related to the frontier, beyond which white settlement was sparse and indigenous reception a possibility. Enslaved blacks often struck out for the backwoods to seek refuge in otherwise inhospitable, inaccessible, mountainous terrain. One early retreat center was St. Augustine in Florida, founded as a Spanish position around 1565. Beginning in the late seventeenth century, Carolina slaves fled to St. Augustine and the neighboring village of Gracia Real de Santa Teresa Mose, or Fort Mose, for asylum; those involved in the famous Stono Rebellion of 1739 may have also been headed for St. Augustine, where they could acquire their freedom as a result of

Spanish–English hostility. St. Augustine continued as a problem for English planters through the colonial period, after which their focus shifted to the growing challenge of runaways among the Seminoles (a term meaning "runaways"). Like the Carib and Arawak, blacks either intermarried with or established separate but linked villages among the Seminoles. Africans and Seminoles became culturally fused, establishing a fortified position of their own, Fort Blount. The number of runaways among the Seminoles rose so dramatically that Carolina and Georgia planters demanded a federal response, especially after a Georgia army was repulsed in 1812. The United States government intervened; no less than Andrew Jackson himself led the charge, attacking Fort Blount in July of 1816. Confronted by the Americans, some Seminoles switched sides and became slavetraders, but this is only part of a more complicated story. When the United States claimed Florida in 1821, Africans and Native Americans responded by retreating even further into the swamps and forests of Florida. The so-called Seminole Wars ensued, lasting until 1842.

In colonial Louisiana, maroon communities were established in the cypress swamps, *laciprière*, where they grew their own crops, gathered berries and nuts, and sold baskets and squared cypress logs to outsiders. Like their counterparts elsewhere, the maroons also raided nearby establishments to supplement their provisions. By the end of the American War of Independence, maroons controlled virtually the whole of the Bas du Fleuve, the area between the mouth of the Mississippi River and New Orleans. As the maroons were in defensible terrain and the white population minimal, there was not much the latter could do for a significant period of time. The dynamics of the area began to change by the middle of the eighteenth century, such that in 1784 St. Malo, leader of the maroons, was captured and hanged along with many of his followers, signaling the beginning of the end of an era.

There were also maroon communities in the Dismal Swamp, between Virginia and North Carolina, where at one point nearly 2,000 runaways lived. In South Carolina and Georgia, maroons both traded with whites and raided their establishments. White fear of insurrection led to a number of laws passed, calling for the destruction of these communities and the killing of their leaders. Maroons invariably enjoyed relations with the enslaved on farms and plantations, and planters frequently complained that maroon influence was corrupting their slaves, inspiring them to rebel. As a result, expeditions were launched all over the South to rein in the maroons. Their numbers were reduced here and there, but on the whole maroons continued through the Civil War.

A major feature of North American society not necessarily true elsewhere in the Americas was the bifurcation of the republic between slaveholding and free states. The existence of the latter presented another option for the enslaved. The organized procession of escaping to the North, referred to as the Underground Railroad, was therefore a means to another kind of existence. Those who escorted and facilitated the runaways, the conductors or operators, numbered at least 3,200. The greatest of all, Harriet Tubman, would actually hire herself out as a domestic servant for several months to support her work. An extraordinary individual, she alone was responsible for conducting at least 300 persons to freedom, threatening to shoot any who succumbed to fear and attempted to turn back. The Underground Railroad was so effective that 100,000 persons may have escaped between 1810 and 1850, creating such a problem that in 1850 the country passed the Fugitive Slave Act, granting slaveholders the right to arrest and return runaways from any state in the Union.

Finally, the ultimate maroon formation developed in the Guyanas. Maroons in French and British Guyana were eradicated by the end of the eighteenth century, but those in Suriname continue to the present, representing a legacy of more than 300 years. Formerly called "Bush Negroes," these people escaped the littoral plantations of Surinam in the late seventeenth and early eighteenth centuries and moved into the interior, where they fought long and hard against a colonial military. Treaties were signed and broken, but the Surinamese maroons continued on, living in states of self-sufficiency except for their reliance on certain manufactured goods, like firearms. Principally informed by African cultures, various cultural groupings emerged out of the maroon communities, with the Juka (Djuka) and the Saramaka as the most prominent. Their lifestyles have been the subject of significant anthropological investigation.

### Everyday–Every Way Resistance

Somewhere between forming maroon communities and collectively taking up arms to dismantle the slaveocracy were vast numbers of slaves who found other ways to resist, and that on a regular basis. Some eventually joined the maroons, while others ultimately took up the gun. Many did neither; instead they used other methods to contest both the substance and the implications of slavery.

Although many blacks challenged slavery, there were those who did not. There were individuals who felt inferior to whites, who believed they were under the Hamitic curse and could expect nothing better in life. Certainly there were those who desired and appreciated any degree of recognition from whites. Not everyone resisted; some capitulated. The seemingly endless accounts of conspiracies betrayed are proof of this.

But many, perhaps most, did resist, and resistance assumed many forms, covert and overt, sporadic and continuous, direct and indirect. It is probably a mistake to think of resistance as a continuum, ranging from "sassing massa" in the lower register to becoming maroons and organizing revolution in the highest. First of all, individuals who experienced any substantial length of life may have made any number of decisions, and over time they would have exhibited various behaviors that were different and even contradictory. Some may have resisted at certain times of their lives and cooperated during others, while there were surely those whose actions were consistent (one way or the other). Second, any demonstrable action of resistance was not only the product of the individual's will and disposition but also the result of several calculations. In addition to determining the likely success of any given action, the individual had to define the meaning of success itself. What of consequences for family and friends? What of separation from family and friends? What of other options less risky and without the drama? These were only some of the meditations of folk engaged in rebellion, and it may be wrong to conclude that those who remained with family were less opposed to slavery, or less valiant, than those who ran away.

In many ways, simply surviving with most of your body and mind intact was an act of resistance, especially where Africans were imported and worked to death in a few years. To beat the odds, to start a family, to see your sons and daughters develop and mature, and to impart to them something of your guidance and wisdom were all acts of defiance, and though difficult, must have taken place, as the considerable population of African-derived persons in the contemporary Americas attests.

On the other hand, accounts of mothers allegedly killing their young infants, or even choosing to not have children (or sex), suggest that not all saw survival as resistance, and they underscore the relative and mutable nature of opposition. Infanticide remains an open question;

scholars disagree over the evidence and the degree to which it was practiced. Less open to debate is the use of birth control, often accomplished by prolonging lactation through breast-feeding; and the incidence of abortion, practiced throughout the Americas and especially in the Caribbean, where knowledge was largely derivative of African procedures and involved the use of herbs, shrubs, plant roots, tree bark, lime, mango, papaya, yam, manioc, frangipani, and the less popular employment of sharp sticks and stalks. Caribbean planters were convinced that enslaved women were inducing miscarriages and were turning to older women and obeah practitioners for assistance. The use of abortifacients may have been a deliberate strategy to deny the slaveocracy the labor it needed; it may also have been out of recognition of a very high infant mortality rate, in the Caribbean largely the result of such diseases as peripneumonic fevers and infant tetanus, or the "jawfall." In the United States, scholars have offered sudden infant death syndrome as an alternative explanation to infanticide, especially in those instances in which mothers were said to have accidently rolled over and suffocated their infants during sleep. Whatever the causes of miscarriage and infant mortality, it would seem that the protection of young life, as well as its termination, were both viewed as viable options.

That preservation and destruction of life may have both been consistent with resistance underscores that slavery, above all else, was a theater of the absurd, and that the enslaved faced an almost impossible navigation in a sea of dilemma. Indeed, the predicament characterized the enslaved condition; any action, be it adversarial or compliant, would likely engender unpleasant consequences. If the slave runs, she will suffer the loss of her family, and they may well be punished as coconspirators; but if she stays on this plantation, there is the certainty of unending ignominy at the end of a whip.

Women were probably more familiar with the dilemma than men; it was most likely their constant companion. Women throughout the Americas were more valued as producers than reproducers, but this observation cannot obscure the fact that they were also female and that they were objectified sexually.

The rape of African women is well established in the literature throughout the Americas; it was necessarily violent in nature. Untold numbers of girls and women were made to endure the violation, sometimes repeatedly, and this fact alone may help explain the incidence of abortion and infanticide. But what about the woman who was

FIGURE 5. Female slaves in Brazil, 1830s. From Jean Baptiste Debret, *Voyage Pittoresque et Historique au Bresil* (Paris, 1834–39), vol. 2, plate 22. Print Collection, Miriam and Ira D. Wallach Division of Art, Prints and Photographs, The New York Public Library, Astor, Lenox, and Tilden Foundations.

not subjected to physical coercion, but rather felt psychological and social pressure to yield in exchange for an improved lifestyle? What if she could alleviate the backbreaking monotony of fieldwork for both herself and her children, or her aged mother, by agreeing to compromise? Was it always a compromise? What if she were already free, of mixed ancestry, and lived in a place like New Orleans, where she would have been more valued than women not of mixed ancestry, and where her status would be considerably elevated by entering into *plaçage*, a socially recognized relationship in which she lived as a homemaker with a white suitor and in a marriage-like condition (not quite marriage though; the suitor was probably married to a white woman in France or on some plantation)? Her children would receive a decent education, and perhaps even travel to Paris to further it. Given such circumstances and options, was there a "right" course of action? Was there one consistent with "resistance?" In the final analysis, is it really possible to extract the element of coercion, in whatever form, from such relations? These queries have particular relevance in the case of Sally Hemings, described as "mighty near white . . . very handsome, long straight hair down her back," who, according to published

DNA test results, most likely had at least one child, and possibly as many as six, by her master, the illustrious Thomas Jefferson.

Ultimately, many problems flowing out of some fundamental predicament were related to the question of family. In the end, although some persons made decisions and conducted their lives as individuals, so many more proceeded out of a familial context. It was the African family, therefore, that informed the decision to resist, the modalities of that resistance, the when, where, how, and degree of that resistance. People acted in concert; they moved in groups; they fought in units. Some discussion of the family is therefore in order, before we turn our attention to other dimensions of resistance.

The literature on African families, as historical variables in transition, remains one of the least understood aspects of the heritage of the African Diaspora. There is a tendency to overgeneralize about "the African family," glossing over important ethnolinguistic and even regional differences within Africa. Not all African families were matrilineal (tracing identity and inheritance through the female line); many were patrilineal, and some were bilineal. While polygyny was a possibility in West and West Central African societies, the likelihood of substantial numbers of men having more than one wife was small, since men needed time to build sufficient resources to support multiple wives and their children, which in turn usually meant that men were significantly older than the women they tended to marry, especially a second wife. This also meant that younger men did not always have access to women, given the hurdles of economic preparation and competition from older, established men. Polygyny was therefore a function of status in much of West and West Central Africa, its seeming continuation in the Americas more the result of New World circumstances than Old World traditions. That is, other factors influenced the formation of African families in the Americas. In fact, the disproportionate importation of males to females could only heighten feelings of frustration and competition.

Planters in the Caribbean and Latin America were for a long time unconcerned with the African family, or at least with the ability of the enslaved to replicate their numbers. To be certain, the Code Noir and the Siete Partidas contained provisions encouraging the maintenance of families, and with the support of the Catholic Church they discouraged the dismemberment of families through individual sales. Nevertheless, the reality on the ground was different; planters were solely concerned with the bottom line prior to 1790, when pressures to abolish the transatlantic slave trade forced them to enact measures more favorable to childbearing. New pronatalist policies were therefore embraced at the end of the eighteenth century, such as lightening the workloads of pregnant women as their time drew near and constructing special houses or plantation hospitals for expectant mothers; these efforts were less successful than envisioned.

A strategy to produce a self-sustaining, enslaved population was also adopted in North America. However, the sanctity of the African family was hardly a consideration; North American planters were interested in their slaves' procreating for the purpose of augmenting the labor force. "Family" beyond the mother–child bond was unimportant to these planters; indeed, slave marriages did not enjoy any legal standing, although circumstances in Catholic regions may not have been so antagonistic. Like their counterparts in the Caribbean and Latin America, the enslaved in North America had to struggle to create some semblance of family life, a struggle informed by what the Africans knew of family prior to the Middle Passage. Therefore, the African family in America tended to be extended; that is, relations of significance went well beyond the nuclear arrangement. Uncles and aunts and cousins became very important, as did the reverence for elders. Fictive kinship was also critical, and familial ties were formed on the basis of experiences of common suffering, such as those created among survivors of the Middle Passage, who became relatives for life, even practicing exogamy. Slave marriages were as stable as conditions allowed, but because those conditions frequently changed, partners sold far away from one another often remarried. Such serial marriages point to the importance the enslaved attached to the institution of marriage, rather than the reverse. Abroad marriages were also widespread, in which partners attempted the difficult task of sharing their lives while belonging to neighboring plantations and farms. Enslaved women were therefore often abroad wives and single mothers, while the man's presence in the lives of his wife and children was inconsistent and variable through no fault of his.

Families also participated in cultures, and scholars continue to discuss how African cultures engaged those of Europe and Native America. Africans had to learn aspects of European culture to survive, but they also retained degrees of their own cultures. Further, while the results of such interaction varied with time and place, it was generally the case that European forms adopted by the African-descended population were heavily influenced by African culture. From religion to music to literature to clothing, European sensibility was African-ized and then reembraced, in many instances by those of European as well as African descent. In many ways, this is the essence of American culture.

Religion was a cultural fundamental, and African religions all posited belief in a generally unapproachable supreme being, with whom were associated more accessible, lesser deities as well as the spirits of departed human beings who remain active in the world. Many African religions also practice spirit possession, not unlike the bori practices in North Africa. As culture bearers, Africans through-out the Americas transformed the Christianity of whites by bringing such antecedent beliefs and practices into its adoption, which is pre-cisely what whites had done in Europeanizing a faith originating in the Middle East. In North America, for example, the African-descended gradually adopted a Protestant Christianity consistent with their own conceptual framework. The concept of a Trinity was not shocking or beyond consideration, nor was the idea of an indwelling Holy Spirit. However, the stiff, placid liturgical styles of the various churches were altered substantially to accommodate the full expression of the Holy Ghost, within which dance and ceremony were in every way consis-tent with African notions of spirit possession. The ring shout, featuring worshipers moving counterclockwise in an ever-quickening circle, was derivative of West Central African and West African practice and was widespread in North America. In these and other ways, Christianity itself was first converted, facilitating the subsequent conversion of the African to its main tenets.

Africans also entered the Americas speaking their own languages, which, like religion, both altered European languages and were al-tered by them. For the most part, complete African languages were gradually silenced in the Americas, although significant portions re-mained in areas where groups were isolated, or where the preservation of African religions required linguistic familiarity. More widespread, however, was the tendency for Africans to take European languages and infuse them with African structure, cadence, and terms, a pro-cess that began with Portuguese and continued with Spanish, English, French, Dutch, and other such tongues. The degree of Africanization depended upon several factors, but the end result spanned a contin-uum, from speaking the European language with an African accent, to changing the syntax of what remained an essentially European idiom, to so altering the language and infusing it with African content that it

**FIGURE 6.** Dance steps and movements, Trinidad, 1830s. From Richard Bridgens, *West India Scenery*. Trinidad (London, 1836), plate 22. General Research Division, The New York Public Library, Astor, Lenox, and Tilden Foundations.

became unintelligible to Europeans, achieving a Creole or *patois* status, at which point it was as much African as European, if not more. This occurred all over the Diaspora, so that "black English" or "ebonics," with which North Americans are most familiar, is not simply a function of contemporary social disadvantage but is also the product of identifiable historical processes.

For the enslaved to insist upon the retention of their culture was not necessarily, in and of itself, resistance to enslavement. Many pursued African-derived cultural forms because it was all they knew; it was the substance of their lives and was not necessarily laden with political content. But the close identification of the African with slavery, such that by the nineteenth century the only slaves were those of African descent, combined with their dehumanization and the rejection of Africa as a site of civilization, meant that resistance for the enslaved was multidimensional. One resisted not only the physical status of slavery but also the devaluation of the African person, which is about culture in the final analysis. As it became impossible to separate slavery from the African, so the fight against slavery and the insistence on African cultural forms became one and the same struggle for many – but of course, not for all. Many blacks had become enamored of European ways and saw little value in anything African. For them, deliverance from slavery required a simultaneous rejection of African culture, the source of their woes.

From a sense of who they were in relation to each other and to Africa, the enslaved engaged in all manner of resistance. Slaveholders and overseers were sometimes killed, often through the use of poison, or they were seriously injured and maimed. Work slowdowns and stoppages, misinterpreted throughout the Americas as an outgrowth of the "innate laziness of the Negro," were common. Sabotage was a related mechanism of resistance, as enslaved workers deliberately torched fields and destroyed equipment. Food and provisions were regularly confiscated, often through the offices of domestics working in the big house, who never forgot their cosufferers and were constantly on the lookout for opportunities to collude. Blacks acquiring their freedom often aided those remaining in slavery. Persons hired out by slaveholders did their best to shield their actual earnings. Those allowed to sell produce in the markets, such as market women in eighteenth-century Charleston, monopolized certain goods and controlled the prices, charging as much as 150 percent more than their initial outlay, thereby extorting additional revenues from their white customers while keeping the extra money for themselves and their fellows. So well had they mastered the essentials of capitalist entrepreneurship, so expansive was their sense of autonomy, that these women, as many as several hundred by the mid-eighteenth century, reached a point where they were unafraid to tell whites just what they thought of them. Regarded as "insolent" and "impudent," these market women dared to openly sass and make fun of their white customers. The charge of insolence resonates with the very same characterization of enslaved women elsewhere, and it provides an extraordinary moment in American history.

But perhaps the most fundamental expression of resistance was absconding. Running for freedom was widespread throughout the Americas. As there could be no maroons without this initial step, flight was essential to the development of an alternative, independent community. Escape to marronage can be viewed as the ultimate form of absconding, but there was yet another, far more unalterable voyage from which there was no return. Suicide was common throughout the Diaspora, men as well as women, African born as well as creole. The former understood suicide as a return voyage to Africa, a means of reversing sail. There are collections of stories in the United States and in the Caribbean (and doubtless in Latin America as research will

FIGURE 7. Loading coal on a steamer, St. Thomas, 1864. From John
Codman, *Ten Months in Brazil* (Boston, 1867), facing p. 20.

uncover) that make reference to "flying Africans," who became fed up with slavery and took wings and "flew back to Africa" or, in other folklore, marched in groups to the seashore, where they mounted into the sky and flew away, back to their homeland. The commission of suicide was no light matter, as it was an abominable act worthy of the greatest condemnation in many African societies; recourse to this form of resistance was a direct indication of the depth of suffering and despair.

Sometimes abscondees stayed away for just a few days or a few weeks; just enough time to clear their heads or experiment with the idea of escape. Specific incidents, rather than the overall concept of slavery, may have triggered the decision to leave: a particularly brutal beating, the sale of a spouse or child, some unbearable humiliation. Perhaps the runaway simply wanted to obtain better working conditions, or some other concession, and temporary flight drove the point home. However, often the design was much more permanent, the decision much more final. In such instances the enslaved stole away under various scenarios and traveled under every imaginable arrangement. The old fled as well as the young, though in far fewer numbers. Persons belonging to the same ethnolinguistic grouping ran away together; persons belonging to differing groups did the same. The African-born joined the creole, and from the runaway slave advertisements it is not always clear which of the two was in command. A few individuals from the same family disappeared, while whole families would on occasion risk the danger. Very dark-complexioned persons conspired with very light-skinned ones, whereas other bands were exclusively composed of persons from either category. While statistically there were more males than females in flight (at least in North America), there are plenty of instances in which groups were all female, some with small children in tow, many still nursing. It was the support of women, who remained to care for the children and who maintained the family, that often enabled men to run in the first place, and it was frequently a network of women who kept them alive as they moved from safe haven to safe haven. In sum, there was no circumstance under which the enslaved would not bolt.

For those intending a more permanent stay, the question of destination generates a number of responses. While many headed for maroon communities, others made their way to towns and cities, where they had a better chance of blending in and achieving anonymity, a possibility enhanced by vocational skills. In these and many other instances, those absconding were seeking to reconnect with family and friends, and often enough the runaway ads describe persons "escaping" to another plantation, where it was believed they had relatives. Some of the more striking cases involved newly arrived Africans heading for the coast, or toward some body of water, with the apparent intention of returning to Africa or some other place, as was true of Jamaica during the last quarter of the eighteenth century, when runaways sought to escape to Cuba by way of canoe. Taken together, these and other vignettes create a more complete picture of an enslaved world on the move, in constant motion. It is the portrait of a hemisphere engaged in an enormous enterprise of industry, agriculture, and commerce largely fueled by the labor of the enslaved, whose restlessness constituted an ever-present threat to these vast, interwoven operations. Africans were never comfortable or complacent in slaveholding America; they could never sit still.

## Facing the Enemy

The decision to directly confront the very fount of oppression, rather than create spaces of autonomy, stirs the imagination like no other. In sixteenth-century Hispaniola and elsewhere in Spanish-claimed territories, Africans revolted with regularity, actions that often resulted in the first American maroons. In Antigua, a 1736 conspiracy engulfing the whole of the island was led by Court (or Tackey), along with Tomboy. An Akan speaker and a creole, respectively, they were assisted by Obbah (Aba) and Queen, both Akan women who provided critical leadership in facilitating the Damnation Oath, a ceremony derived from Akan traditions in which the insurrectionists committed themselves by drinking rooster blood, cemetery dirt, and rum, among other elements. Court had been crowned by 2,000 of the enslaved as the "king of the Coromantees," the basis of which was the Akan *ikem* ceremony, a tradition preparing participants for war. Queen, in turn, may have been Court's principal advisor, playing the same role as the queen-mother or *ohemaa* in Akan society. While the conspiracy was exposed before it could be executed, planters were astonished that not only the enslaved but many free blacks and so-called mulattoes were also implicated. Some eighty-eight enslaved males were executed and forty-nine expelled from the island.

A few decades following Tackey's insurgency in Antigua, conspiracies and revolts erupted throughout the circum-Caribbean: Bermuda and Nevis in 1761, Suriname in 1762, 1763, and 1768–1772; British Honduras in 1765, 1768, and 1773; Grenada in 1765; Montserrat in 1768; St. Vincent in 1769–1773; Tobago in 1770, 1771, and 1774; St. Croix and St. Thomas in 1770; and St. Kitts in 1778. Yet another Tackey led a revolt in Jamaica in 1760, two decades after the British–Maroon peace treaty. With Abena presiding as the Akan queen-mother in Jamaica, over 1,000 slaves raised havoc for six months; some sixty whites died, compared with 600 of the enslaved after Tackey was killed by the maroon leader Captain Davy of Scotts Hall. Well organized and widespread, the revolt was Akan based, incorporating participants from a number of parishes. Taking an oath similar to the 1736 Antiguan Damnation Oath, the Akan sought to destroy slavery and replace it with a society based upon West African models. They found succor in the example of the Windward and Leeward maroons, and they sought to extend the freedoms the maroons enjoyed. However, as irony would have it, it was the Leewards and Windwards who, in compliance with the 1739 treaty, fought alongside the planters to end the 1760 revolt; they would do the same in the revolts of 1761, 1765, and 1766, all Akan-led conspiracies betrayed by informants. The Leewards, particularly the Accompong and Trelawny Town groups, were rewarded with twice as much money as were the Windward groups of Scotts Hall, Moore Town, and Charles Town, whose participation was considerably less enthusiastic.

Maroon opposition to these revolts would eventually return to haunt them. The enslaved could not help but feel ambivalent, at best, toward the maroons, unsure if they were friend or foe. Conversely, the maroons had become contemptuous of the slaves but never comfortable in their role as treaty partners with the British. They were wary of the planters and the colonial government, concerned about the latter's continual encroachment and attempts to bring the maroons under their jurisdiction. Tensions came to a head in 1795, at the height of the Haitian Revolution, when conflict erupted between the Trelawny Town maroons and the local government of Montego Bay of St. James Parish. The Trelawny Town War ensued until the following year, with minimal slave support for the maroons. Indeed, the other Leeward group, the Accompong, fought against the Trelawnys on the side of the British, whereas the Windwards, as a whole more distrustful of the planters and more independent, offered the British little in the way of assistance. In the end, the Trelawnys were defeated and some 568 were deported, first to Nova Scotia in June of 1796 and ultimately to Sierra Leone. Their land, some 1,500 acres, was seized by the British.

The war against slavery in Jamaica continued, but the end of the eighteenth century saw an important development in the insurrection movement. An uprising led by Cuffy, another Akan speaker, was this time composed of several ethnolinguistic groups in addition to the Akan. This represented a heightened awareness of similarities among the enslaved, and it suggests they were moving away from specific African groups to a broader sense of African-derived commonality. The zenith of this new corporate expression took place in 1831–1832, when some 20,000 slaves from all ethnolinguistic backgrounds, together with the Jamaican-born slaves or creoles, waged a widespread war against the slaveocracy. The best organized of all of Jamaica's slave revolts, it proved to be the most costly to repress; it was a critical factor in the eventual collapse of slavery in the British Caribbean, together with major uprisings in Barbados in 1816 and Demerara (what is now Guyana) in 1823.

Similar kinds of disturbances, attributed again to the Akan, were taking place in eighteenth-century New York City. The port had a significant slave population during the period: Between 1700 and 1774, at least 6,800 slaves were imported, 41.2 percent of whom were born in Africa. Before 1742, 70 percent came from Caribbean and American sources, with thousands arriving from Barbados and Jamaica, underscoring the interconnectedness of enslaved populations throughout the Americas. After 1742, however, 70 percent came directly from Africa. This turnabout was related to the revocation of the asiento after 1750, when Spanish markets were closed to English slavers and traders flooded New York and other English colonies with captives. The enslaved loaded and unloaded at docks, slips, and warehouses along the East River, labored in shipbuilding and construction industries, ferried between Long Island farms and the city, contributed to public works, served as domestics, and sold so much produce in the city streets that the Common Council curbed their activities in 1740.

Those from Jamaica and other Caribbean locations would have been aware of slave revolts and unrest in the islands; some had in fact been shipped to New York because of their participation. It is not surprising, then, that the Akan played prominent roles in the New York City rebellion of 1712, when "some Negro slaves of ye Nations of Carmantee and Pappa plotted to destroy all the White[s] in order to obtain their freedom." Nine were killed and five or six wounded before the uprising ended; twenty-one were executed by hanging, burning, or being broken at the wheel. Six ended their own lives. The conspiracy of

1741 involved similar participation from these and other ethnolinguistic groups, when it was believed (partially informed by white paranoia) that some 2,000 slaves were poised to torch the city. Sixteen blacks and four whites (judged coconspirators) were hanged, thirteen blacks were burned at the stake, and another seventy-one were expelled from the island following mass hysteria and a sensational trial.

Brazil experienced many slave insurrections that, like those in Jamaica and to a lesser extent New York City, tended to be organized along ethnolinguistic lines. In particular, the northeastern province of Bahia was a hotbed of discontent, notorious for slave revolts in the first half of the nineteenth century, and it is there that a multiplicity of identities arising from the intersection of a variety of elements that included racial intermixing, free versus slave statuses, urban versus rural settings, and religious adherence can be discerned. The Hausa, Muslims from what is now northern Nigeria, had been implicated in a revolt in Bahia in 1807, when the Hausa near the city of Salvador were accused of a conspiracy to capture ships and reverse sail to West Africa. Enslaved and free Hausa plotted together, and the two leaders of the conspiracy were executed. Two years later, in January of 1809, almost 300 slaves, again mostly Hausa, attacked the town of Nazaré das Farinhas in search of food and weapons. The attack was beaten back and eighty-three persons were captured, women and men. The 1809 revolt saw increased non-Hausa participation, in the form of "Jêjes" or Aja–Fon–Ewe from Dahomey and "Nagôs" or Yoruba from what is now southwestern Nigeria. Between 1810 and 1818 were three more revolts of significance, the second of which involved Nagôs under Hausa leadership headed by a *malomi* or *malām*, a Muslim religious leader. The revolts continued with regularity through the 1820s to 1835.

It was in the latter year that the insurrection of the *Malês* took place, a term referring to African Muslims who were by then mostly Nagôs rather than Hausa. Islam had become an important religion in Bahia, but it was not the dominant religion among blacks, nor were all Nagôs Muslim. In January of 1835, up to 500 Africans, enslaved and free, mostly Muslim but also non-Muslim, took to the streets of Salvador under Muslim leadership. The plan called for the conspirators to link with the enslaved in the surrounding plantations, but betrayal forced them to begin the uprising prematurely. Brutally repressed with over seventy killed, the Malê revolt revealed the importance of Islam and an impressive level of Arabic literacy among the participants, who wore

distinctive clothing, maintained their own religious schools, and observed Islamic rituals such as fasting Ramadan. The 1835 revolt also
suggests that participating Africans rejected the notion of race, preferring their own ethnolinguistic identities. The rebels sought to kill not
only whites but also "mulattoes" and crioulos (creoles or Brazilian-
born blacks), a reflection of not only racial ambiguities but also significant cultural differences. The 1835 revolt, therefore, was a Muslim-
led, mostly Nagô effort that targeted whites and Brazilian blacks while
also rejecting Africans from Congo and Angola for cultural and religious purposes. In the end, hundreds were sent to the galleys, imprisoned, lashed, or expelled from Bahia, with some returning to West
Africa. In such a context, a single, all-inclusive definition of blackness
would have been highly elusive.

As unrelenting and courageous as the Brazilian and Caribbean uprisings were, the single most far-reaching revolt in the New World took
place in Saint Domingue. Although the former uprisings were crucial
to the eventual abolition of slavery, the Haitian Revolution stands apart
as the only revolt to militarily defeat the slaveocracy and colonialism,
and it is the only revolt that ended slavery directly. That the enslaved
and their free black allies freed themselves sent shock waves throughout
the Americas, striking terror in the hearts and minds of slaveholders all
over. Word of the revolution also reached the ears of cosufferers from
Virginia to Bahia, and it served as a model for one of the most important conspiracies in North America. News traveled not only through
slaveholder conversations and newspapers but also through black seamen, underscoring that blacks regularly plied the seas in ships other
than slavers. But in addition to information were enslaved individuals
themselves, either expelled from Saint Domingue or in the company
of slaveholders fleeing to other parts. So it was that on the island of
Curaçao, as one example, several of the enslaved from Saint Domingue
joined Tula in his 1795 revolt against the Dutch.

The repercussions of the 1789 French Revolution were far-
reaching, to say the least. In Saint Domingue, white planters took
advantage of the new situation to agitate and maneuver for greater autonomy of their own. Although there were serious political differences
between them over developments in France, they became one in resist-
ing attempts of affranchis (free blacks and so-called persons of color)
to join their ranks and enjoy equal liberties. The enslaved, observing
the dissension and rancor, began to realize that all this talk of freedom
and liberty, combined with the unstable situation on the ground, was

a unique opportunity to do something about their own freedom. The enslaved on several plantations in the North began holding clandestine meetings in the woods, initially broken up by the maréchaussée (hunters of runaway slaves) and the execution of leaders. The meetings nevertheless continued, and by August 22, 1791, the date of the revolution's commencement, leaders from northern plantations had been meeting for weeks, planning the wide-scale revolt. At the Lenormand de Mézy plantation in Mourne-Rouge, they finalized their plans to set it off.

The leaders of the conspiracy included Boukman Dutty, a voodoo priest, Jean-François, and Georges Biassou; the first two apparently had some maroon experience. In an instructive example of how relatively privileged persons were not necessarily narrowed by that privilege but could instead see the larger picture, Toussaint L'Ouverture, the eventual leader of the revolution, was a black affranchi and a coachman. He was in the background in the early days, serving as a link among the leaders. Women played important roles as well, and their ranks included Cécile Fatiman, a voodoo high priestess or *mambo* severally described as a "green-eyed mulatto woman with long silken black hair." In the dense forest of Bois-Caïman, she and Boukman officiated a solemn voodoo ceremony for the conspirators that was not unlike the Damnation Oath in Antigua and Jamaica, again demonstrating the centrality of African religions.

At ten o'clock on the morning of August 22nd, the enslaved arose and torched plantation after plantation in the North, destroying everything in their path. By the eighth day of the insurrection, some 184 sugar plantations had been destroyed in seven parishes, rising to 200 sugar and 1,200 coffee plantations by September's end. By the end of November, some 80,000 out of 170,000 enslaved in the North had burst their chains, attacking both symbol and substance of power. This initial eruption was soon channeled into more manageable military order, as the insurrectionists were organized into bands under officers answering to Jean-François, who assumed the generalship following Boukman's capture and decapitation by the French, his head stuck on a pole and displayed in le Cap's public square. After initially indicating a willingness to settle for less than full freedom, the revolution's leadership was forced by the masses to persevere in the fight.

The Haitian Revolution would take many unpredictable, bewildering shifts and turns. Unlike those in the North, the enslaved in the South and West of the island were not as organized or cohesive, and they were overshadowed by the politics of the free blacks and gens de couleur (persons of color or mixed ancestry). Matters spun out of control, with free blacks and gens de couleur teaming up to fight white planters in the South. The enslaved were enlisted to fight on both sides and therefore fought each other. Further developments and the realization that the gens de couleur were also slaveholders, even more so than whites, led the enslaved in the South to come together and fight for their own interests. The combination of insurrection and conflicts between Britain, France, and Spain led the French to abolish slavery throughout Saint Domingue on October 31, 1793. For the most part, however, little changed for the exslaves. Although they could no longer be whipped or tortured, they were still landless, legally bound to the plantations of former slaveholders. Many continued to run away or commit acts of sabotage.

In the meantime, Toussaint had emerged as leader of the forces in the North, under whom served Dessalines, Henri-Christophe, his brother Paul, and his adopted nephew Moïse. By 1798, after further intervention by the British, Toussaint had taken control of both the North and the West, with the South under the control of Rigaud, leader of the mixed race elite. Civil war (or fratricide) ensued, with Rigaud and those under his command suffering defeat. By 1801 and the termination of the civil war, Toussaint was the single leader of a slaveless Saint Domingue, but it remained a French colony. Continuing conflict with France eventually led Toussaint to accept an invitation to a meeting to negotiate a settlement, where he was promptly arrested and shipped to France. He would remain in the French Alps for the rest of his life, dying of consumption, in isolation. His lieutenant Dessalines, now commander of a unified black and mixed race army, went on to defeat the French and to declare independence on January 1, 1804. The island would henceforth be called Haiti, its original Arawak name.

The Haitian Revolution stands as a crowning achievement of those Africans determined to deliver themselves from American slavery. In the short term, however, the fall of slavery in Saint Domingue ironically led to the expansion of the institution elsewhere in the attempt to replace the island as a leading sugar producer. As for Haiti itself, those who struggled so valiantly against tyranny have only met with a U.S.-led policy of ostracism and indifference ever since. The island's poverty endures.

The struggle in Haiti was joined by forces to the north, on the North American mainland, where there were a number of revolts. One of the more striking examples was the prior Stono Rebellion of 1739, when a contingent took up arms twenty miles west of Charleston, South Carolina and marched through the countryside wrecking havoc. South Carolina at this time had a black population of some 39,000 (compared with 20,000 whites), 70 percent of whom were from West Central Africa. The revolt was put down after several days and the deaths of thirty whites and forty-four blacks.

Another development was the response of those of African descent to the American War of Independence, a conflict financed by black labor. Blacks fought on both sides of the war with the hope of ensuring their freedom, so it is not inaccurate to characterize their participation as a slave revolt coinciding with, or taking advantage of, an anticolonial struggle. Those who fought with the colonies, some 5,000 out of 300,000, were mostly from the North and only entered American ranks after considerable vacillation by the Continental Army, which under George Washington had forbade the participation of blacks, only to later amend that policy. Most of the colonies also reversed themselves and allowed for both enslaved and free blacks to serve (with the exceptions of Georgia and South Carolina). The cause of the colonies' reversal was the November 7, 1775 declaration of Lord Dunmore, governor of Virginia, freeing all slaves and indentured servants who bore arms on the side of the British. As a result, it is estimated that Georgia lost 75 percent of its enslaved population (of 15,000), while Virginia and South Carolina combined may have lost some 55,000 slaves; it is not clear precisely how many of these actually fought for the British, but even if they only ran away and did not formally join the British, their actions still represented a significant defection.

Blacks who fought for the British had every right to do so. Indeed, the Declaration of Independence, that oft-quoted articulation of a desire for freedom and equality, absolutely ignored the plight of the enslaved. This comes as no surprise, since many of the Declaration's signatories were themselves slaveholders. In a surreal echo of the second-century Greek physician Galen, Thomas Jefferson, principal architect of both the Declaration and the Constitution, reveals his deep-seated reservations and overall racist sentiments concerning the African in his *Notes on the State of Virginia* (1781–1782):

> The first difference which strikes us is that of colour.... And is this difference of no importance? Is it not the foundation of a greater or less share of beauty in the two races? Are not the fine mixtures of red and

white, the expressions of every passion by greater or less suffusions of colour in the one, preferable to that eternal monotony, which reigns in the countenances, that immoveable veil of black which covers all the emotions of the other race? Add to these, flowing hair, a more elegant symmetry of form, their own judgment in favour of the whites, declared by their preference of them, as uniformly as is the preference of the Oranootan for the black women over those of his own species... They are more ardent after their female: but love seems with them to be more an eager desire, than a tender delicate mixture of sentiment and sensation. Their griefs are transient. Those numberless afflictions, which render it doubtful whether heaven has given life to us in mercy or in wrath, are less felt, and sooner forgotten with them. In general, their existence appears to participate more of sensation than reflection... Comparing them by their faculties of memory, reason, and imagination, it appears to me, that in memory they are equal to the whites; in reason much inferior, as I think one could scarcely be found capable of tracing and comprehending the investigations of Euclid; and that in imagination they are dull, tasteless, and anomalous.... This unfortunate difference of colour, and perhaps of faculty, is a powerful obstacle to the emancipation of these people. Many of their advocates, while they wish to vindicate the liberty of human nature, are anxious also to preserve its dignity and beauty. Some of these, embarrassed by the question "What further is to be done with them?" join themselves in opposition with those who are actuated by sordid avarice only. Among the Romans emancipation required but one effort. The slave, when made free, might mix with, without staining the blood of his master. But with us a second is necessary, unknown to history. When freed, he is to be removed beyond the reach of mixture. (*Notes on the State of Virginia*, W.W. Norton and Co., 1972, pp. 138–143)

This distillation of racism into its two core components – the rejection of African somatic form and the dismissal of African comparable intelligence – is notable for both its inimitable style and devastating effect. For Jefferson, the racial chasm was unbridgeable, a certitude that could only encourage rebellion.

Smaller revolts followed the American War of Independence, but in August of 1800, Gabriel Prosser and Jack Bowler met with an army of over 1,000 of the enslaved six miles outside of Richmond, Virginia. Having planned their assault for months, they marched on the city only to be thwarted by a powerful storm and the previous betrayals of two slaves, by whom the governor, fully informed of the conspiracy, called out the militia. Many were arrested and thirty-five executed; Prosser himself was captured in late September and also killed.

The Denmark Vesey conspiracy of 1822 also developed in an urban setting – Charleston – and demonstrates the interconnectedness of the African Diaspora by the early nineteenth century. Vesey, born either in the Caribbean or Africa, was a fifty-five-year-old seafarer who had purchased his freedom in 1800. Like Toussaint, he lived relatively well as a carpenter in Charleston, but he became persuaded by the suffering of the masses that there was more to life than his personal comfort. Organizing a revolt that took into consideration differences among the enslaved, he formed columns of distinct groups, such as the Igbo and Gullah (West Central Africans, Gola from West Africa, or both). African religious practices and Christianity were both observed out of respect for diversity. Vesey evoked the Haitian Revolution, predicting that help would arrive from that island and Africa itself, if only those in and around Charleston would take the initiative. All of this suggests that Vesey's followers, possibly as many as 9,000, could grasp his vision of a black world, in which the cause of freedom transcended divisions of birthplace and language. But the refrain is all too familiar: Made aware of the conspiracy by informants, white authorities preempted the revolt and arrested suspects; thirty-five blacks were hanged and forty-three deported to either Africa or the Caribbean.

David Walker may have been in Charleston at the time of the Vesey conspiracy; something certainly inspired him to pen his famous anti-slavery *Appeal* in 1829, in which he called for a general uprising in clear language. Walker died in Boston under very suspicious circumstances the following year, but Nat Turner attempted to answer his summons, launching a large-scale revolt in August of 1831 in Southampton, Virginia. A religious man and mystic, Turner interpreted that year's solar eclipse in February to be the divine signal for the apocalypse, and he launched the revolt on August 21. Within twenty-four hours, some sixty whites were killed, including Turner's owner and family. When the smoke cleared, over 100 of the enslaved had been killed in combat, and another 13 were hanged (along with three free blacks). Captured on October 30, Turner was executed on November 11. The revolts would continue in less dramatic fashion, only to flare up one more time just before the Civil War, when John Brown's company of less than fifty men, including several blacks, raided the federal arsenal at Harpers Ferry, Virginia on October 16, 1859. John Brown's leadership, reminiscent of the Zanj revolt in ninth-century Iraq under 'Alī b. Muḥammad, points to the fact that whites were involved in a number of these uprisings, usually in supportive roles. Federal and state

**FIGURE 8**. Hanging a slave, South Carolina, 1865. From *Harper's Weekly* (Sept. 30, 1865), p. 613.

troops overwhelmed Brown's small force, killing many and hanging others. On December 2, John Brown was also hanged, but only after his self-sacrifice and total identification with the enslaved had caused a sensation throughout the South.

## Slavery's End?

The cumulative effect of all of these acts, large and small, was to undermine the institution of slavery throughout the Americas. Resistance increased slavery's costs, affecting the bottom line while raising the level of danger. Resistance also emboldened the oppressed, making the entire system increasingly unmanageable. Slavery expired with a whimper in some places, while in others it required herculean efforts to subdue. In the end, the antislavery struggle of the enslaved themselves was fundamental to abolition.

But abolition was a long process informed by other factors as well. Throughout the Americas there were those, black and white, who opposed the slave trade or slavery and fought for their destruction by way of antislavery publications (pamphlets, newspapers, novels, and slave narratives) and government petitions, seeking legislative means to this end. In North America, antislavery sentiment became significant following the American War of Independence, as whites struggled with Enlightenment ideas and the Bible. Manumission and antislavery societies, first organized by the Quakers in 1775, were in every state from Massachusetts to Virginia by 1792, in tandem with similar forces in Britain. A direct consequence of their agitation was the passing of legislation in 1807 (effective in 1808) by both Britain and the United States outlawing the transatlantic slave trade. The trade continued illegally and without significant efforts on the part of the United States to enforce the ban, but the story with Britain was different. While maintaining its slave-based colonies in the Caribbean, Britain gradually committed its naval capabilities to interdicting the trade. They had some success, but it was not possible to police all nations and parties trafficking in such a vast ocean. The real effect of the ban in the United States, where the westward expansion of commercial agriculture required labor, was the acceleration of the domestic slave trade.

Antislavery literature included the important 1789 publication of Olaudah Equiano's *The Interesting Narrative of the Life of Olaudah Equiano, or Gustavus Vassa*. Antislavery sentiment in the United States intensified after 1815, resulting in such papers as white abolitionist William Lloyd Garrison's *Liberator*, first appearing in January 1831, and religious treatises such as James G. Barney's *Letter to the Ministers and Elders* in 1834 and Theodore Weld's *The Bible Against Slavery* in 1837. Black abolitionists had their own newspapers, including the first black newspaper, *Freedom's Journal*, published in 1827 by John Russwurm and Samuel Cornish. Others included the *National Watchman*, published by Henry Highland Garnet and William G. Allen, and the *North Star*, begun by Frederick Douglass in 1847. Important slave narratives included Douglass's own story, first published in 1845 and subsequently revised, while the most prominent antislavery novel was Harriet Beecher Stowe's 1852 *Uncle Tom's Cabin*. Selling more than 300,000 copies in its first year of publication, its description of the horrors of slavery was also dramatically translated to the stage. Whether in print or theater, the effect was electrifying.

As just one example of organized antislavery activity outside of the United States, Brazil also witnessed the development of a significant abolitionist movement. Before 1850, independence leader José Bonifácio de Andrada e Silva spoke out against slavery, although his protests were rejected by Brazil's ruling class. In the late 1860s, a number of antislavery societies were created, consisting for the most part of persons of mixed ancestry and relative privilege. Perhaps the most important was Antônio Frederico de Castro Alves, who recited his poetry before large gatherings and was involved with two antislavery societies in Salvador and Recife prior to his death in 1871. José do Patrocínio of Rio de Janeiro, whose father was a Portuguese priest, was a former slave who achieved his freedom and went on to purchase two newspapers, turning them into antislavery organs. In 1880, Patrocínio would be instrumental in the creation of an antislavery umbrella organization called the Abolitionist Confederation, and he was crucial in making the debate over slavery much more public. The more elite Brazilian Anti-Slavery Society was founded by Joaquim Nabuco and intellectual André Pinto Rebouças in 1880, and it was the organization through which *The Abolitionist* newspaper was begun. A final example of leading Brazilian abolitionists was Luís Anselmo da Fonseca, a medical professor who published *Slavery, the Clergy, and Abolition*, the most influential critique of slavery of the period, in which he took both the Catholic Church and free black Brazilians to task for their complicity in slavery.

One of the more arresting developments to come out of the antislavery campaign was the movement to repatriate the African-descended population to Africa. These efforts reveal how participants in the same enterprise came with entirely different assumptions and motivations. For Africans and their descendants, the opportunity to return to Africa represented the possibility to reverse sail and reconnect, to escape the oppressive, racist atmosphere of the Americas and start over as pioneers, or to fulfill a missionary zeal to bring the Christian gospel to "benighted heathens." Whites who supported repatriation were divided. Those in Britain were interested in relocating the "black poor" to Africa, where they could both improve their lives and facilitate British interests in "legitimate" (nonslave) trade. Whites in the United States, on the other hand, were entirely cynical in their approach, advocating the project to rid the land of free blacks, thereby actually strengthening slavery. Men like Thomas Jefferson and Abraham Lincoln were convinced that Africans could never become the equal of whites, and that repatriation to Africa, or deportation to the Caribbean, was the best solution for resolving "the freedman question." This is consistent with the fact that whites could be opposed to the slave trade but not slavery, or, if they were opposed to slavery, were not necessarily advocating full citizenship rights for blacks; these attitudes were evident in the U.S. North, where blacks, though technically free, suffered from a range of discriminatory laws, practices, and even violence.

Whatever their various impulses, repatriation to Africa from Britain and Canada, the latter the destination for Jamaican maroons and a refuge for blacks who fought for the British during the American War of Independence, began in 1787 and centered on the British settlement at Sierra Leone. These initial groups would be joined, beginning in the nineteenth century, by captives taken from slavers bound for the Americas, the result of the British effort to outlaw the trade. Sierra Leone received thousands of such recaptives, reaching a peak in the 1840s. As for the United States, repatriation became an organized, state-sanctioned enterprise beginning in 1817 with the founding of the American Colonization Society, which in 1822 began a colony in what would become Monrovia, Liberia. Money was raised to finance the voyages, and by 1830 some 1,420 persons had sailed to Liberia. All told, not more than 15,000 blacks participated in the return, to which can be added recaptives liberated from slavers by the American navy. The scheme was opposed by abolitionists, white and black, but in both Sierra Leone and Liberia, the return of Africans and their descendants from the Americas would have a profound effect upon the future course of those nations. Fundamentally, the cultures of the returnees had been altered by the experience in the Americas; they did not necessarily identify with Africans who had never left the continent. Stratification developed largely along lines of cultural differences between the returnees and the indigenous population, with the former arrogating privilege and power for themselves. It was a recipe for disaster, the consequences of which continue to reverberate.

While many Africans and their descendants returned to the continent by way of American and British government and private assistance, others financed their own way. In North America, Paul Cuffe, possibly of Akan (but also of Native American) descent, personally transported thirty-eight persons back to Africa in 1815, financing the entire enterprise himself. Perhaps even more spectacular was the return of people from Brazil and Cuba to West Africa, particularly to what is now southwestern Nigeria and Benin. Those not sent back as conspirators were usually members of *cabildos* (in Cuba) and *irmandades* (Brazil), fraternal organizations based upon purported membership in ethnolinguistic groups. These brotherhoods pooled their resources to pay for such return voyages, among other things. Rather than blending in upon their return, persons originally taken from the Bight of Benin (many of whom were Yoruba, Fon, and Ewe) often formed their own settlements along the coast and became known as *amaros*. Similarly, some of the Yoruba and Fon–Ewe rescued at sea by the British and brought to Sierra Leone later returned to southwestern Nigeria and Benin, where they were referred to as *saros*. Perhaps the New World experience had changed them, like it had the "Americo-Liberians." There is great irony here: People who voluntarily returned to Africa wound up distancing themselves from Africans, or perhaps it was the indigenous peoples who rejected the returnees. Rejection and self-containment may have even been mutual. In any case, the recovery of life prior to the slave trade proved challenging.

One by one, and over a long stretch of time, the various polities throughout the Americas dismantled the machinery of slavery. The people of Haiti freed themselves in 1791. Next came many of the colonies under Spanish control, where wars of independence were organized as early as 1808. As would be true of the United States and Cuba, black soldiers made their own contributions to the independence efforts, fighting as well for an end to slavery. General José de San Martín, who led much of South America in their struggle against Spain, was authorized by both Argentina and Chile to grant freedom to slaves enlisted in his armies, resulting in the mobilization and manumission of thousands. The scope of these manumissions was limited, as those who would become freedmen or *libertos* could only do so after serving extended terms in the army; one term, for example, required that they continue to serve for two years after all hostilities had ended. While some deserted, others stayed the course; in the invasion of Chile in 1816 to fight the Spanish, half of San Martín's army were exslaves, recruited from Buenos Aires and western Argentina and serving in all-black units. These soldiers paid dearly; they fought with San Martín in Chile, Peru, and Ecuador between 1816 and 1823, returning to Argentina with only 150 of the original 2,000. Nevertheless, some had risen to the rank of officer, a feat duplicated in Mexico, where African-descended leaders José Maria Morelos and Vicente "El Negro" Guerrero provided important leadership. In what is now Colombia and Venezuela, the "great liberator" Simón Bolívar, who in 1815 requested and received military assistance from Haiti, favored abolition, though he was ambivalent about freed Africans becoming full members of society. Abolition was opposed by Colombia and Venezuela's mining interests, for whom 55 percent of the 38,940 enslaved still toiled as late as 1830. As a result, slavery was officially abolished in Chile, the countries of Central America, and Mexico in 1823, 1824, and 1829, respectively, but not until 1852 in Colombia. Ecuador followed suit that year, then Argentina and Uruguay (1853), Peru and Venezuela (1854), Bolivia (1861), and Paraguay (1869).

Emancipation in the British Caribbean, achieved through the resistance of the enslaved, was supported by British abolitionists under William Wilberforce's leadership in the late eighteenth and early nineteenth centuries. Initially waging a campaign of "amelioration" to improve the conditions of the enslaved, these abolitionists soon lobbied for the interdiction of the transatlantic trade and the end of slavery itself. Prominent among them were Olaudah Equiano and Ottobah Cugoano, who published his *Thoughts and Sentiments of the Evils of Slavery* in 1787. The cumulative effect of antislavery forces was the passing in Parliament of the Emancipation Act of 1833, ratified the following year, which ushered in the Apprenticeship period in the English-speaking Caribbean. Under these provisions, children under six years of age became free, while all others were to work for their former slaveholders for another four years, after which all would be emancipated in 1838. For their losses, slaveholders received significant compensation.

Slavery in Canada, a modest institution in Nova Scotia, New Brunswick, and Lower Canada, was also destroyed by Parliament's 1833 Act, following its demise in Upper Canada (now Ontario) in 1793. Slavery in what remained of the French and Danish-held Caribbean was abolished in 1848, while the Dutch afforded the same to their colonies (Aruba, Bonaire, Curaçao, St. Maarten, St. Eustatius, and Saba) in 1863. It would take a major civil war, however, for the institution to be abolished in the United States. Some 186,000 blacks enlisted in the Union Army, 93,000 of whom came from seceding states, and over 38,000 died in the war. Initially opposed to using black troops, the Union acquiesced in August of 1862, more than a year after the war began. The enslaved also advanced their own liberation by crossing Union Army lines and offering to work for wages. On the other side, the Confederacy used slaves for much of the vital infrastructural work, such as repairing railroads and bridges, manufacturing firearms and powder, and constructing fortifications. They were the cooks for the Confederate Army, and they attended the wealthy soldiers, cleaning their clothes, polishing their swords, and running errands. A few blacks also fought with the South, a last-ditch effort resulting from an act of desperation on the part of the Confederate government, enacted in March of 1865, by which time all was lost; the Confederacy surrendered at Appomattox the following month. But before placing the South in too cynical a light, we should recall that President Abraham Lincoln preceded the Confederacy in embracing expediency. In issuing the Emancipation Proclamation, initially floated on September 22, 1862 but not put into effect until January 1, 1863, Lincoln sought to deny the Confederacy its labor base and main support for the war. The Proclamation only applied to those in the Confederacy, and it did not emancipate the enslaved in states loyal to the Union or in territory under Union occupation. It was not until the war's end and the ratification of the Thirteenth Amendment on December 18, 1865 that the formerly enslaved were freed.

The culmination of the American Civil War brought into focus the remaining Spanish-held territories of Puerto Rico and Cuba as slave-holding societies. A military junta seized power in Spain in 1868 and issued a Cuba-directed decree freeing children born to enslaved mothers. The abolitionist Segismundo Moret, appointed minister of the colonies in 1870, convinced the Spanish legislature to pass the Moret Law that year, which in effect reinforced the 1868 decree. The Moret Law affected the fortunes of Puerto Rico, whose enslaved population by 1872 was less than 2 percent of its labor force; the Spanish legislature abolished slavery in that island in 1873 without compensating slaveholders.

The British abolition and interdiction of the slave trade, combined with the end of slavery throughout the Americas (except for Brazil), made it more difficult for Cuba to import captives. Further mechanization of sugar manufacturing decreased reliance upon slave labor, while the eruption of three major slave revolts in 1842–1843, followed by the repression of an 1844 conspiracy known as *La Escalera* ("The Ladder," where those charged with insurrection were tied and beaten), certainly underscored its unreliability. However, the fatal blow to slavery was struck during the Ten Years' War (1868–1878), when Cuba attempted to throw off the Spanish colonial yoke. As was true of both the American War of Independence and the American Civil War, whites fought for their reasons and blacks fought for those same reasons as well as their own, particularly for freedom. Slavery became more of an issue as the war progressed, but initially it was fought in the name of Cuban nationalism. These two different yet related issues would coalesce to place Cuba's greatest military leader, Antonio Maceo, on the horns of yet another dilemma. The son of a free African Cuban, Maceo delivered stellar service to the Cuban struggle for independence, but he was suspected by white revolutionaries of harboring secret plans to establish a black republic on Cuban soil, à la Haiti, a fear encouraged by the Spanish. Maceo was joined by such men of African descent as Quintín Bandera, Guillermo Moncada, and Policarpo Pineda (or Rustán) as military leaders in the Ten Years' War, and they were joined by thousands of enslaved infantry. The war ended with the Pact of Zanjón and the defeat of the nationalists. Spain manumitted 16,000 slaves to quell further trouble, but Maceo rejected the Pact precisely because it did not manumit all the enslaved. The Guerra Chiquita (Little War) ensued in eastern Cuba from 1879 to 1880, in part waged by blacks and those of mixed ancestry over their lack of power and slavery's continuation. Quickly suppressed as a result of a lack of support by white Cubans, Spain further undermined the spirit of the rebellion by declaring the end of slavery in 1880 and the start of the *patronato* or apprenticeship which, like the policy in the British Caribbean, required former slaves to work for former slaveholders for the next eight years. Because there were few *patrocinados* left in Cuba by 1885, Spain declared the end of the apprenticeship in 1886. The enslaved's fight for freedom from both slavery and colonial rule would deeply influence the concept of race in Cuba.

Brazil was the last to abolish slavery. In contrast to both Cuba and the United States, there was no all-consuming conflagration within which the enslaved fought for multiple purposes, with the possible exception of the Paraguayan War of 1865–1870. It was during that war, waged against Paraguay by Brazil, Argentina, and Uruguay, that Brazil offered freedom to those who enlisted. Although this war was important to the demise of Brazilian slavery, more critical was the steady diminution in the slave population stemming from resistance, mechanization, and the abolitionist campaign in that country. The ban of the transatlantic trade, initially agreed to in 1817 by the Portuguese, was finally enforced after 1850, although the clandestine trade continued. The 1860s through the 1880s saw a significant increase in the number of slaveholders killed by the enslaved, the number of (mostly small-scale) uprisings, and the number fleeing from slavery, particularly in the coffee regions around Rio de Janeiro and São Paulo. The surge of activity pressured the government to pass the Rio Branco Law of 1871, or Law of Free Birth, manumitting the children of enslaved mothers, and a sexagenarian law passed in 1885 granting freedom to those reaching sixty years of age. The effect of resistance and legislation was the precipitous decline in the percentage of the enslaved, from 50 percent of the total population in 1822 to 5 percent in 1888. In that year the Golden Law was enacted, officially abolishing a slavery in Brazil that had been practically ended by the enslaved themselves.

The close of the nineteenth century saw the end of an institution throughout the Americas, but by the time slavery was finished in Cuba and Brazil, another chapter had begun elsewhere in the Caribbean and the northern mainland. The question for all concerned was this: How free would freedom be?

## Games People Play

The most arresting, startling, critical, and indisputable fact concerning the whole of the Americas and their respective processes of emancipation was that, whether slaveholders were compensated for their losses or not, the enslaved themselves received virtually nothing. It is therefore the case that past and present development in the Americas was based upon an institution whose labor came free of charge. Many contemporary African countries may be presently indebted, but the Western world is historically indebted and ironically so, as it extracted free labor in exchange for costly suffering from Africans and their descendants, stolen from Africa. Does this historical debt require some contemporary resolution from those in the Americas and Europe, who obviously were not "there" in the eighteenth and nineteenth centuries but whose lives and economies continue to benefit from a foundation laid by slavery?

A review of postemancipation societies, beginning with the British Caribbean, demonstrates a certain continuity of experience between slavery and freedom. The Apprenticeship, 1834 to 1838, began the process by which the status of some 80 percent of the British Caribbean population changed. During the four-year transition period, former slaves were still required to work for former slaveholders in exchange for wages, and they were bound to the plantations by means of so-called pass laws that restricted their mobility. It became clear, therefore, that the apprentices themselves would have to take action to transform the significance of freedom from an abstraction of colonial decree to the substance of lived experience. This they did by asserting as much control over their labor as possible; they used their free time (a quarter of the week) as they saw fit, often withholding it from desperate employers. They also refused to work in some instances, resorting to sabotage in others. While wary of the legal system, they yet sought to clarify their freedom in the courts.

Following apprenticeship, blacks were keen to negotiate a freedom that afforded the conditions of their labor as much flexibility as possible, and provided their families as much autonomy as possible, including the opportunity to relocate, both within the island of their residence and to different islands as well. Many vocationally skilled and semiskilled workers moved to urban areas, while others migrated from lower-wage areas such as Barbados and the Leeward and Windward islands to higher-wage sites, such as Trinidad and British Guyana. Negotiations, work stoppages or strikes, and violence accompanied efforts to receive equitable, acceptable salaries. Conflict with employers determined to reduce wages produced major strikes in Jamaica in 1838–1839 and 1841, Guyana in 1842, and Trinidad in 1843. While wages were important, the African-descended also fought for task work and jobs that did not require contracts, both of which maximized their choices and enhanced their liberty. They could better control their time on the plantations, have more time to cultivate their own provision grounds and participate in the market, or pursue supplemental economic endeavors. They insisted on shorter weeks for women and children than men, allowing women more time to work the provision grounds and pursue huckstering in the market.

Attempts to define the terms of freedom, severely handicapped by the absence of any meaningful compensation for slavery, were resisted within ten years of emancipation by former slaveholders. They responded by seizing the courts and imposing a series of restrictions on movement, squatting, and the use of plantation property. They succeeded in lowering wages and reestablishing their ownership of provision grounds. Increased educational access was a glimmer of hope, but this was severely restricted to a few privileged families and individuals, leading to even more class divisions among blacks.

The former slaveholder backlash resulted in a period of renewed oppression, contiguous with enslavement. Those of African descent responded in ways similar to their resistance to slavery; cultural opposition took the form of a reinvigorated embrace of African-influenced religions, while the folklore, memorials, and the language itself evinced a deep-seated anger. The cultural worked in tandem with the political,

FIGURE 9. Thatched houses, Barbados, 1898. From Robert T. Hill, *Cuba and Porto Rico* (New York, 1898), facing p. 396.

and violent revolts against reconfigured oppression broke out all over the Caribbean. These included the 1844 Guerre Nègre in Dominica, the Angel Gabriel Riots of Guyana in 1856, the 1862 Vox Populi Riots of St. Vincent, the 1876 Belmanna Riots of Tobago, and the Confederate Riots of Barbados of the same year. Perhaps the most representative of these uprisings were the Morant Bay Disturbances of 1865 in Jamaica, led by the lay preacher Paul Bogle.

In 1865, the people of Stony Gut, a St. Thomas Parish farming village located on land leased by blacks following apprenticeship, faced desperate economic times, a condition exacerbated by royal and colonial government indifference. Refusing to continue paying rent to the magistrates of Morant Bay, these black farmers claimed squatters' rights. The local planters tried to evict them, and Bogle, leader of the Stony Gut community, called for revolt. Following the rescue of a fellow farmer on trial in Morant Bay, members of Stony Gut violently resisted the arrest of the rescuers. In a response bearing clear resemblances to Akan-based uprisings during slavery, Bogle and his followers took an oath and administered it to others, and on October 10 they marched into Morant Bay with drums beating and conch shells blaring, crying "Cleave to the black, color for color." Vowing to kill repressive whites while saving white sympathizers, they took control of

St. Thomas Parish for three days. After death and destruction, Bogle was captured with the assistance of – who else? – the maroons, and he was hanged on a British gunboat on October 24, along with over 1,000 other blacks.

By the 1870s, then, many in the British Caribbean had been forced to return to dependence on the plantations as a consequence of both planter countermeasures and the disruption of trade resulting from the American Civil War. They suffered rates of unemployment, lowered wages, and a surge in food prices that placed them in conditions not very far removed from those characterizing slavery. Their continued resistance, however, establishes this response as a principal theme in the history of the African Diaspora. Their experience would be echoed in the mainland of the United States.

## Freedom's Tease

The close of the Civil War ushered in Reconstruction (1865–1877), the quintessential saga of the rise and fall of a people's dreams and aspirations, as promising and progressive social policies introduced at the period's beginning were ultimately reversed and crushed by the period's end. Some 4 million people had been emancipated, but as was true of the British Caribbean, the precise meaning of their emancipation was undefined and contested. A war-torn South, struggling to regain an economic footing while wrestling with the implications of freedom, initially attempted to resolve both by controlling black labor. Again, not unlike the Caribbean, southern whites adopted legislation collectively known as the Black Codes, seeking to ensure black worker availability. The Black Codes were similar to the Slave Codes in that they proscribed black movement, limiting where they could rent or own property and forcing them to work for white employers by means of vagrancy laws. Black life in the workplace and society in general was regulated, and opportunities for blacks' participation in the political process were denied. The dawn of Reconstruction was pretty bleak.

Determining that Andrew Johnson, Lincoln's successor following the latter's assassination in April of 1865, was content to allow white home rule in the South, Congress convened in December of 1865 and wrested control of Reconstruction away from the executive branch, inaugurating the subperiod known as Radical Reconstruction. With the exception of a cooperative Tennessee, the South was divided into five military districts governed by martial law; no southern state would be admitted into the Union until it ratified the Fourteenth Amendment granting blacks citizenship. In March of 1865 the Bureau of Refugees, Freedmen, and Abandoned Lands was established. Better known as the Freedmen's Bureau, the agency oversaw efforts to relieve not only blacks but also whites of intense suffering. To that end, the Bureau created forty-six hospitals by 1867, and by 1869 dispensed food rations to 5 million whites and 15 million blacks. The Bureau intervened in disputes between black workers and employers, and it helped thousands resume work under better conditions. "Freedmen's" courts were created to adjudicate cases deemed inappropriate for local tribunals. Perhaps what was more important was that the Bureau promoted the education of freedpersons and created day, evening, Sunday, and vocational schools. The African-descended of all ages sat in the same classroom, eager to finally read the Bible for themselves. Colleges were also established with Bureau assistance during this time, including the Hampton Institute and Fisk, Howard, and Atlanta Universities. Hundreds, if not thousands, of whites from the North volunteered as teachers, and by 1870 there were some 247,333 students in over 4,000 schools.

In addition to such measures, the Reconstruction Act of 1867 enfranchised southern blacks and loyal whites while disfranchising a large number of disloyal whites. Constitutional conventions were held in 1867 and 1868 in which blacks participated, constituting the majority in South Carolina while equaling the white delegation in Louisiana. Black delegates helped craft the most progressive state constitutions the South had ever known, with such features as the abolition of property qualifications for the franchise and elective office. Blacks went on to hold public office, especially in South Carolina, where they controlled the lower house of the legislature for a period, contributed two lieutenant governors, and served in the state supreme court from 1870 to 1876 in the person of Jonathan Jasper Wright. Between 1868 and 1896, Louisiana saw thirty-eight black senators and ninety-five representatives elected to the state legislature; of its three black lieutenant governors, P. B. S. Pinchback served as acting governor for forty-three days. At the national level, of the twenty blacks elected to the House of Representatives between 1869 and 1901, South Carolina supplied the largest number with eight. There were also two black senators, Blanche K. Bruce and Hiram R. Revels, both of Mississippi; no African descendant would again serve in that capacity until the election of Edward Brooke of Massachusetts in 1966.

Although these developments were significant, they did not address the fundamental economic difficulties of freedpersons. The notion of "forty acres and a mule" for every black family stems from an 1865 military order by General Sherman, by which certain sea islands and a thirty-mile tract of coastal land south of Charleston were designated for freedperson settlement. Households were assigned forty-acre plots and a pack animal (if no longer needed by the Union Army), and by 1865 some 40,000 freedpersons had received 400,000 acres of land. But in February of 1865, Congress stripped the Freedmen's Bureau of the authority to assign such lands, and President Johnson soon rescinded all such land titles. Some of the many displaced were helped by the Southern Homestead Act of 1866, which provided those in five southern states, both black and white, the opportunity to secure homesteads. By 1867, blacks owned 160,960 acres in Florida, and they acquired over 350,000 acres in Georgia by 1870.

However, in the larger scheme of things, the vast majority of the 4 million freedpersons received nothing, and they were forced by economic necessity to return to plantations they had worked prior to the war, lands owned by former slaveholders. They were then required to work for either monthly wages or as sharecroppers; in the former instance, the wages in 1867 totaled less than what had been paid to the enslaved who had been hired out. As for sharecropping, it was a nefarious system that kept black labor in place, bound to the land like serfs, because at year's end they were always in debt to plantation and farm owners who manipulated the records or "cooked the books." Thus, the reality for too many was an economic arrangement similar to an institution supposedly abolished. Sadly but predictably, the South's production of cotton rebounded from its wartime lows, and by 1880 was higher than it had ever been.

Just as sharecropping was another form of exploitation, even slavery under a different name, so the South resurrected another institution echoing the activities of the antebellum patty-rollers. The institution made the reimposition of white control possible and was, simply put, state-sponsored terrorism. In reaction to Radical Reconstruction, white southerners unleashed a widespread, unrelenting campaign of sheer horror, aimed at driving blacks, along with their white supporters, out of the political process and back to the plantations, where they were to be immobilized and "put in their place." As early

**FIGURE 10.** Black family, Beaufort, South Carolina, 1862. Library of Congress, Prints and Photographs Division, LC-B8171-152-A.

as 1866, organizations such as the Regulators and the Black Horse Cavalry emerged, terrorizing blacks throughout the South. After 1867 the number of these clandestine societies mushroomed to include the Pale Faces, the Rifle Clubs of South Carolina, the White Line of Mississippi, the White League of Louisiana, the White Brotherhood,

the Knights of the White Camelia, and the Knights of the Ku Klux
Klan. Together with the Black Codes, these terrorist organizations
were quite effective in intimidating a defenseless population, and they
worked with white politicians to resist and gradually overturn progressive legislation through murder, mutilation, rapine, and confiscation. With the North weary of the fight for black citizenship, the federal government's decision to remove federal troops from the South
in 1876 opened wide the floodgates for white supremacists. By such
requirements as the poll tax, proof of literacy and ability to understand any part of the constitution, ownership of property, grandfather clauses, and by vulgar physical threat, blacks were removed from
the polls in dramatic fashion. By 1910, state constitutions rewritten
to include such requirements had disfranchised blacks in North and
South Carolina, Louisiana, Georgia, Mississippi, Alabama, Virginia,
and Oklahoma. Jim Crow laws, legislating separate and segregated
spaces for blacks and whites in public and private places, became fixtures on the legal landscape, upheld by the Supreme Court itself in its
1896 *Plessy v. Ferguson* decision; they would remain until the civil rights
gains of the 1960s. By the dawn of the twentieth century, the vestiges
of slavery were apparent throughout the South, home to 90 percent
of all the African-descended in the United States. For another 100
years following slavery's abolition, black folk suffered another form of
legal, state-supported discrimination and oppression, and again they
endured the exploitation of their labor, the destabilization of their families, and the curtailment of their potential. All, it would seem, simply
because they were black.

## Another Way

The different yet parallel experiences of those of African descent in the
United States and the Caribbean suggest that de facto slavery in the
postemancipation period was a powerful factor in the development of
race and racial consciousness in these societies. The denial of opportunity and pervasiveness of black suffering, white arrogation of privilege
and power, and the mediating role disproportionately played by those
of mixed ancestry rendered racial identity a meaningful category of social significance. Blackness, well established during slavery, acquired
an even greater quality of immutability, as the end of legal slavery failed
to significantly alter the very real predicament of the formerly enslaved.

A consideration of postslavery Cuba, however, suggests that the concept of race was neither universal nor unchanging throughout the Americas; it was relative to the unique circumstances of a given society. Cuba's struggle for independence from Spain, coming on the heels of the abolition of Cuban slavery, forged a collective identity in that island that attempted to merge color and nationality. That is, the African-descended felt loyal to both their blackness and their Cubanness; the two were not easily separated and were uniquely linked to their white Cuban compatriots. Evidence for this view of racial identity can be found in the words of the black general Guillermo Moncada, military leader in both the Ten Years' War and the Guerra Chiquita, who argued for the existence of a "Cuban race." The context for Moncada's statement was war with Spain, without which Cuba's racial relations may have conformed to North American and British Caribbean patterns. The notion of a "Cuban race" was in conversation with the idea of a *raza de color* (race of color) or *clase de color*, created by African-descended Cubans to combine blacks (morenos) and those of mixed ancestry (pardos) into a unified category, with the result that morenos and pardos were both often called *negros* (blacks). But even those who embraced the idea of a raza de color saw themselves as fully Cuban and vigorously fought for their rights as such.

The end of slavery in Cuba resulted in continuing despair for the majority of the formerly enslaved. As was true elsewhere, they received nothing. Some moved to urban areas; others fled the sugar plantations of the island's western sector in search of land to farm on their own. However, most remained where they had been, on or near their former plantations, where they worked for either wages or tenancy. Wages were uncertain and individual lives quite precarious, however, as the Cuban sugar industry was in crisis, suffering from competition, in addition to other factors. Laborers had also been displaced by an influx of more than 100,000 Spaniards between 1882 and 1894, most of whom wound up working in rural areas, where the devastation of two wars between 1868 and 1880 remained a formidable challenge. By the early 1890s, therefore, the situation for blacks in Cuba was not unlike their counterparts in the United States and the Caribbean.

Desperate economic conditions further fueled the flame of resistance to Spanish rule and the drive for independence. To counter the insurgency, Spain held aloft the example of Haiti and warned that independence efforts would devolve into racial conflict. Led by the writings of José Martí, the response of Cuban intellectuals of all shades was to develop a concept of transracial nationalism in Cuba. Their work aimed at rewriting the black insurgent as raceless compatriot and hero rather than black, vengeful menace, an effort greatly assisted by black and mixed race journalists and writers, including Juan Gualberto Gómez, Martín Morúa Delgado, and Rafael Serra y Montalvo. It was through such individuals, along with black newspapers, that the struggle for black civil rights was simultaneously waged, and the establishment of such organizations as the Directorio Central de las Societies de la Clase de Color allowed black and mixed race organizations to coalesce. Their creation points to the fact that black leaders did not necessarily agree on the best way to achieve a common Cuban identity, as some advocated black political organizations and others (such as Antonio Maceo) did not.

Led by Martí's Cuban Revolutionary Party, the independence movement again took up arms in February of 1895, Antonio Maceo was again a principal general, and black participation was again both significant and crucial. Racial equality was enunciated by independence leaders as the ideological underpinning of the movement. Achieving rapid success, the insurgents suffered a major setback when Maceo was ambushed and killed in Havana province in December of 1896. Hopes that Spain would be more amenable to Cuban independence revived with the assassination of the Spanish prime minister in August of 1897 and the fall of Spain's conservative government. The American entry into the conflict in April of 1898 launched the Spanish-American War, ending with an American victory that August. The Americans would remain in Cuba for three and a half years, until the Cubans had satisfactorily demonstrated to the Americans their "fitness to rule," certified by Cuba's acceptance of the 1901 Platt Amendment (which granted the United States the right to intervene in Cuba whenever the former deemed necessary).

American interventionism was a blow to Cuba's transracial experiment, as Americans introduced Jim Crow to Havana, complete with segregated fighting units. The black Cuban's pride in both her blackness and her nationality would be tested, therefore, as some white Cubans were encouraged by North American racism to forego the principles of Martí.

The irony in the Spanish-American War is difficult to overlook. African Americans from the United States enthusiastically supported Cuban independence out of an identification with Cubans, who they viewed as largely black or of mixed ancestry and therefore similar to themselves. After all, both groups were just out of slavery. Four all-black units saw action in Cuba and probably saved Theodore Roosevelt's Rough Riders from annihilation at Las Guasimas. Those very same black American soldiers, however, suffered discrimination in a service for which they were prepared to give their lives. They could not even get to Cuba without first passing through a gauntlet of hate-filled white mobs in the American South, protesting their transit. For those black American soldiers, a raceless American nationalism was unimaginable.

## Suggestions for Further Reading

Resistance and emancipation literature has amassed rapidly. An introduction to themes in the Caribbean is provided by Hilary Beckles and Verene Shepherd, eds., *Caribbean Freedom: Society and Economy From Emancipation to the Present* (Kingston, Jamaica and London: Curry, 1993). In addition to aforementioned works by C. L. R. James and Carolyn Fick, there is Mavis Campbell, *The Maroons of Jamaica, 1655–1796: A History of Resistance, Collaboration, and Betrayal* (South Hadley, MA: Bergin and Garvey, 1988); Jean Fouchard, *Les marrons de la liberté* (Paris: Éditions de L'École, 1972); Michel-Rolph Trouillot, *Silencing the Past: Power and the Production of History* (Boston: Beacon Press, 1995); Michael Craton, *Testing the Chains: Resistance to Slavery in the British West Indies* (Ithaca, NY: Cornell U. Press, 1982); David Barry Gaspar, *Bondsmen and Rebels: A Case Study of Master–Slave Relations in Antigua, With Implications for Colonial British America* (Baltimore, MD: Johns Hopkins U. Press, 1985); and Thomas C. Holt, *The Problem of Freedom: Race, Labor, and Politics in Jamaica and Britain, 1832–1938* (Baltimore, MD: Johns Hopkins U. Press, 1992).

For Brazil and Latin America, see Emilia Viotti da Costa, *The Brazilian Empire: Myths and Histories* (Chicago: U. of Chicago Press, 1985) and *Crowns of Glory, Tears of Blood. The Demerara Slave Rebellion of 1823* (New York: Oxford U. Press, 1994); Rafael Duharte Jiménez, *Rebeldá esclava en el caribe* (Veracruz: Gobierno del Esatado de Veracruz, 1992); João José Reis, *Slave Rebellion in Brazil: The Muslim Uprising of 1835 in Bahia*, trans. Arthur Brakel (Baltimore, MD: Johns Hopkins U. Press, 1993) and *Death is a Festival: Funeral Rites and Rebellion in Nineteenth-Century Brazil*, trans. H. Sabrina Gledhill (Chapel Hill: U. of North Carolina Press, 2003); Rebecca J. Scott, *Slave Emancipation in Cuba: The Transition to Free Labor, 1860–1899* (Princeton, NJ: Princeton U. Press, 1985); Ada Ferrer, *Insurgent Cuba: Race, Nation, and Revolution, 1868–1898* (Chapel Hill: U. of North Carolina, 1999); Louis A. Pérez, *The War of 1898: Cuba and the United States in History and Historiography* (Chapel Hill: U. of North Carolina, 1999); Aline Helg, *Our Rightful Share: The Afro-Cuban Struggle for Equality, 1886–1912* (Chapel Hill: U. of North Carolina, 1995); and Jane Landers, *Black Society in Spanish Florida* (Urbana and Chicago: U. of Illinois Press, 1999). Richard Price, *Maroon Societies: Rebel Slave Communities in the Americas* (Baltimore, MD: Johns Hopkins U. Press, 1979), remains useful, while Pierre Verger, *Trade Relations Between the Bight of Benin and Bahia from the 17th to 19th Century*, trans. Evelyn Crawford (Ibadan, Nigeria: Ibadan University Press, 1976) provides fascinating insights into cultural ties between West Africa and Brazil.

As for the United States, W. E. B. Du Bois, *Black Reconstruction* (Millwood, NY: Kraus-Thomson, 1963) remains a standard and remarkable work, as is C. Vann Woodward, *The Strange Career of Jim Crow* (New York: Oxford U. Press, 1955) and Leon F. Litwack, *Been in the Storm So Long: The Aftermath of Slavery* (New York: Knopf, 1979). There is a lot of work on rebellions. Herbert Aptheker, *American Negro Slave Revolts* (New York: International, 1970) has been an important source for many years. Eugene D. Genovese, *From Rebellion to Revolution: Afro-American Slave Revolts in the Making of the Modern World* (Baton Rouge: Louisiana State U. Press, 1979), organizes slave revolts in a progression with which not all scholars agree, but is nonetheless valuable especially concerning Denmark Vesey, an example of which is Douglas R. Egerton, *He Shall Go Out Free: The Lives of Denmark Vesey* (Madison, WI: Madison House, 1999). An instructive scholarly debate on Vesey entitled "Forum: The Making of a Slave Conspiracy" can be found in *William and Mary Quarterly* 58 (no. 4, October 2001): 913–976 and 59 (no. 1, January 2002): 135–202. The journal *Slavery and Abolition* is also an excellent source for materials on slave insurrection. Peter P. Hinks, *To Awaken My Afflicted Brethren: David Walker and the Problem of Antebellum Resistance* (University Park: Pennsylvania State U. Press, 1997) is a related though overlooked investigation of David Walker, and suggests a possible, indirect link between him and Vesey.

The movement of black sailors and their contributions to resistance can be read about in Peter Linebaugh and Marcus Rediker, *The Many-Headed Hydra: Sailors, Slaves, Commoners, and the Hidden History of the*

*Revolutionary Atlantic* (Boston: Beacon Press, 2000). Black mariners and revolt are also taken up in Julius S. Scott, "The Common Wind: Currents of Afro-American Communication in the Era of the Haitian Revolution," (PhD dissertation, Duke University, Durham, NC 1986). Jeffrey W. Bolster, *Black Jacks: African American Seamen in the Age of Sail* (Cambridge: Harvard U. Press, 1997) also contributes to the subject of black seafarers.

Regarding culture and resistance, one should consult such works as Gwendolyn Midlo Hall, *Africans in Colonial Louisiana: The Development of Afro-Creole Culture in the Eighteenth Century* (Baton Rouge: Louisiana State U. Press, 1992); Margaret Washington Creel, *"A Peculiar People": Slave Religion and Community Culture Among the Gullahs* (New York: New York U. Press, 1988); and Albert J. Raboteau, *Slave Religion: The "Invisible Institution" in the Antebellum South* (New York: Oxford U. Press, 1978). Alex Bontemps, *The Punished Self: Surviving Slavery in the Colonial South* (Ithaca, NY and London: Cornell U. Press, 2001) presents slavery as predicament, an idea borrowed here. Certainly the work of Sterling Stuckey, *Slave Culture: Nationalist Theory and the Foundations of Black America* (New York: Oxford U. Press, 1987) has been critical to the uncovering of a resilient African culture's role in resistance to slavery and racism in the United States.

# CHAPTER 7

# Reconnecting

Two striking aspects of the first half of the twentieth century concern the large-scale and widespread circumventions of the African-descended throughout the Americas, and their persistent efforts to reconnect in meaningful ways with Africa. The former was in response to economic need and incentive; the latter was motivated by political, philosophical, and religious considerations. Whatever the motive, people were not forgetting their African ancestry, but endeavoring to remember and sustain it. In these ways, they were reversing sail in their minds and hearts, if not with their bodies.

While reconnecting to Africa, those of African descent were also redefining themselves as a series of communities related yet distinct from each other, a consequence of differing local circumstances and histories. Reconnections and redefinitions took place during periods of rapid industrialization, organization and theorization of labor, emerging struggles against empire, world war, women's rights movements, the rise of allegedly scientific racism, and the division of the world into eastern and western camps. Members of the African Diaspora played significant roles in all of these developments.

From this complex period of interpenetrating influences and experiences arose a cultural efflorescence throughout the African Diaspora. Notable works of art, literature, and scholarship, as well as political and religious innovations, resulted from this intercontinental cross-fertilization of ideas and experiences. The components of the African Diaspora were therefore in extensive dialogue, a conversation reverberating to the present day.

## Boats and Trains

The latter quarter of the nineteenth century had been a tremendous disappointment to most throughout the African Diaspora, their hopes of full freedom dashed by the realities of debt peonage, rural wage labor, peasant impoverishment, and either wide-ranging, systematic, state-backed terrorism or a heavy-handed colonialism favoring a few while disparaging many. Whether on an island or mainland, most people were trapped, virtually incarcerated in an economic and political system from which there seemed no escape.

Changes in the international economy, combined with two world wars, created cracks in the prison through the demand for labor. The problem, however, was that those meeting the demand were required to relocate to places hundreds, if not thousands, of miles from their lands of birth, resurrecting the dilemma of opportunity at the cost of family. Conditions were so desperate, however, that many made the sacrifice. The African Diaspora during the first half of the twentieth century was therefore characterized by perpetual motion, in both hemispheres.

The peasant majority in the Caribbean remained locked in a struggle to bypass the power of the planters through strategies of self-reliance. In Barbados and Antigua, they invariably continued to reside on or near former plantations, providing labor in exchange for occupancy. In Cuba, most remained in the countryside as wage laborers on sugar plantations or as squatters in new areas, and in the latter instance were not unlike many in Haiti, where many plantations had been dismantled and divided into smallholdings of one or two acres. Timber and minerals were extractive industries financed by American and European interests in various islands, but after the First World War (1914–1918) the focus shifted to petroleum in Trinidad, Aruba, and Curaçao, and bauxite (for aluminum) in Jamaica and Guyana. The region's economy was strengthened by these two exports until 1929, when the depression contributed to perennial unemployment.

As a consequence, the Caribbean emerged as the quintessential region of migratory activity. Divided into several phases, the first of the region's major redistributions took place between 1835 and 1885, when activity centered on the islands themselves. Persons from economically depressed areas, such as Barbados, sought opportunities elsewhere, especially in Trinidad and Tobago and British Guyana.

About 19,000 left the eastern Caribbean for Trinidad and British Guyana between 1835 and 1846; from 1850 to 1921, some 50,000 emigrated to Trinidad, Tobago, and British Guyana from Barbados alone. Destinations during this initial phase were not limited to the islands, as 7,000 from Dominica, for example, left for the goldfields of Venezuela.

Such considerable flight of labor caused concern within the sugar industry, resulting in government recruitment of workers from outside the Caribbean. In response, labor was drawn from two sources: The first consisted of so-called postemancipation Africans, or persons seized from slave ships and taken to Sierra Leone and St. Helena in West Africa. Some 36,120 were subsequently spread throughout the British-held Caribbean between 1839 and 1867, where their arrival also reinvigorated cultural ties to Africa. The second source was Asia, principally the Indian subcontinent (but also China), from where approximately 500,000 indentured laborers were imported between 1838 and 1917 to such places as Jamaica, Trinidad, Grenada, Martinique, St. Lucia, and St. Vincent. The influx has resulted in certain ongoing tensions, but the Asian presence has also left cultural impressions upon those of African descent, ranging from religion (principally in the form of Islam) to music to culinary tastes.

A second migratory phase originating within the Caribbean between the 1880s and the 1920s was both intra-Caribbean as well as an outmigration. Destinations included Panama, Cuba, the Dominican Republic, Costa Rica, and the United States, as well as other Central American sites. It was the construction of the Panama Canal, however, that laid the foundation for this important phase.

The United States' acquisition of the Panama Canal in 1903 was part of an imperialist expansion that began with the Spanish-American War and the U.S. seizure of Cuba and Puerto Rico. The American presence in Panama was followed by a treaty with Haiti in 1915, giving the Americans control over the island's finances and internal security for ten years, a period that actually lasted nineteen, complete with U.S. occupational forces. In 1916 the marines landed on the other side of the island in the Dominican Republic, guaranteeing the preservation of American economic interests there until the present day. Finally, the 1917 purchase of the Virgin Islands from the Danes created an American lake in the Caribbean; de facto American colonialism was therefore extended over a significant portion of the African Diaspora in the Americas. With such military and political control established, American and European economic interests proceeded unencumbered.

By 1903, some 44,000 from the Caribbean were already working on the Panama Canal, mostly from Barbados and Jamaica. By the time the canal was completed in 1914, from 150,000 to 200,000 from the Caribbean had labored on the canal, as many as 30,000 from Barbados alone. Stated differently, those of African descent built the Panama Canal. While the contract workers were mostly men initially, they were joined by women who began arriving in Panama in increasing numbers, eventually evening out the sex ratio. The women worked as domestics and cooks and laundry women, reflecting a general surge in the percentage of women emigrating from the Caribbean through the first quarter of the twentieth century. It was on the canal site that Caribbean workers were introduced to North American Jim Crow, for although they performed every imaginable job associated with the canal's building and operation, they did so in segregated fashion, living in segregated housing. When the canal was completed, the United Fruit Company transported thousands of the unemployed to its banana and sugar plantations and railroads in Costa Rica, Honduras, Cuba, and the Dominican Republic. Cuba alone took in 400,000 Jamaicans and Haitians between 1913 and 1928, and, as is true of Panama, a significant community of their descendants remain in Cuba.

Taking jobs in other parts of the Caribbean and Central America was not an entirely effective strategy, however, as the economies of these areas declined during the First World War. The United States, already a focus for many who had worked in Panama, became the destination for others. Those who had come directly from Panama paid for their and their loved ones' voyages with "panama money," highly esteemed because of the horrific human costs associated with it – thousands had died or were permanently maimed in constructing the canal. These workers and their families were for the most part illiterate, according to some accounts, whereas those from the Caribbean who joined them later were from a different social stratum and were either literate or in possession of marketable skills. By 1930 over 130,000 had arrived in U.S. urban areas, including Miami and other Floridian cities, but their major port of call was New York City, where some 40,000 took up residence in Harlem between 1900 and 1930, providing a substantial proportion of the professional and entrepreneurial classes. Most were from the English-speaking islands, but they also came from Cuba, Puerto Rico, and the Dominican Republic. The Caribbean presence and contribution to New York City, dating back to colonial times, has therefore been crucial to its development as an economic and cultural mecca.

Emigration from the Caribbean continued after the Second World War. Bauxite and petroleum were still the region's leading industries, but bananas replaced sugar as the leading export of a number of islands. The rise of agribusiness, combined with increased mechanization, resulted in the collapse of plantation agriculture and heightened unemployment, forcing people to again seek work elsewhere. Haitians went to the sugar fields of the Dominican Republic; both Haitians and Dominicans came to Florida along with others from the Caribbean and Central America; Puerto Ricans and (eventually) Dominicans undertook major migrations to New York City. Those from the English- and French-speaking islands also relocated to cities in Britain and France, and they would find their way to Canada in a movement that became much more significant in the 1950s and 1960s.

In North America, blacks already in the United States joined Caribbean immigrants. The Great Migration between 1916 and 1930 witnessed more than 1 million leave the South for the North, with over 400,000 boarding trains between 1916 and 1918. This was an intense period of relocation, involving such push factors as economic despair (related to the ravages of the boll weevil) and white racism in the South. The latter element had become particularly pernicious, as more than 3,600 people were lynched between 1884 and 1914, the vast majority black southerners. Pull factors centered on the high demand for labor in the North, occasioned by global war and the precipitous decline in foreign immigration from Europe, from 1.2 million in 1914 to 110,000 by 1918. The Second World War had a similar effect, and in the 1940s an additional 1.6 million black southerners are estimated to have left for the North as well as the West (especially the Los Angeles and San Francisco–Oakland areas), a figure that does not include movement to the South Atlantic and Gulf coasts, where many found jobs in defense-related industries. Such migratory activity continued in the 1950s and 1960s, when 2.9 million are estimated to have left the South. The movement north would transform the majority of African Americans into urban dwellers, so that by 1950, some 52 percent of African Americans were living in cities and large towns (a figure that would increase to 81 percent by 1980).

Paralleling the economic experiences of those in North America and the Caribbean were those of the African-descended in Brazil. As the 1835 Malê revolt revealed, the politics of racial identity in Brazil were complicated; by the late twentieth century, over 100 options would appear on the Brazilian census, such was the fusion of African,

European, and native elements. To speak of "black" Brazilians therefore is to employ terms both unstable and ever evolving. The percentage of Brazilians with African ancestry is undoubtedly much higher than official estimates allow, as many ostensibly white Brazilians admit to having had a "foot in the kitchen" (a reference to long-standing white male access to black female domestics). Discounting such persons, the concept of black Brazilians is used here to denote those of discernible African descent (well over half of the current Brazilian population) who may or may not have embraced the classification of *prêto* (black) or *pardo* (mixed), or who may have appropriated such categories for some purposes and not others, or whose identification with blackness was no barrier to their simultaneous embrace of alternative identities. Reference to black Brazilians also recognizes a pervasive reality that darker-skinned people have historically been disadvantaged, however they defined their individual identities, and that poverty and ignorance and disease were historically concentrated in the squalor of their existence. This was true not only of Brazil but also the entire western hemisphere.

In the sugar-producing northeast, black Brazilians remained as wage laborers and tenants on the plantations, but in the coffee region of the southeast there was considerable migration to the rapidly developing cities of São Paulo and Rio de Janeiro. There, they ran into the issue of *embranquecimento*, or "whitening," an effort to increase European immigration and thereby achieve so-called civilized status as a nation, equal to that of North America and Europe. As one example of this idea-turned-policy, some 90,000 Europeans immigrants, called *colonos*, arrived in Brazil between 1886 and 1889. The policy's implications for São Paulo were dramatic: By 1894, colonos outnumbered Brazilians in a variety of industries and accounted for 79 percent of all manufacturing workers. By 1940, colonos controlled 44 percent of the city's earned industrial capital and far outnumbered those of African descent in São Paulo, who made up only 12.6 percent of an estimated 1.3 million. Factory jobs were reserved for European immigrants, while those of African descent were forced to accept menial, low-wage jobs.

Regarding world war, black folk participated as both combatants and civilians. As an example, when the United States entered World War I in 1917, some 400,000 blacks went into military service. Emmett J. Scott, Booker T. Washington's secretary at the Tuskegee Institute in Alabama for eighteen years, served as a special assistant to the secretary of war, advising him on matters relating to blacks. His presence, however, could not alter the deep-seated hatred of and discrimination against blacks; while represented in almost every branch of the army save the aviation corps' pilot section, they could not serve in the marines, and only as menials in the navy. Black soldiers were assaulted by white civilian mobs in a number of incidents throughout the country, resulting, for example, in a (white) riot in Houston in 1917. Those who made it overseas were largely relegated to serving as stevedores and laborers, while those who were allowed to actually fight suffered disproportionate casualties. At war's end, a bloody race riot in East St. Louis in 1918, in which forty blacks were killed, presaged the famous Red Summer of 1919, in which twenty-five race riots erupted from June to the end of the year. The competition for jobs was one factor precipitating the flare-ups, one of the worst of which took place in Chicago in July and August, leaving 23 blacks and 15 whites dead, with 537 injured and over 1,000 (mostly black) left homeless. As for the Second World War, discrimination remained but was less of an impediment. Approximately 1 million black men and women served in the United States military, over 700,000 in the army, and perhaps a half-million overseas. One of the more dramatic developments was the formation of the 99th Pursuit Squadron of the U.S. Army Air Corps, the famed Tuskegee Airmen, 450 black pilots who were later incorporated into the 322nd Fighter Group and flew combat missions in Europe, contributing significantly to the war effort.

The African-descended from British and French colonies also participated in both world wars under the flags of the respective colonial powers, joining the African-born in European theaters of war. The French were particularly active, recruiting nearly 200,000 for the First World War, mostly from West Africa. Both wars were also fought on African soil, especially the second, and though it was Le Clerc's all-white division that was given the honor of liberating Paris, more than half of de Gaulle's Free French were African or Arab.

## Organizing Black Labor

Blacks in the United States had perhaps the largest percentage of industrial workers in the African Diaspora in the early twentieth century; by 1910, over 350,000 of them were in factory jobs in both the North and the South. Even so, black labor was virtually banned by all-white labor unions, making it very difficult to acquire skills and experience in certain vocations. The Knights of Labor had accepted 60,000 black workers as early as 1886, but the Haymarket Square riots of the same year discredited the organization as a foreign-controlled entity. The American Federation of Labor permitted widespread discrimination against blacks, leading the latter to form their own unions, including the Associated Colored Employees of America and the Association of Afro-American Steam and Gas Engineers and Skilled Workers of Pittsburgh. Efforts at self-organization intensified following the First World War, and the American Negro Labor Congress held its inaugural meeting in Chicago in 1925 to mobilize. Perhaps the most significant union of this type, the Brotherhood of Sleeping Car Porters and Maids, or Pullman Porters, was also founded in 1925 by A. Philip Randolph. The 1930s and 1940s would witness a broad campaign by the Congress of Industrial Organizations to unionize black workers throughout the South, resulting in the Steel Workers Organizing Committee, the International Union of Mine, Mill, and Smelter Workers, and the Food, Tobacco, Agricultural, and Allied Workers, names indicative of a wide range of industries reliant upon black labor. These efforts point to the complexity of black life in the American South, as Marxist-influenced unionization often called upon local churches and benevolent societies for their support. Blacks who joined unions maintained their religious values, suggesting a multidimensional analysis of social realities.

In the English-speaking Caribbean, membership in industrial unions was severely limited, although there was some development between 1919 and 1929, the result of a robust regional economy based upon bauxite and oil. However, the ensuing depression wiped out these gains. Increased unemployment and British seeming indifference resulted in an activism in the 1930s that was interested not only in workers' rights but also the end of colonial rule. The Butler Riots of 1937 in Trinidad are an example of the period's unrest, as workers joined Grenadian T. B. U. Butler's rival union to counter one supported by industry and colonial authority, and reacted violently to the refusal of the American-owned oil company to restore pay cuts after the company had rebounded from a momentary drop in revenues. A 1938 workers' revolt in St. Thomas Parish, Jamaica, site of Paul Bogle's 1865 assault on Morant Bay, involved some 1,400 machete- and stick-wielding persons whose protests were likewise put down by the state. In similar fashion, sugar industry workers vehemently reacted to the loss of wages and work throughout the islands in the 1930s.

In Brazil, individual choice of identity did not shield the discernibly African-descended person from discrimination, and racial barriers to industrial jobs meant that black Brazilians found it difficult to organize labor unions. Their response was to develop trade associations focusing on social security and retirement benefits, much like self-help societies. Brazilian trade associations tended to be segregated, reflecting occupational divisions along racial lines. For example, artisans and barbers were traditionally "black" occupations going back to slavery, and these professions were represented organizationally by the Artisans' Philanthropic Union Beneficent Society and the Barbers' Union Beneficent Society, both associations of *homens de côr*, or people of color. Although not a trade association, the Sociedade Protectora dos Desvalidos, or the Society for the Protection of the Needy, was critical in that it offered benefits to blacks of all trades.

## Faiths New and Renewed

While those of African descent were fighting to recreate themselves as free workers, they were also developing religious traditions that can be placed into three streams. The first extended a process that began with the African's initial contact with European Christianity, whereby the religion was steadily Africanized both liturgically as well as theologically. The second stream, also continuing from previous periods, involved practices developed in Africa and transferred to the Americas, where they were renewed with some alteration but remained identifiably African. The third stream saw the creation of new religions, typically taken from the fabrics of Islamic-Judeo-Christian traditions and woven into entirely novel patterns, informed by a vision of Africa as a historical power and, at least in one instance, a future destination. While the following examples are taken from specific regions, the streams of religious tradition they represent are not territorially limited but can be found flowing elsewhere in the Americas.

The first stream is more a river, in that Christianity contains a range of African influences often inversely proportionate to class: the higher the class, the lesser the African influence. The practices of hoodoo and voodoo, analogues derivative of West and West Central African religions, permeated the beliefs of peasant and working class black Christians in the American South, whose religious services were in any event charged with song and dance and possession in the Holy

Ghost. In the English-speaking Caribbean, Christianity was often infused with substantial African content and connected with obeah, the use of supernatural powers to inflict harm, and *myalism*, the employment of spiritual resources and herbs to counteract witchcraft and other evil. The religions of *convince* and *kumina* also developed, the former involving respect for the Christian deity, but also an active veneration of the spirits of African and maroon ancestors by practitioners known as Bongo men. Kumina, otherwise known as *pukumina* or *pocomania*, also venerates ancestors, who rank after sky gods and earth deities.

The second stream is most prominently represented in Brazil and Cuba, where many were adherents of renewed African religions. Enslaved Africans entering Brazil maintained the concept of distinct ethnolinguistic groupings by pursuing, as one strategy, religious traditions peculiar to their lands of origin. In the complex society that would become Brazil, the reality was that groups intermingled, borrowing ideas from one other while retaining the concept of distinct communities, or *nações* ("nations"). As the black population became predominantly crioulo (Brazilian born) and stratified along lines of color gradation during the nineteenth century (with prêtos or "blacks" and pardos or intermediate shades as the basic divisions), persons born in Bahia and elsewhere began to choose a nação. This was significant, as those who made such choices were also choosing an African identity and an African religion. The various nações, such as the Nagôs (Yoruba) and Jêjes (Aja–Ewe–Fon), maintained distinctive religious traditions, which can collectively be referred to as *candomblé*. The various African traditions, associated with specific nações, were centered upon sacred spaces known as *terreiros*, where rituals were held. Originating in private houses, the terreiros expanded to separate plots of land during the first half of the twentieth century, facilitating the pursuit of candomblé as a way of life with minimal outside interference. In this way, the terreiros became epicenters of not only African religion but also African culture. Women were the principal leaders of candomblé, and perhaps the most famous of the terreiros in Bahia, Ilê Iyá Nassô or Engenho Velho, was founded around 1830 by women from the Yoruba town of Ketu. Terreiros were established in the late nineteenth and early twentieth centuries by women of considerable financial means, including Eugenia Anna dos Santos, or Aninha, who founded the terreiro of Ilê do Axe Opô Afonjá in 1910. Hers is a fascinating example of the mutability of ethnic identity in Bahia, as she was initiated into the

Nagô tradition at Ilê Iyá Nassô, but her African-born parents were not Yoruba.

All of these various candomblé houses were associated with *irmandades*, brotherhoods and sisterhoods that were mutual aid societies, providing burial benefits and unemployment assistance at a time when state relief either did not exist or was woefully insufficient. Examples include the Bôa Morte (Good Death) sisterhood and the Senhor dos Martírios (Lord of the Martyrs) brotherhood of the Nagôs, and the Bom Jesus das Necessidades e Redenção dos Homens Prêtos (Good Jesus of the Needs and Redemption of Black Men) of the Jêjes. The affiliation of the brotherhoods or sisterhoods with specific terreiros underscores an important feature of candomblé: its connection to the Catholic Church. Indeed, the multiple orishas or deities of candomblé, such as Eshu, Yemanja, Oshun, and Shango, are associated with the various saints and principal figures of Catholicism, which was useful when candomblé needed concealment.

Other African-centered religions include West Central African *macumba* near Rio de Janeiro, and elsewhere the practice of *umbanda*. Together with convince, kumina, and candomblé, these religions feature the common elements of African spiritual entities, sacrifice, drumming and singing, and spirit possession. They parallel the Cuban experience, where research is revealing the importance of such clandestine religious organizations as the *abukuá*, a society originating in the Cross River area of southeastern Nigeria and Cameroon. Cuba is also a center of Yoruba or *lucumí* influence, apparent in the practice of *santería*. Divisions among the African-born and their descendants, which like Brazil eventually became a matter of choice, were equally preserved in Cuba's system of *naciones*, supported as they were by the respective *cabildos*, the functional equivalents of the Brazilian irmandades. Yoruba-based religion can also be found in Trinidad in the religion of *Shango*, in which the Yoruba gods Shango, Yemanja, Eshu, and Ogun are worshiped along with deities of Trinidadian origin.

The third stream of religious expression is just as dynamic as the first two. Perhaps its most innovative example is the Rastafarian movement. The onerous economic struggle in the Caribbean not only produced emigration, labor unionism, and social unrest, but also conditions in which the sufferers reenvisioned themselves within an international context. Incessant emigration and subordination to the colonial empire generated within the Caribbean a transnational perspective, contributing specifically to the belief among the downtrodden in Jamaica that there was a special connection between the Diaspora and Ethiopia. Leonard Percival Howell, experienced in foreign travel, returned to Jamaica in 1932 to proclaim that black Jamaicans should no longer offer their loyalty to England, but to the emperor of Ethiopia, Ras ("Lord") Tafari Makonnen, crowned in November of 1932 and given the throne name Haile Selassie I. The idea that a black man was a sovereign ruler, at a time when most of African descent were under colonial rule in both Africa and the Americas, stirred the collective African imagination. Howell, Archibald Dunkley, and Joseph Hibbert further held that because black Jamaicans belonged to an African nation under Haile Selassie, they should not pay taxes to England.

The 1935 Italian invasion of Ethiopia was a watershed event in the history of the African Diaspora. All around the world, people of African descent were scandalized by the occupation of this ancient, Biblically related land, and they rallied to support the Ethiopian cause. A remarkable, formative moment, the response to the invasion demonstrated the importance of Africa to the struggles of persons thousands of miles and hundreds of years removed from its shores. The invasion also strengthened the position of Howell and his associates. In 1937 the Ethiopian World Federation was founded by a Dr. Malaku Bayen in New York City to promote Ethiopia's liberation, linking it to the fortunes of black folk everywhere. The Federation elevated Haile Selassie as the "Elect of God" and maintained that Africans were the Twelve Tribes of Israel, a claim based upon the Beta Israel and the ancient *Kebra Nagast*.

The British persecuted and imprisoned Howell and his followers, who in 1940 had established a commune at Pinnacle in the hills of St. Catherine, Jamaica. Released from prison in 1943, Howell led a process through which the tenets of the Rastafari were gradually worked out. Haile Selassie acquired divine status and the capitalist, imperialist system was identified as Babylon, its rejection symbolized by "dreads" or locking of the hair, apparently in emulation of Kenya's Land and Freedom Army (or "Mau Mau") in the 1950s, and by the use of ganja and the pipe, both introduced to the Caribbean from India. Africans and their descendants were the true Israel, and Ethiopia the promised land, to which the Rasta would eventually return. The Pinnacle would be repeatedly raided by the authorities, and Howell would be placed in a mental asylum more than once. Nevertheless, the Rastafari movement became an international phenomenon, influencing the anticolonial struggle and giving rise to a deeply political and spiritual reggae.

While the Rastafari borrowed from Judeo-Christian traditions, innovations in the United States engaged these traditions as well as Islam, forging movements that, while entirely novel in theory and practice, were politically similar to the Rastafari in their anticolonialism and advocacy for the black poor. Specifically, the Moorish Science Temple of America, possibly founded in Newark, New Jersey by Noble Drew Ali as early as 1913, offered the startling proposition that African Americans were in fact Moors from Morocco, and as such were part of a larger "Asiatic" community of persons that essentially included everyone except Europeans. The claim of Moorish ancestry, like the Rastafari, linked the Diaspora back to Africa, but the Asiatic identification suggests a concern that was not limited to Africa. Unlike the Rastafari, Noble Drew Ali never advocated a physical return to Morocco. As Moors, his followers adopted Islam as their religion, but it was unorthodox; Noble Drew Ali penned his own *Circle Seven Koran*, drawing upon metaphysical beliefs foreign to conventional Islam. Noble Drew Ali died under mysterious circumstances in 1929, by which time another neo-Islamic movement was taking root. The Nation of Islam, founded in Detroit by W. D. Fard Muhammad in 1930, certainly employed Noble Drew Ali's notion of an international Asiatic identity, but it went much further in its denunciation of Europeans, identifying them as "devils." Indeed, the Nation rejected the principles of sanctioned religion as such, dismissing the idea of an afterlife and the conception of God and Satan as spiritual beings, positing instead that just as whites were devils, blacks were divine, with W. D. Fard Muhammad as Allah. The Nation's identification with Africa was not as strong as the Moors and the Rastas, however, for although members were given an "X" or an equivalent variable to represent the African name lost through enslavement, the original home of blacks was not Africa but Mecca, from where they later migrated to "East Asia" or Egypt, and then to other parts of the African continent. The Nation embraced a variant of Islam in conflict with many of the latter's central tenets, including the claim that Elijah Muhammad, W. D. Fard Muhammad's successor after the latter's disappearance in 1934, was a messenger of God. With the death of Elijah Muhammad in February of 1976, the movement splintered into several factions, with some either embracing or moving toward orthodoxy.

The racialism of the Nation of Islam reversed the assumptions and values of the day. Blackness, long associated by whites with evil, immorality, filth, and worthlessness, became the embodiment of holiness, cleanliness, morality, and self-confidence. The Nation's emphasis on hard work and economic self-reliance was the means by which a disproportionate number of its members achieved middle-class status, and it provided a model for black economic development. At the same time, the Nation's early years were very much influenced by global conflict and by its support of Japan during the Second World War. An early form of black nationalism, the Nation saw white racism as a phenomenon separate from capitalist venture, condemning the former while embracing the latter; indeed, the Nation was generally opposed to leftist movements, and in this way it differed in quality from the more radical Rastafari.

The Nation of Islam and the Moorish Science Temple of America were also mutual aid societies, but there were others in the Americas not so directly tied to religion. To be sure, Freemasonry enjoyed a significant white following, but the Masons, Odd Fellows, Order of the Eastern Star, and Sisters of Calanthe were parallel secret societies with large black memberships, providing significant assistance in times of need, while organizations such as the Ancient Sons of Israel and the Independent Order of St. Luke issued insurance policies to cover sickness and death. Those in and from the Caribbean often had their own mutual aid networks, and the *sou sou*, a fund into which members paid regularly and out of which they could draw when necessary, was a common societal feature. Beneficial and insurance societies such as the Young Mutual Society of Augusta, Georgia and the Workers Mutual Aid Association of Virginia were not secret societies, but they provided similar services through the collection of weekly dues. Hospitals, orphanages, and homes for the elderly were also established. But as important, if not more so, was the extensive assistance provided by black churches, efforts supported in varying degrees by white congregants of mainline denominations, especially concerning education. In a nutshell, black folk throughout the Diaspora drew upon what meager resources they had, their activities animated by belief systems reaching back to an ancient African past.

## Conceptualizing the Solutions

Just about everything black people did and said carried political implications. Their labor, religion, and mutual support systems all addressed social and economic relations of power. Black folk revealed views on social policy with their benevolent societies; they communicated their sense of community through religion; and they protested economic conditions through strikes, riots, and stoppages. These were all significant, but black folk also articulated political views in clear and explicit terms. Political developments within the African Diaspora require greater attention to individuals as leaders of the masses, but the participation of the latter was just as critical.

As early as Denmark Vesey and David Walker, black leaders of the highest caliber have consistently displayed an awareness that the plight of their particular community was somehow tied to similar communities elsewhere. Eventually referred to as pan-Africanism, connections between these communities varied, but it was rare for a visionary to not have a sense of a more broadly defined, African-derived community extending beyond geopolitical boundaries. The last quarter of the nineteenth century through the first half of the twentieth saw the growth of this principle among the leadership. Their activities, in conjunction with labor migrations, advances in technology, and the reality of empire itself, helped disseminate the concept of an African Diaspora among working class blacks. Reconnecting to Africa and others in the Diaspora, initially envisioned as an intellectual quest or an ideological campaign, often led to concrete action, albeit limited.

Early leaders of pan-Africanism, many of whom were Christian ministers, included Henry Highland Garnet, whose grandfather was Mandinka and whose immediate family escaped Maryland slavery in the 1820s. In his 1843 *Address to the Slaves of the United States*, Garnet called for armed revolt against the slaveocracy, citing Toussaint L'Ouverture as an example to be emulated (Frederick Douglass, who initially opposed Garnet's call for revolt, later reversed his position). Garnet further revealed a diasporic perspective in predicting that the islands of the Caribbean would eventually be "ours" (a reference to blacks in the Caribbean, not North America), and by his organization of the Cuban Anti-Slavery Committee in 1873. He completed the circle in his voyage to West Africa in 1882, where he died and remains buried. His contemporaries Alexander Crummell, Martin R. Delany, and Henry McNeil Turner all favored black emigration to either Africa or Central and South America, convinced that they would never receive the "full free" in the United States. Edward W. Blyden, born in St. Thomas, Virgin Islands, repatriated to West Africa beginning in the 1860s, where he became a leading force in establishing educational institutions in Liberia and Sierra Leone. While Anna Julia Cooper, born to an enslaved mother and a white slaveholder, cannot be categorized as a back-to-Africa emigrationist, her 1892 *A Voice from the South* established connections between racial and gender inequalities in the United States and downtrodden populations beyond its borders.

Perhaps the quintessential expression of diasporic political consciousness was the creation of the Universal Negro Improvement Association and African Communities League (UNIA) under Marcus Garvey. Born in Jamaica on August 17, 1887, Garvey learned the printing trade before joining the tens of thousands who left the Caribbean for work in Central America. Traveling to London in 1912, he came across the pan-Africanist ideas of the Egyptian Dusé Muhammad, editor of the *African Times and Orient Review*. Upon his return to Jamaica, he founded the UNIA in 1914, in which his wives Amy Ashwood and later Amy Jacques Garvey would play prominent roles. Venturing to the United States in 1916 to raise money for the UNIA and to meet Booker T. Washington (who, unknown to Garvey, had died the previous year), he incorporated the UNIA in New York state in 1918, establishing his headquarters in Harlem. Garvey's "back-to-Africa" movement was much more involved than a simple call for repatriation. Facing colonialism in both the Caribbean and Africa, he advocated the dismantling of European and American empire and the reconstruction of black societies everywhere. His businesses, such as the Black Star Line, were launched to promote trade between black communities in the Americas. His official organ, the *Negro World*, was the most widely circulated black publication in the world, appearing in English, French, Spanish, and Portuguese, and was edited from 1923 to 1928 by T. Thomas Fortune, former editor of the New York *Age*. By 1921, Garvey had achieved international recognition, his parades through Harlem, along with his annual August conventions, attracting thousands from all over the world. His initial backers included A. Philip Randolph (who would later withdraw his support) and Ida B. Wells Barnett, champion of the antilynching campaign, while Madame C. J. Walker, cosmetics entrepreneur and multimillionaire, provided some financial backing. Centered in Harlem, the UNIA was the literal embodiment of pan-Africanism, and in time it established 996 branches in forty-three countries, including Cuba, South Africa, Europe, and even Australia. Its membership is difficult to calculate, but it conceivably numbered in the hundreds of thousands.

Familiar with racism and light skin privilege, Garvey instilled pride in persons with dark skin, thick lips, broad noses, and nappy hair. He originated the Red, Black and Green flag of pan-Africanism and black nationalism, and he taught that hard work and discipline were the keys to success. His overall message was a much-needed balm, but there were problems in the organization. Succinctly put, his advisors were not up to the task, and his investments were poorly advised. There were also elements within the American black community appalled by his back-to-Africa message, at his ability to raise substantial sums of money, at his rapid ascent. Some were sincerely concerned that Garvey was a charlatan, but others were driven by the politics of xenophobia and personal ambition. For them, Garvey was an outsider with an accent, a dark-skinned West Indian who had come to Harlem, the center of the black world, and virtually taken over. His critics became even more alarmed after Garvey met with the Ku Klux Klan in 1922, their anxiety converging with that of the federal government, the latter concerned about the implications of Garvey's antiracist, anticolonial activities. Britain also was uneasy with Garvey, and together with the United States covertly opposed the UNIA's attempt to acquire land and establish a presence in Liberia. The "Garvey Must Go" campaign resulted in his indictment on mail-fraud charges in 1921 and conviction in 1923. In 1925 he began serving a five-year term at the federal penitentiary in Atlanta, Georgia. His sentence was commuted in 1927 by President Coolidge following a campaign for his release by the national black press. Garvey would return to Jamaica, and from there to London, where he died in 1940. The UNIA still exists though in much truncated form, as Garvey's efforts at revitalizing it were largely unsuccessful.

One of Garvey's principal critics was W. E. B. Du Bois. Born in Great Barrington, Massachusetts, Du Bois's long life span (1868 to 1963), his training at Fisk, Harvard, and Berlin, and his unparalleled intellect positioned him to make incredible contributions to the struggle of black folk and the downtrodden throughout the earth, for whom he continues to serve as an exemplar of the scholar-activist. As early as 1897 he founded the American Negro Academy with other black intellectuals, including Alexander Crummell. Between 1896 and 1914 he led the annual Congress on Negro Problems at Atlanta University. In 1903 he published *Souls of Black Folk*, challenging, among other things, Booker T. Washington's emphasis on vocational training, his public deemphasis of the struggle for social and political equality, and his extraordinary influence in the decision-making process affecting black people, otherwise known as the "Tuskegee Machine." Instead,

Du Bois proposed a vigorous campaign for full citizenship led by a black "talented tenth," in whom he would express great disappointment later in life.

Du Bois, at the head of a similarly minded group, met in Niagara Falls, Canada in June of 1905. Four years later, the Niagara Movement became institutionalized in the founding of the National Association for the Advancement of Colored People (NAACP), whose leaders included Ida B. Wells Barnett (but not Monroe Trotter, publisher of the Boston *Guardian*, who disagreed with the inclusion of whites). In 1911, the National Urban League was founded, likewise an multiracial organization dedicated to improving the social and economic plight of blacks. It was in such a context, with national organizations already in place and fighting to improve conditions for those of African descent, that Marcus Garvey entered the picture.

Du Bois concluded that Garvey did not understand North American race relations, and he saw him as a menace. It did not help that both men engaged in personal invective. They differed from each other in a number of ways, but one of the greatest ironies of the period is that both were committed to the struggles of black people on an international scale. As longtime editor of the *Crisis*, official organ of the NAACP, Du Bois published articles and information that covered the whole of the African Diaspora, and in that way paralleled the range of Garvey's *Negro World*. A series of several Pan-African Congresses, begun in 1900, saw Du Bois's organizational involvement in 1919, 1921, 1927, and 1945. These congresses, convened to marshal opposition to colonialism and racism, were not unlike Garvey's annual conventions, and the two men's efforts were often confused in the media. Du Bois would go on to incorporate a Marxist analysis into a powerful critique of capitalism, while Garvey remained an unabashed capitalist enthusiast. Disillusioned with developments in the United States, Du Bois relocated to Ghana in 1960, joined the Communist Party, and renounced his American citizenship; he died in Ghana on the eve of the August 27, 1963 March on Washington. Tensions between Du Bois and the Garvey camp lessened when Amy Jacques Garvey and Du Bois collaborated in organizing the 1945 Manchester Pan-African Congress. The tempestuous reality of Du Bois and Garvey as pan-Africanist pioneers was symbolically reconciled on African soil under Kwame Nkrumah, independent Ghana's first president. Having studied in the United States at Lincoln University, Nkrumah's pan-Africanist vision for Africa was directly inspired by both men.

The Caribbean contribution to pan-Africanism and the concept of the African Diaspora was therefore highly significant. In addition to Garvey and Blyden, Trinidadian Henry Sylvestre Williams called the first Pan-African Congress in London in 1900, and he collaborated with Dr. Robert Love of Jamaica to establish branches of the Pan-African Association in Jamaica in 1906. Deeply disturbed by the 1935 Italian invasion of Ethiopia, Jamaican Harold Moody transformed his League of Coloured Peoples from an educational organization to a decidedly political one, while Trinidadians George Padmore and C. L. R. James responded by founding the International African Service Bureau in London in 1937, along with the future president of Kenya, "Burning Spear" Jomo Kenyatta. Padmore, born in 1902, had attended Fisk and Howard universities, dropping out of the latter's law school in 1928 and joining the U.S. Communist Party to combat imperialism. A gifted writer, Padmore became editor of the influential *Negro Worker*, rising to prominence in the Communist International, for which he wrote *The Life and Struggles of Negro Toilers*. But four years before establishing the Bureau with James, he exited the Communist Party over differences concerning race. Padmore would control the Bureau until it became the Pan-African Federation in 1944, and he was instrumental in recruiting many of the organizers for the Manchester Congress the following year. Having published the insightful *How Britain Rules Africa* in 1936, he continued to write articles for a number of publications, including the *Crisis*, the *Chicago Defender*, and the *Pittsburgh Courier*, demonstrating the international dimension of the black media during this period. Padmore's influence as a journalist writing on labor strikes in Trinidad and the Caribbean in 1937 and 1938 was far-reaching, exposing the relationship between foreign capital and colonial rule in the increasingly desperate plight of the peasant turned wage laborer. He would precede Du Bois in Ghana, where in the 1950s he served as an advisor to Nkrumah.

C. L. R. James, another towering scholar-activist whose work continues to influence, left Trinidad in 1932 with only a high school education. In 1938 James published *The Black Jacobins*, the seminal work on the Haitian Revolution, simultaneously igniting a scholarly revolution by inaugurating a movement in which history is written "from the bottom up," or from the perspective of the working and downtrodden classes. His 1938 *History of Negro Revolt* centered people of African descent in world history, emphasizing the vital role they must play in future global struggles. As was true of *Black Jacobins*, James demonstrated how the African-descended could take ownership of ideas originating in Europe and forge them into implements of liberation in his 1963 publication concerning cricket, *Beyond a Boundary*.

No less important was North American Paul Robeson, born at a time (1898) when the memory of slavery was quite fresh, his father having escaped it at the age of fifteen. Raised in Princeton, New Jersey, Robeson graduated from Rutgers and then Columbia Law School after stellar accomplishments both academically and athletically. While his acting and singing careers began during in law school, he traveled to London in 1927 to study at the London School of Oriental Languages. There he met James, Padmore, Kenyatta, and Nnamdi Azikiwe, first president of Nigeria, and would later recall "I discovered Africa in London." Robeson studied African languages and read widely on Africa, adding to his understanding of art and spirituality in the African Diaspora. His 1934 publication, *What I Want from Life*, is one of the most incisive inquiries into the collective psyche of the African-derived, emphasizing the importance of retrieving an African-centered identity. During his travels to the Soviet Union and Spain in the 1930s, he developed a deeper appreciation of the plight of the downtrodden, and he began to stress the need to coordinate anticolonial and antiracist struggles throughout Africa, the African Diaspora, and Asia. He became increasingly radical as his singing and acting careers soared, helping to establish in 1937 what became the Council on African Affairs (CAA) and serving as its chair for most of its existence after 1942.

Perhaps the CAA's most important work was in South Africa, where it supported the African National Congress. Robeson's anticolonial activities intensified after the Second World War, but following the CAA's "Big Three Unity" rally in June of 1946 at Madison Square Garden in New York City, attended by 19,000 people and led by Robeson, Du Bois, Mary McLeod Bethune, and others, Cold War politics caused a major split in African American leadership. As early as 1942, the FBI had begun investigating the CAA for subversive activities, and by 1948 a previously receptive white media joined the NAACP under Walter White in denouncing Robeson (and Du Bois, who was dismissed from the NAACP that same year). Concerned with the influence of Robeson and Du Bois in West Africa and elsewhere, the U.S. government revoked Robeson's passport in 1950. Robeson would suffer a fate similar to that of Du Bois, virtually forgotten by his people who owed him so much, reaching the end in 1976.

Notwithstanding the complexities of racial identity in Brazil, consciousness of a larger black world managed to develop there as well. In São Paulo, black newspapers such as *A Liberdade*, *O Menelick*, and *O Alfinete* ("The Pin"), published early in the twentieth century, initially featured community news and information, social commentaries, and reports concerning racial discrimination. These earlier newspapers gave way to *O Clarim da Alvorada* ("The Clarion of Dawn") and *Progresso* in the 1920s, and *A Voz da Raça* ("The Voice of the Race") in the 1930s. Under the leadership of cofounder José Correia Leite, *Clarim* sought to unify the African-descended community by examining the challenges of the day and by emphasizing African Brazilian history. At the same time, the first African Brazilian activist organization in São Paulo was founded, the Centro Cívico Palmares, its name a tribute to the famous quilombo. Correia Leite was a member of the Palmares organization and connected *Clarim* to both an activist agenda and a diasporic vision, as *Clarim* published articles from the *Chicago Defender* and Garvey's *Negro World*. Robert Abbott, publisher of the *Defender*, visited Brazil in 1923, and subsequently he began sending his paper to *Clarim* and to *Progresso* (the Garvey influence apparently came through an English teacher in Bahia named Mario de Vasconcelos, who sent translations of *The Negro World* to the offices of *Clarim*).

Black Brazilian consciousness took a momentous step forward in September of 1931, when the Frente Negra Brasileira, or Black Brazilian Front, was founded under the leadership of Arlindo Veiga dos Santos and others. A civil rights organization as well as a benevolent society, the Frente Negra launched *A Voz da Raça*. However, schisms between the Frente Negra and other sectors of the African Brazilian community arose as a result of Vega dos Santos' autocratic style of leadership and embrace of fascism. Dissolved (along with all political parties) by the imposition of the *Estado Novo* (New State) under Getúlio Vargas in November of 1937, the Frente Negra nevertheless remains a critical turning point in the effort both to unify the African-descended population in Brazil and to connect them with blacks elsewhere. A similar movement developed in Cuba, where the Cuban Independent Party of Color was established in 1907 by Evaristo Estenoz and Pedro Ivonet. Fighting for equality of treatment from a government under heavy American influence, they were opposed by others of African descent such as Juan Gualberto Gómez, who saw their race-based efforts as divisive and anti-Cuban. The party was outlawed in 1910, Esenoz and Ivonet were arrested, and the ensuing revolt by aggrieved party members brutally repressed by President José Miguel Gómez (with American backing). Unlike members of the Frente Negra, thousands of party members were slaughtered, including women and children. The aspirations of African Cubans would suffer for many years to come.

## Efflorescence

Black folk have always maintained a dynamic and vibrant life of the mind. Not even slavery, Reconstruction's failure, and the rise of state-sponsored terrorism in the American South could stamp out their creativity and scientific genius. Individuals of distinction followed in the footsteps of the mathematician, astronomer, almanac maker, and surveyor Benjamin Banneker (d. 1806), discovering how to intellectually transcend the impediments of racism. While Banneker, greatly responsible for the design of the District of Columbia, had been free-born, the slave-born George Washington Carver (d. 1943) developed hundreds of applications for such plants as soybeans, sweet potatoes, and peanuts, and he was instrumental in aiding the South's flagging agriculture from his laboratories at Tuskegee Institute. Elijah McCoy (d. 1929) was also familiar with slavery, his parents having escaped the institution in Kentucky to Canada, Elijah's birthplace. Eventually settling in Detroit, McCoy accumulated nearly sixty patents, his steam engine lubricator so celebrated that it became "the real McCoy," a standard by which such machinery would be measured. Freeborn Granville T. Woods (d. 1910) also held over sixty patents, and he played a major role in the development of the rail by creating a telegraph system that allowed communication between trains and stations. Likewise, Norbert Rillieux (d. 1894), son of a slave woman and a planter in Louisiana, received an education in France and made contributions to industry with his invention of an evaporating process to refine sugar. Perhaps as significant was the accomplishment of Rebecca J. Cole (d. 1922), the second black female physician on record in the United States, who received her medical degree in 1867. Edward A. Bouchet (d. 1918) was also highly educated, receiving a doctorate in physics from Yale in 1876. Lewis Latimer (d. 1929) held patents for an electric lamp and a carbon filament for light bulbs, and he was a member of Thomas Edison's laboratory. Madam C. J. Walker (d. 1919) became wealthy as an innovator of female hair care techniques.

The preceding are just some of the African-descended who made significant contributions to science and industry. They would be accompanied or succeeded by such individuals as Roger Arliner Young (d. 1964), who in 1940 became the first black woman to receive a doctorate in zoology from the University of Pennsylvania and who went on to publish significant research; Dr. Daniel Hale Williams (d. 1931), who performed the first known successful open heart surgery, in 1893; Dr. Ernest E. Just (d. 1941), noted zoologist; Howard Medical College professor Ruth Ella Moore (1903–1994), the first African American woman to earn a doctorate in bacteriology from Ohio State University, in 1933; and Dr. Charles Drew (d. 1950), a leading expert in blood plasma and a pioneer in the creation of blood banks. While most of these notables were formally educated, there were many others who never had the opportunity to grace academic halls, but who nonetheless had formidable knowledge of the medicinal properties of plants and herbs, or had unusual insight into the habits of animals and insects, or knew the movements of the constellations from years of observation. They were also scientists, though uncelebrated.

Regarding cultural production in the African Diaspora, the plastic arts, music, dance, and literature were tightly interwoven with labor and politics, reflecting as well as influencing. Whatever the political circumstances, black folk have consistently lived in strikingly beautiful and uniquely innovative ways. In the beginning of the twentieth century, however, black artists and writers and musicians began to experience a notoriety previously unknown by their ancestors. The "discovery" of black aesthetics had the effect of intensifying cultural production, otherwise referred to as a renaissance. We should not approach the phenomenon uncritically. Black intellectuals debated the purpose of black cultural production, whether it should always have redeeming social value and be of use in the overall struggle to "uplift" the poor and oppressed. Further complicating black art were questions relating to white patronage, whether it was merely supportive or more intrusive. Issues of authenticity were also present, as the relatively privileged, in some instances, sought to interpret for a white audience the experiences of the downtrodden. Twin considerations of white patronage and class difference therefore raise this question: How representative of the black masses was the cultural work of a small black elite?

We can begin this discussion in Harlem, where the early-twentieth-century arrival of immigrants from the English-, French-, and Spanish-speaking Caribbean merged with that of blacks migrating from the

American South to create an atmosphere of tremendous energy. The rise of the UNIA and the NAACP invigorated the black community, as did other organizations whose leaders addressed throngs of listeners from their stepladders on Harlem's various street corners, charging the air with an expectancy that looked to move beyond the legacies of slavery to a new day. Harlemites vigorously debated alternative visions of the future, thrilled with the thought that they could at least dream a better future, a world in which increasing emphasis was placed on similarities between the African-descended rather than differences.

It was in such a context that the Harlem Renaissance, also called the New Negro Movement, began to flourish, spanning the 1920s and early 1930s, having been slowed by the depression of 1929. The idea was that a different kind of black person was emerging out of the shadows of the past, a person much more assertive and demanding of his rights. Black writers in particular achieved recognition during this period, benefiting from a growing American interest in urban life and social challenges.

For many scholars, the Renaissance began with Jean Toomer's *Cane* (1923), an excursion into issues of race from which Toomer took a detour as his life unfolded, opting to explore mysticism instead. Jessie Fauset, who supported Toomer's development as a writer, was herself a major figure of the period, serving as literary editor of the *Crisis* from 1919 to 1926. Like Toomer, Fauset's *There is Confusion* (1924) and *Plum Bun: A Novel Without a Moral* (1929) both examine interracial questions, in particular the notion of light-skinned blacks "passing" for white. Fauset also played a role in the rise of Langston Hughes, often referred to as the "Poet Laureate of the Negro Race." Author of "The Negro Speaks of Rivers," Hughes published *Weary Blues* in 1926 and *Not Without Laughter* in 1930, demonstrating his versatility as both poet and novelist. *The Big Sea*, his 1940 autobiography, is an important source for what is known about the Renaissance. Countee Cullen was also a poet of tremendous talent, publishing *Color* in 1925, containing his most famous poems, "Heritage" and "Incident." The second black person to win a Guggenheim Fellowship, he followed *Color* with *The Ballad of the Brown Girl* and *Copper Sun*, both in 1927. Though ending in divorce in 1930, his 1928 marriage to Du Bois's only child Yolande demonstrates the interconnectedness of the period's black intelligentsia.

James Weldon Johnson had been active prior to the emergence of Jean Toomer. Secretary of the NAACP for a time, Johnson published *Fifty Years and Other Poems* in 1917, followed in 1922 by *The Book of*

*Negro Poetry.* His *Autobiography of an Ex-Coloured Man* was reissued in 1927, the same year that *God's Trombones* appeared, in which the oratorical style of the black preacher was poeticized (and immortalized). Perhaps the most recognized figure of the Renaissance, Johnson was later joined in prominence by the celebrated Zora Neale Hurston, whose insight into the lives and culture of the black peasantry and working class, particularly her depiction of women and their struggles in black southern communities, is exemplified in such works as *Jonah's Gourd Vine* (1934) and *Their Eyes Were Watching God* (1937). An anthropologist, she also studied African-based religions in the American South and Haiti; *Tell My Horse* (1937) remains an important discussion of the latter, while her autobiographical work, *Dust Tracks on a Road* (1942), is a reflective as well as stinging critique of American policies.

In 1925, Alain Locke published a major compilation of nonfiction prose called *The New Negro*; among those who would become prominent later, but who participated in the Renaissance at an early age, was Sterling Brown, whose 1932 collection of poetry, *Southern Road*, was a significant landmark. Du Bois himself contributed to the literary movement through his creative writing, including *The Quest of the Silver Fleece* (1900) and *Darkwater* (1920), and by editing the works of others.

Writers from the Caribbean were also among the leaders of the literary outpouring; Nella Larsen was possibly among them, as her mother may have come from the Caribbean. Her novels *Quicksand* (1928) and *Passing* (1929), however, correspond more closely to issues raised in the work of Jessie Fauset. More clearly fitting this category was the Jamaican Claude McKay, who in 1924 published the classic *Home to Harlem*. He was joined by Eric Walrond, from British Guyana, who worked for a number of black journals before publishing his *Tropic Death* in 1926. As writers explored connections among African-descended populations and Africa's meaning for the Diaspora, tensions sometimes developed; McKay, for example, became alienated from black American intellectuals. For all of his disaffection, however, he contributed greatly to the creation of a diasporic intellectual network, maintaining a lively correspondence with North American and Caribbean thinkers during his stay in Europe from 1922 to 1934. For his part, Walrond helped to publish the writings of the Martinicuan René Maran in *Opportunity*, a journal of the Urban League, for whom Walrond worked at one point. Mention of *Opportunity* allows for the general observation that black periodicals of the day, including Garvey's *Negro World* and Du Bois's *Crisis*, were instrumental in promoting the literary renaissance, as they regularly published short works of fiction as well as poetry.

In addition to creative writers, New York City was either home or way station for a constellation of other black intellectuals and artists, including the prominent sociologist E. Franklin Frazier, political activist and organizer Hubert Harrison, journalist J. A. Rogers, and bibliophile Arthur (Arturo) Schomburg, the last three from St. Croix, Jamaica, and Puerto Rico, respectively. Arna Bontemps occupied several stations as poet and novelist (for example, his 1936 *Black Thunder*), but he was also a researcher and scholar. All of these people lived at a time when the artwork of Henry Ossawa Tanner enjoyed great notoriety in Europe and the Americas, the sculpture of Meta Warrick Fuller was critically acclaimed, and the artwork of Aaron Douglas was attracting ever-widening attention. Black film companies such as the Lincoln Motion Picture Company, established in 1916, and that of Oscar Micheaux, created in 1918, sought to counter the racist depictions of the film industry. Blacks in the theater and musicals included Paul Robeson's 1924 leading role in Eugene O'Neill's *All God's Chillun Got Wings*, and the 1921 debut of *Shuffle Along*, written and produced by Eubie Blake, Noble Sissle, Aubrey Lye, and F. E. Miller. All of these activities were enlivened by the music of the period, jazz (discussed in Chapter Eight). New York City, Chicago, New Orleans, Kansas City, and several other sites experienced the music, but Harlem as the focal point of concurrent movements was a most extraordinary place and certainly a cultural capital.

Paris was another. Blacks from the Americas came to the city, including North American soldiers who chose to remain in France at the end of the First World War. A number of musicians alighted as well, either passing through or electing to settle in the Montmartre section of the city, the center of the black American expatriate community. Paris, for much of the twentieth century, served as a refuge for black Americans seeking to escape virulent American racism, and it was a place where the appreciation of jazz allowed musicians to make a living. No doubt the greatest examples of this were Sidney Bechet and Josephine Baker. Bechet, a pioneer in a jazz form closely associated with New Orleans, went back and forth between the United States and France until he finally settled in the latter in 1950, only to die nine years later. In contrast, the dancer, singer, and actor extraordinaire Baker arrived in Paris in 1925 and remained there for most of her life until her death in 1975, having acquired French citizenship in 1927 and later serving the French Resistance in the Second World War. In addition to Claude McKay, writers and intellectuals who spent significant time in Paris included Anna Julia Cooper (the first African American to achieve the doctorate at the Sorbonne), Langston Hughes, Jessie Fauset, Nella Larsen, Alain Locke, and Countee Cullen. Henry Ossawa Tanner was the most illustrious black artist living in Paris, but also studying in France was sculpturer Augusta Savage, known for her *Lift Every Voice and Sing*; Nancy Elizabeth Prophet, who worked in stone and wood, producing *Head of a Negro* and *Congolaise*; Hale Woodruff, perhaps best known for his *Amistad* murals in the Talladega College Library (Alabama); Palmer Hayden, whose paintings of everyday life are represented in *The Janitor Who Paints*; and Aaron Douglas, regarded as the "Dean" of black painters. His work graced the *Crisis*, as it also illustrated Johnson's *God's Trombones*. Douglas was deeply influenced by African art, and it was in France, ironically, that these artists were exposed to such art, source of cubism's genius. Like Paul Robeson, they traveled to Europe to either discover or develop a more intimate relationship with African culture.

Related to, yet independent of, the African American experience in Paris was the rise of *négritude*, a movement largely consisting of French-speaking and French-writing individuals who posited the idea that people of African descent throughout the world possessed an essence distinguishing them from non-Africans, a difference that was expressed culturally. Négritude writers sought to explain the reasons why blacks were nearly everywhere under European domination, and they found their answer in the idea of négritude or "blackness." Briefly, négritude maintains that the African-descended seek a harmonious rather than exploitative relationship with their environment; that they are warm, sensual, and artistically creative, and therefore susceptible to the ruthless. Needless to say, not all in Africa or the Diaspora subscribed to such views, and many rejected them outright. Nonetheless, négritude was an important concept whose influence remains discernible. A distaste for colonial rule was shared by students in Paris from Africa and the Caribbean, who began organizing when sisters Paulette, Jane, and Andrée Nadal of Martinique held weekly literary salons from 1929 to 1934. Persons from Africa, the Caribbean, and North America met (usually on Sundays) to discuss art and politics, and to dance. In 1929, Paulette Nadal and the Haitian dentist Leo Sajous started a monthly

**FIGURE 11.** Nicolás Guillén, Afro-Cuban poet and editor of *Mediodía*, Madrid, Spain, September 1937. Photographs and Prints Division, Schomburg Center for Research in Black Culture, The New York Public Library, Astor, Lenox, and Tilden Foundations.

publication in both French and English entitled *Revue du Monde Noir*, in which writers from all over the Diaspora and Africa were featured. The *Revue* folded in less than a year, but it was replaced by *Légitime Defense*, published by another group of students from Martinique. In 1935, students began the journal *L'Etudiant Noir*, and among them were those who would become leading intellectuals. Léopold Senghor, prolific writer and future president of Senegal, was a participant, as was Aimé Césaire of Martinique, who in 1939 published the highly influential *Cahier d'un retour au pays natal* ("Notes on Return to My Native Land"), an anticolonial classic that also presented the concept of black cultural unity. Other négritude writers included Jacques Roumain, Léon G. Damas, Etienne Léro, and Birago Diop.

In tandem with négritude and the New Negro Movement, Spanish-speaking artists developed what was called *negrismo*. African Cuban poet, writer, and journalist Nicolás Guillén is a prominent example, whose works celebrate African beauty while depicting black struggle over the centuries. His 1929 collection of poems, *Cerebro y Corazón* ("Brain and Heart"), was a major contribution and signaled his lifelong commitment to social and political change. Guillén was joined in the negrismo movement by poet Luis Palés Matos of Guayama, Puerto Rico, whose 1937 *Tuntún de pasa y grifería* ("Drumbeats of Kink and Blackness") also focused on race. That Palés Matos was phenotypically "white" drew criticism, and his subsequent poetry reflected different issues. African Cuban poet Marcelino Arozarena Ramos was a third major voice in the literary movement, but perhaps the quintessential artist of the period was the Cuban painter Wilfredo Lam. Born of a Chinese father and a mother of African, European, and indigenous ancestry, Lam's work developed an intense engagement with African themes, perhaps owing to both his background and his personal participation in santería.

## Suggestions for Further Reading

Much of what is contained in this chapter is related to suggested materials for the previous two, as works often venture into multiple periods and subjects. In addition to these and to the numerous works referred to in the text, a good place to find more about migrations is Irma Watkins-Owens, *Blood Relations: Caribbean Immigrants and the Harlem Community, 1900–1930* (Bloomington and Indianapolis: Indiana U. Press, 1996), a book that also moves into early-twentieth-century Harlem and Marcus Garvey. It can be complemented by Winston James, *Holding Aloft the Banner of Ethiopia: Caribbean Radicalism in Early Twentieth-Century America* (London and New York: Verso, 1998). Concerning indentured Africans, see Monica Schuler, *"Alas, alas Kongo": A Social History of Indentured African Immigration Into Jamaica, 1841–1865* (Baltimore, MD: Johns Hopkins U. Press, 1980), and Maureen Warner-Lewis, *Guinea's Other Suns: The African Dynamic in Trinidad Culture* (Dover, MA: Majority Press, 1991).

Labor movements are covered in such works as Robin D. G. Kelley, *Hammer and Hoe: Alabama Communists During the Great Depression* (Chapel Hill: U. of North Carolina Press, 1990), and Joe William Trotter, Jr., *Black Milwaukee: The Making of an Industrial Proletariat, 1915–1945* (Urbana: U. of Illinois Press, 1985). Trotter has also edited a useful volume on migration in *The Great Migration in Historical Perspective: New Dimensions of Race, Class and Gender* (Bloomington: Indiana U. Press, 1991). Relating labor and political developments in the United States through the mid-twentieth century is Penny M. Von Eschen,

*Race Against Empire: Black Americans and Anticolonialism, 1937–1957* (Ithaca, NY and London: Cornell U. Press, 1997). In *Freedoms Given, Freedoms Won: Afro-Brazilians in Post-Abolition São Paulo and Salvador* (New Brunswick, NJ: Rutgers U. Press, 1998), Kim D. Butler provides insight into both labor developments and African-based religions in her discussion of Brazil. This can be read together with Philip A. Howard, *Changing History: Afro-Cuban Cabildos and Societies of Color in the Nineteenth Century* (Baton Rouge: Louisiana State U. Press, 1998), and Michael G. Hanchard, *Orpheus and Power: The Movimento Negro of Rio de Janeiro and São Paulo, Brazil, 1945–1988* (Princeton, NJ: Princeton U. Press, 1994).

There is a lot of literature on the Harlem Renaissance. One can begin with Arna Bontemps, ed., *The Harlem Renaissance Remembered* (New York: Dodd Mead, 1972); Nathan Huggins, *Harlem Renaissance* (New York: Oxford U. Press, 1971); and David Levering Lewis, *When Harlem Was in Vogue* (New York: Knopf, 1981). Regarding négritude, see Janet G. Vaillant, *Black, French, and African: A Life of Léopold Sédar Senghor* (Cambridge: Cambridge U. Press, 1990); Femi Ojo-Ade, *Leon Gontran-Damas: The Spirit of Resistance* (London: Karnak, 1993); and Léopold Senghor, *Négritude, arabisme et francité: réflexions sur le problème de la culture* (Beirut, Lebanon: Éditions Dar al-Kitab Allubnani, 1967). Tyler Stovall's *Paris Noir: African Americans in the City of Light* (Boston and New York: Houghton Mifflin, 1996), although primarily concerned with black Americans in Paris, also discusses négritude, as does Brent Hayes Edwards, *The Practice of Diaspora: Literature, Translation, and the Rise of Black Internationalism* (Cambridge, MA: Harvard U. Press, 2003).

One could focus on any number of influences in the Harlem Renaissance, and the Garvey phenomenon was certainly one key. Edited by Amy Jacques-Garvey, *Philosophy and Opinions of Marcus Garvey,* 2 vols. (New York: Arno Press, 1968–69) is a classic distillation of his views. For context, see Tony Martin, *Race First: The Ideological and Organizational Struggles of Marcus Garvey and the Universal Negro Improvement Association* (Dover, MA: Majority Press, 1986), and Rupert Lewis, *Marcus Garvey: Anti-Colonial Champion* (Trenton, NJ: Africa World Press, 1988). Robert A. Hill has edited primary documents relating to the Garvey movement in *The Marcus Garvey and Universal Negro Improvement Association Papers,* 9 vols. (Berkeley: U. of California Press, 1983–). For a work linking Garvey with related movements in the Caribbean, see Horace Campbell, *Rasta and Resistance: From*

*Marcus Garvey to Walter Rodney* (Trenton, NJ: Africa World Press, 1987). An excellent work on the Nation of Islam is Claude Andrew Clegg III, *An Original Man: The Life and Times of Elijah Muhammad* (New York: St. Martin's Press, 1997).

Women played major roles in the Garvey movement, along with other formations. See Ula Yvette Taylor, *The Veiled Garvey: The Life and Times of Amy Jacques Garvey* (Chapel Hill: U. of North Carolina Press, 2002); Barbara Bair, "Pan-Africanism as Process: Adelaide Casely Hayford, Garveyism, and the Cultural Roots of Nationalism," in Sidney Lemelle and Robin Kelley, eds., *Imagining Home: Class, Culture and Nationalism in the African Diaspora* (London and New York: Verso, 1994); Adelaide M. Cromwell, *An African Victorian Feminist: The Life and Times of Adelaide Smith Casely Hayford, 1868–1960* (Washington, DC: University Press, 1986); and Gerald Horne, *Race Woman: The Lives of Shirley Graham Du Bois* (New York: New York U. Press, 2000).

Regarding W. E. B. Du Bois, see Arnold Rampersad, *The Art and Imagination of W. E. B. Du Bois* (New York: Shocken Books, 1990); Manning Marable, *W. E. B. Du Bois: Black Radical Democrat* (Boston: Twayne, 1986); and David Levering Lewis, *W. E. B. Du Bois: Biography of a Race, 1868–1919* (New York: Holt, 1993). On C. L. R. James, see Anthony Bogues, *Caliban's Freedom: The Early Political Thought of C. L. R. James* (London and Chicago: Pluto Press, 1997), and Paul Buhle, *C. L. R. James: The Artist as Revolutionary* (London and New York: Pluto Press, 1988).

Works that bypass the nation-state in their analyses of anticolonial struggle include the foundational W. E. B. Du Bois, *The World and Africa: An Inquiry Into the Part Which Africa has Played in World History* (New York: International, 1965); C. L. R. James, *A History of Pan-African Revolt* (Washington, DC: Drum and Spear, 1969), 2nd ed., revised; Cedric J. Robinson, *Black Marxism: The Making of the Black Radical Tradition* (Chapel Hill: U. of North Carolina Press, 1983); and P. Olisanwuche Esedebe, *Pan-Africanism: The Idea and Movement, 1776–1963* (Washington, DC: Howard U. Press, 1982).

# CHAPTER 8

# Movement People

Movement has long been a principal characteristic of the African Diaspora. The period from 1945 to 1968 was an important era of "movement," a term that, in contrast to involuntary transatlantic transfers and reluctant labor migrations, came to signify organized campaigns to reverse the legacies of slavery and discrimination. Black people were indeed on the move, fighting racism and colonialism globally. In concert with each other and the aspirations of the similarly downtrodden, the period witnessed the persistence of a defiance made manifest with the first slave revolt, the continuing quest for the full free.

The period after the Second World War created new conditions for freedom's struggle. Nazi Germany's defeat discredited racism and brought the concept of empire under increasingly unfavorable light. Returning African veterans further fueled anticolonial protests, adding to the costs of maintaining colonies. Europe, seat of colonial power in Africa, was superceded by the United States and the Soviet Union as the two world superpowers, neither with territorial claims in Africa. The new Cold War facilitated the anti-imperial struggle while transforming parts of Africa into an East–West theater of conflict. Egypt's Gamel 'Abd al-Nāṣir took power in 1952 and ended British military control of the Suez Canal in 1956, the year of Sudan's independence. In fact, the 1950s saw a number of African colonies held by the British, French, and Belgians achieve a generally peaceful transition to independence, in contrast to the more turbulent transition in Kenya from

1952 to 1963. With the exception of Zimbabwe, Nambia, and South Africa, the rest of the continent became independent by 1975, although often via war.

Africa's independence movement took place concurrently with parallel developments elsewhere, especially in India and China, and it was also unfolding at a time of tremendous unrest in the United States, the Caribbean, and Latin America. The imagination of the African Diaspora was especially captured by five developments in Africa: Ghana's independence under Kwame Nkrumah in 1957; the bloody struggle of Jomo Kenyatta and the Kenyan Land and Freedom Army (the so-called Mau Mau) against the British, culminating in Kenyan independence in 1963; Congo's independence (1960) and the assassination of its first prime minister, Patrice Lumumba (1961); the Algerian War (1954–1962), a particularly grim, intense struggle against the French; and the ongoing antiapartheid campaign in South Africa. Like Senegal's Léopold Senghor, many anticolonial leaders had studied in Europe and the United States and had been influenced by Garvey, Du Bois, Padmore, and others. This was true not only of Nkrumah, who envisioned a United States of Africa as a part of his pan-Africanism, but also Nnamdi Azikiwe, who also studied at Lincoln University and the University of Pennsylvania and had Nkrumah as a student while teaching in Ghana. Azikiwe (or "Zik") became Nigeria's president in 1963 and the father of Nigerian nationalism; he was a pragmatic leader and unifier of disparate groups. Thus the dawn of African independence included illumination from the Diaspora, and the effect of simultaneous conflict in Africa and the Diaspora were closer cultural and political links between the two.

## Freedom and Fire

Technological advances, especially in mass media, were important components of American social movements of the 1950s and 1960s. Social protest formed around various issues, including the Vietnam War and the feminist movement, but the struggle for civil rights and the rise of the black power movement, broadcast nightly on television for all to see, exposed America's principal fault line, the fundamental divide of race, which would preoccupy much of American domestic policy for the remainder of the century.

Racial segregation suffered serious assault in the U.S. military during the Korean War, when black and white troops began fighting in integrated units. The U.S. Supreme Court overturned the 1896 *Plessy v. Ferguson* ruling with its 1954 *Brown v. Board of Education* decision, and the steady surge of southern blacks north and west saw some modification of employment and housing discrimination. Black participation in the franchise was increasing, and in 1954 the House of Representatives included three black men – Adam Clayton Powell of New York, Charles Diggs, Jr. of Michigan, and William Dawson of Illinois. But such modest gains were far from characterizing the experience of a growing number of blacks trapped in what were to become rapidly expanding urban ghettoes; indeed, Chicago politicians, for example, planned the construction of vast, high-rise housing projects on its south side to minimize the amount of land a swelling black population would require. Unemployment, inadequate housing, substandard education, and restricted access to quality health care resulted in rising crime and festering resentment. Both in the North and South, black folk were catching hell.

Organizations such as the Congress of Racial Equality (CORE), founded by Bayard Rustin and James Foreman in 1942, pioneered nonviolent protest against discrimination in public accommodations, and the successful Baton Rouge, Louisiana bus boycott of 1953 preceded the more famous 1955 bus boycott in Montgomery, Alabama, a nonetheless crucial campaign ignited by the refusal of Rosa Parks, a member of the NAACP, to yield her seat to a white man. The strategy of CORE and the NAACP was to fight both in the courts and in the marketplace, making discrimination illegal and costly. The 1956 Supreme Court decision declared Alabama bus segregation laws unconstitutional, and it signaled the emergence of twenty-seven-year-old Dr. Martin Luther King, Jr., who had led the boycott while pastoring Dexter Avenue Baptist Church. In soon founding the Southern Christian Leadership Conference (SCLC) to challenge segregation throughout the South, King exemplified an Africanization of Christianity, as he drew deeply from the well of black experience to fashion the religion into an implement of liberation.

That Ghana's independence and congressional passage of the Civil Rights Act both occurred in 1957 was no coincidence. The Act, establishing a commission to help defend blacks' voting rights while monitoring abuse of their civil liberties, reflected increasing awareness in the U.S. government that its treatment of African Americans now carried international significance. But the struggle was far from over, as President Eisenhower evinced little interest in enforcing the Act. Black students pressed the issue by launching the sit-in movement, beginning in Wichita, Kansas in 1958 but bursting on the national scene in February of 1960, when four students attending North Carolina Agricultural and Technical College in Greensboro, North Carolina sat at a lunch counter and were refused service. Sit-ins, involving black and white students, erupted all over the South that spring and summer, only to be followed by CORE's Freedom Rides in 1961, involving students using public transportation to test interstate antidiscrimination laws. The Student Nonviolent Coordinating Committee (SNCC), newly formed with the encouragement of NAACP veteran Ella Baker, also contributed freedom riders, but SNCC and SCLC met with stiff opposition in Albany, Georgia in 1961, followed in 1963 by the brutality of city commissioner of public safety Bull Connor in Birmingham, Alabama.

Albany and Birmingham were setbacks, but on August 28, 1963, the March on Washington drew hundreds of thousands, the highlight of which was King's "I Have a Dream" speech. W. E. B. Du Bois had died in Ghana the day before, perhaps a symbolic passing of the torch. For all of their differences, King and Du Bois shared a powerful critique of American capitalism and imperialism, emphasizing their concern for the working classes of all races. King's detractors within the black community, focusing on his method of nonviolent protest and civil disobedience, would subsequently brand him an accommodationist and an integrationist, who sought acceptance and inclusion into the American mainstream. There is some truth in such an assessment, but any serious review of King's writings and speeches would also find that his vision of a nonracist America was directly related to his call for a redistribution of resources and eradication of poverty. Like Anna Julia Cooper, King was one of the few to make connections between imperialism, industrialism, and domestic policy, calling for an end to corporate greed and the Vietnam War.

The history of the civil rights movement is often written with an emphasis on leaders, especially men. But the movement was borne by the labor of women who cooked and sold chicken dinners, answered the phones, ran the endless errands, cleaned up after the meetings, and were still able to march in the streets as well as help plan strategy. As for leaders, Fannie Lou Hamer joined Ella Baker as one of the most electrifying, male or female, in her capacity as cofounder of the Mississippi Freedom Democratic party and powerful orator. Ann Moody, activist in SNCC, CORE, and the NAACP; Daisy Bates, leader of the movement in Little Rock, Arkansas; and Jo Ann Robinson, cofounder of the Montgomery Improvement Association are just a few of the other prominent movement women.

In response to the March on Washington in August, the death of four little black girls in the bombing of a Birmingham church in September, and the assassination of President Kennedy in November, President Johnson signed into law the Civil Rights Act of 1964, a comprehensive set of legislation aimed at relieving discrimination in public housing, accommodations, education, and voting. Resistance to such reforms in Selma, Alabama led the SCLC and SNCC to organize a march from that city to Montgomery; on "Bloody Sunday," March 7, 1965, state troopers viciously assaulted some 600 marchers on Selma's Edmund Pettus Bridge. On August 4, Johnson again responded with the Voting Rights Act of 1965, but by then the pattern was clear: Before the federal government would act, participants in the civil rights movement had to pay dearly in lives, sacrifice, and commitment.

King, though in communication with the larger African Diaspora and supportive of anticolonial struggles, is not often characterized as a pan-Africanist; this may be due to his universal appeal, his commitment to nonviolence, and his engagement with ideas not primarily concerned with the Diaspora, perhaps most notably those of Mahatma Gandhi. Malcolm X, a King critic for part of his life, was on the other hand the quintessential pan-Africanist, the very embodiment of the Diaspora. In accepting the Nation of Islam's teachings while in prison, Malcolm was in some ways returning to his origins, as his parents were Garveyites. That his mother was from the Caribbean also meant he shared a bond with the Diaspora beyond the rhetorical. He turned from a life of crime and became the Nation of Islam's most public and articulate spokesman, an ardent advocate of black nationalism and a student of the larger black world. In keeping with the Nation of Islam's principles, Malcolm rejected King's vision of an integrated America, calling for racial separation instead. Malcolm viewed nonviolence as counterintuitive and ineffective, a position from which he never wavered. However, Malcolm renounced the racism of the Nation of Islam once he split with that organization and embraced orthodox Islam in early 1964. At that time he made the pilgrimage to Mecca, after which he returned to Africa to meet with heads of state and students. Having made a brief trip to Egypt and Saudi Arabia in 1959, he spent nearly half of 1964 in Africa and the Middle East.

It was Malcolm who repeatedly raised the issue of American involvement in the assassination of Lumumba, and it was he who kept the plight of the Congo and other African nations in the forefront of his followers' consciousness. He consistently spoke out against apartheid in South Africa, and he supported the anticolonial struggle in Kenya and elsewhere. In imitation of the Organization of African Unity, Malcolm created the Organization of Afro-American Unity. While events in Africa were high on his agenda, he was also careful to address developments involving the African-descended in Latin America, the Caribbean, and Europe. It was his ambition to coordinate the struggle for freedom in the United States with those elsewhere in Africa and the Diaspora, and to that end he extended his offer of help to Dr. King and others in the civil rights movement. Cautious for the most part, civil rights leaders began organizing a meeting between King and Malcolm two weeks before the latter's assassination on February 21, 1965.

Malcolm's brilliance and uncompromising fearlessness had a profound impact, and they were the modern basis for the black power movement. Frustrated with the incremental pace of progress, many in the black community began to deemphasize integration as a realistic or even desirable goal, instead focusing on developing the economic and political clout of African American communities. Stokely Carmichael, born in Trinidad, may be the best example of a former SNCC member who, under the influence of Malcolm's philosophy, rejected nonviolence and began to speak of revolution. Later changing his name to Kwame Toure and repatriating to Guinea, it was Carmichael who coined the phrase "Black Power!" In 1967, the Black Power Conference in Newark, New Jersey, in which writer and scholar Amiri Baraka played a vital role, called for an independent black homeland on U.S. soil. In Oakland, California, Huey P. Newton and Bobby Seale founded the Black Panther Party for Self-Defense.

King, who had shifted his efforts to include discrimination in the North, was having trouble containing what he called "this marvelous new militancy." A careful reading of his later writings and speeches reveals his own frustration with intractable racism. Many in the black community, while deeply respectful of King, were beginning to question his approach. A rifle shot ended the challenge to his leadership on April 4, 1968. The perennial threat of "hot summers," having exploded in Watts, Los Angeles in 1965, erupted into multiple conflagrations in both the immediate aftermath of King's assassination and the ensuing summer. Over 100 cities were scorched from several days of rioting, looting, and burning; some have yet to recover.

## Developments in the Caribbean, Latin America, and Europe

From the mid-1960s forward, many of the Caribbean colonies achieved independent status, paralleling events in Africa and Asia. Trinidad's petroleum and natural gas resources distinguished it from the rest of the region, where economies saw agribusiness replace plantations, increasing emigration pressures on the unemployed. In addition to destinations such as New York, Toronto, Paris, and London, emigrants journeyed to rural areas as well. Haitians and Dominicans followed the earlier pattern of migrating to the U.S. and Canada, where they were joined by American southerners and Central Americans in picking fruit and vegetable harvests and working as domestics. Migrant workers often did not come to stay but rather to save enough money to create better conditions for themselves and their families back home. Whether their movement was temporary or permanent, some 300,000 per annum were leaving the Caribbean by the early 1960s.

While pockets of English-speaking blacks have influenced race in places like Costa Rica and Nicaragua, the U.S. empire in the Americas was perhaps a greater factor in that it exported a model of racism contributing to conditions in which the African-descended had the least education, occupied the lowest economic levels, and were without political power. Their plight can be difficult to discern in Latin America, where many cultures do not acknowledge the existence of discrimination, or even race, citing the high rate of miscegenation and mixed marriages as proof.

Race in the Dominican Republic highlights the extent to which it is an arbitrary and politicized concept, and is significantly conditioned by Haiti; the fear of being mislabeled a Haitian led many to undervalue their African heritage. Sixty percent of the country is of mixed ancestry, but those of the upper class are classified as white, illustrating the principle that class "whitens" throughout Latin America, while the 12 percent of "purer" African ancestry are invariably poor.

The idea of a color-blind "Cuban race" has been contested, as African Cubans were the worst educated, eking out an existence in rural backwaters or as unskilled laborers in urban areas. Their situation remained unchanged under Fulgencio Batista, of partial African ancestry himself, who assumed power in 1933 when Cuba was the playground (casinos, etc.) of the United States. Although controversial, there is no gainsaying that since coming to power via armed revolution in 1959, the education, health care, and living conditions of African Cubans have improved dramatically under Fidel Castro.

In Mexico, the 3 percent of the population of African descent are mostly descendants of maroons, with a number of "Afro-mestizo" communities lining Mexico's Gulf and Pacific coasts. Reference to African Mexicans as Afro-mestizos underscores the general Mexican self-description as mestizo while connoting that the African component is an unacceptable part of the meld. Indeed, the African Mexicans themselves, until the recent rise of tourist interest, emphasized their mestizo heritage as a result of the devaluation of both indigenous and African identity.

The theme of the invisible African also emerges in South America's southern cone. Argentina is the best example, where significant numbers of Africans imported through the eighteenth century seemingly disappeared by the end of the nineteenth. Black participation in frequent wars, horrendous living conditions, and Argentina's nineteenth-century policy of importing Europeans to whiten the population help explain the decline, as the number of blacks plummeted from 30 percent of the total population in the early nineteenth century to less than 2 percent by 1887. However, remaining African Argentinians continued their mutual aid societies and newspapers, their numbers augmented by the early-twentieth-century arrival of Cape Verdeans. Living in a country proud of its distinctive "whiteness," African Argentinians have lived under considerable duress. Paraguay's African-descended population was similarly decimated by incessant war; by the mid-twentieth century, most were actually descendants of blacks from Uruguay called Cambá Cuá ("place of the blacks" in Guaraní, their adopted language). Rural and few in number, their land has been the target of government appropriation since the 1940s. Uruguay was home to another beleaguered, small community who in 1936 started their own Partido Autóctono Negro (Native Black Party) to agitate for inclusion, an attempt resisted by a government that repressed the African music and dance of *candombe* in the mid-twentieth century. As for Bolivia, the tiny number of the African-descended, concentrated in the Yungas provinces, has continued with such African-influenced practices as *el rey negro*, crowning a king every year in a ceremony similar to those in New England and the Caribbean during slavery.

Venezuela's racial history of the nineteenth and early twentieth centuries resembles that of Argentina, while its subsequent history approaches that of Cuba. African Venezuelans descend from distinct groups and historical moments; they are the descendants of the enslaved, the hispanicized progeny of late-nineteenth-century Caribbean immigrants, and Guyanese blacks maintaining their own culture. While acknowledging the African presence, Venezuelan leaders believed it was inferior and set upon a policy of whitening that also called for blacks to surrender their African heritage in hispanicization. Before 1945, most blacks were uneducated and suffered significant discrimination; they were far from acceptable to the Venezuelan elite. After 1945, however, the party Acción Democrática took power, extolling the triple heritage of Venezuela (African, European, and Native American), and referring to Venezuelans as a *café con leche* (brown-skinned) people, a concept that included the African contribution. The African-descended have since experienced some amelioration of their conditions, with more employment, improved education, and movement of individuals into positions of leadership.

The popular understanding of race in Brazil has been heavily influenced by the work of sociologist Gilberto Freyre, who in the 1930s made the deceptively persuasive argument that Brazil, because of its large African-descended population and extensive racial miscegenation, was a racial democracy, and that race was not an impediment to the individual. Since the 1950s, scholars like sociologist Florestán Fernandes have been busy debunking racial democracy as a myth. Brazilians of African descent have been disproportionately poor and uneducated, achieving significant status only as star athletes and entertainers. Attempts to address these deficiencies included cultural responses, and in 1944 the *Teatro Experimental do Negro* was created under the direction of Abdias do Nascimento. The absence of organization among blacks since the Second World War, however, combined with a repressive military regime from 1964 to 1985, meant that more intense political activity did not commence until the 1970s.

As for Europe, two principal sites for the African Diaspora have been Britain and France. Enslaved Africans arrived in England in the sixteenth century, although references to Africans date as far back as the early third century, when Rome sent a "division of Moors" to help defend Hadrian's wall. By the late eighteenth century, there were as many as 10,000 enslaved blacks (often called "blackamoors") in Britain, mostly in London, Bristol, and Liverpool, which was a major port in the slave trade. Black seamen had become fixtures in the various ports, where they played leading roles in labor struggles. Early-twentieth-century England boasted a small black community numbering in the thousands, but subsequent immigration of colonial subjects from Asia, Africa, and the Caribbean in response to the labor and soldiering needs of two world wars significantly augmented their numbers. Caribbean labor continued to arrive in the 1950s to assist in the rebuilding of Britain's postwar economy, but a growing black presence had the effect of increasing white resentment, xenophobia, and violence over the fear of economic competition. Racial antagonisms helped to shape a black culture or set of black cultures in Britain, emphasizing ties between Africa, Asia, and the Caribbean.

Developments in France were analogous. With expansive territorial claims in both North and West Africa, the Caribbean, and the Indian Ocean, France has long been acquainted with people of African descent. Its conflict with Algeria has profoundly impacted race relations in France, and the experience of the North African immigrant, originally recruited to fill labor needs, has been the most critical of all. Anti-North-African sentiment in France was inflamed not only by the end of the Second World War and the reclamation of jobs by white Frenchmen, but also by the Algerian Revolution. Islam is an important dynamic, as North Africans are highly integrated into the Muslim world. However, North Africans also acknowledge ties to the non-Muslim African world, the best example of which was their acceptance of Martinican Frantz Fanon. A psychiatrist and participant in the struggle against the French in Algeria, his 1963 publication *The Wretched of the Earth* helped to popularize the Algerian Revolution throughout the African Diaspora, establishing it as a model for subsequent revolts. Xenophobia has since been on the rise in France, with North and West Africans as the principal targets.

Since the Second World War, African and African-descended populations have achieved appreciable numerical levels throughout Europe. Italy, Portugal, Spain, the Netherlands, and Germany (via American troops) all have recognizable populations of African-descended individuals, often owing to very different historical circumstances. Even Russia has a black history, though nothing like that of the Americas, which includes the servants of Peter the Great (d. 1725) and other czars. Such great Russian personalities as Alexander Pushkin had direct ties to Africa, as his great-grandfather Abram Hannibal (d. 1781), a major general in the Russian army, was possibly Ethiopian. Imperial Russia's interest in Africa was largely confined to Ethiopia, because of their similar Christian orthodoxies and the strategic location of the latter. Soviet Russia would become a magnet for African university students and visiting black intellectuals, including Claude McKay, Langston Hughes, George Padmore, W. E. B. Du Bois, Paul Robeson, and Harry Haywood, a leading activist and international figure in the Communist Party who in 1978 wrote *Black Bolshevik: Autobiography of an Afro-American Communist*, 1978. They saw in the Soviet Union an alternative model to the pervasive racism of the West.

## Cultural Innovations

In the North America of the 1950s and 1960s, blacks were openly embracing their African heritage while pushing for full equality as Americans. Full lips, nappy hair, and dark skin, once despised, were now celebrated, while such descriptors as "colored" and "Negro" were rejected for "black" and "Afro-American." Long neglected in textbooks as unworthy of formal study, the history and culture of Africa and African Americans began to appear in schools and universities around the country, a concession to growing student demand and new geopolitical realities. In the 1960s and 1970s, black studies programs were inaugurated on majority-white campuses, corresponding to modest increases in the numbers of black college students, while the curricula at such historically black colleges and universities as Spelman, Morehouse, Fisk, Dillard, Morris Brown, and Howard, among others, were infused with African-related content.

In resonance with the call for black power was the black arts movement, led by such writers and poets as Amiri Baraka (Le Roi Jones), who published *Preface to a Twenty-Volume Suicide Note* in 1961, and who wrote and produced *Dutchman* in 1964, founding the Black Arts Repertory Theatre/School that same year; Gwendolyn Brooks, celebrated author of such works as *A Street in Bronzeville* (1945), *Bronzeville Boys and Girls* (1956), *The Bean Eaters* (1960, in which can be found the previously published "We Real Cool"), and *In the Mecca* (1968); Sonia Sanchez, whose period plays and poetry include *Sister Son/ji* (1969), *Home Coming* (1969), and *We a BaddDDD People* (1970); Haki Madhubuti (Don Lee), founder of Third World Press in 1967 and author of *Don't Cry, Scream* (1969); Mari Evans, renowned poet of *Where is All the Music?* (1968) and *I Am a Black Woman* (1970); and Nikki Giovanni, poet and essayist whose first works, *Black Feeling, Black Talk* (1968) and *Black Judgement* (1969) established her as a critical voice. Many were more radical than James Baldwin, whose novels and social commentary *The Fire Next Time* (1963) are often hailed as emblematic of the period. In turn, Baldwin had been in dialogue (and competition) with Richard Wright, whose *Native Son* (1940) and *Black Boy* (1945) identified him as a major writer and thinker. However, Ralph Ellison's *Invisible Man* (1952) remains one of the more profound analyses of race in America.

African American expatriation to France resurfaces with mention of Wright and Baldwin. The former lived in Paris from 1947 to his death in 1960, and his writings from the period suggest an evolving view of race. Baldwin arrived in Paris in 1948, often returning to New York until the period 1957 to 1963, when he remained in the United States as a participant and observer in the civil rights movement while exploring race and homosexuality in such novels as *Go Tell It on the Mountain* (1953) and *Giovanni's Room (1956)*. Chester Himes, author of *Cotton Comes to Harlem (1965)*, part of a detective series featuring protagonists Grave Digger Jones and Coffin Ed Johnson, also came to France in 1953.

While in France, African American writers came into contact with French-speaking black intellectuals who included Alioune Diop, director of the journal *Présence Africain*, and Ousmane Sembene, author and film maker. Senghor and Césaire remained the leaders of the black francophone elite, and they cooperated with Wright and others to form the Congress of Negro Artists and Writers in 1956, a critical meeting of some sixty delegates from twenty-four countries, among whom were Mercer Cook, a scholar of black literature, and Horace Mann Bond, a major figure in higher education and civil rights. Influenced by the philosophy of négritude, the gathering discussed matters of race, colonialism, and culture and contributed to a decolonization effort in dialogue with such non-African intellectuals as Jean-Paul Sartre and Albert Camus.

Caribbean intellectuals in addition to Césaire played a large role in conceptualizing the global African Diaspora following World War II. Edouard Glissant of Martinique laid the theoretical foundations for "Caribbeanness," a response to négritude that emphasizes the multiple influences in Caribbean life and culture. His first novel, *La Lézarde*

("The Ripening," 1958), was followed by a series of works whose critique of négritude is echoed in the poet and writer Derek Walcott of St. Lucia, whose *In a Green Night* (1964) brought attention to his promise. But perhaps the consummate intellectual-activist was Trinidadian Eric Williams, whose *The Negro in the Caribbean* (1942) was followed two years later by the classic *Capitalism and Slavery* (1944). These books, so critical to an understanding of the Western world, came out of a diasporic context, as Williams taught at Howard University between 1939 and 1948. He would go on to serve as Trinidad and Tobago's prime minister from 1962 to 1981, dying in office.

In addition to black literature and scholarship, connections within the African Diaspora were facilitated through music and dance. Indeed, diasporic musical genres would proliferate throughout the twentieth century, engaging and borrowing from each other as well as non-African traditions. In the United States, the sorrow songs and field hollers and spirituals of slavery, all having their roots in African musical traditions, slowly gave way in the late nineteenth century to a profusion of musical expressions. There was continuity of idiom and form, but the content changed. Work songs developed, epitomized by ballads concerning black folk hero John Henry, but like other black folk music these songs remained largely unknown outside the African-descended community. The creation of the Fisk Jubilee Singers in 1867, one year after the founding of Fisk University in Nashville, Tennessee, began to change this, as the group toured the United States and Europe, introducing their spirituals and folk songs and inspiring the development of similar groups. Black minstrel groups, known as Ethiopian minstrels, also toured the country in the last quarter of the nineteenth century with their ballads and comic songs. Black minstrelsy would give way, in turn, to vaudeville, with an expanded repertoire that included operatic scenes and arias.

While some black minstrel troupes were able to expand the genre, minstrelsy on the whole has impeded the progress of the African-descended all over the world. The first minstrel show began on the slave ship, when Africans were forced to dance and sing and hide their suffering. Then, in New York City as early as 1843, whites in black face found a way to commercially benefit from the caricaturing and belittling of slaves and exslaves. This brand of live entertainment, otherwise known as a "coon show," quickly became very popular (Mark Twain was an ardent fan). In 1926, two white men began a radio show called *Sam n' Henry*, which became *Amos and Andy* in 1928.

Its popularity was such that in 1951 a television version using black actors was launched. Black protest led to its cancellation in 1953, but reruns in syndication remained until 1966. The film industry's projection of the coon worldwide not only has facilitated white racism but also has led to misunderstandings between diasporic communities, as blacks outside of the United States have also been exposed to the stereotype of the shiftless, scheming, absurdly ridiculous nigger. The trajectory and legacy of minstrelsy have yet to end, but there is an alternative tradition of serious black theatrical performance, with partial roots in the founding of the African Grove Theatre in New York City in 1821. There, at the corner of Mercer and Bleecker Streets, tragedies, ballets, and operas were performed by blacks, the most famous of whom was Ira Aldridge (1807–1867), an internationally acclaimed Shakespearian actor, touring Europe as far as Russia.

Minstrels employed music, but musical innovation went far beyond minstrelsy. The rise of the "jig piano" in the late nineteenth century, a style in which the left hand takes the place of foot stomping and the right hand delivers syncopated tunes similar to those of the banjo and fiddle, was the basis of ragtime, a genre made famous by Scott Joplin (d. 1917). The term *rag* was synonymous with dance, and ragtime emerged at a time when the cakewalk, a dance of plantation and ultimately African origin, was in vogue. Meanwhile, the blues and the spirituals were being popularized, the distinction between them essentially one of content rather than form. Sacred music was sung through much of the twentieth century by "lining-out," where the leader states the next "Dr. Watts" line (writer of many hymns) to be repeated by the congregation in a slow imploring of the heavens. The blues, focusing on the tragedies and disappointments of the individual (rather than the group), is laced with humor and irony, its ultimate objective the upliftment of the human condition. While its origins go back to an undetermined past, the blues were first popularized by W. C. Handy's 1912 published composition *Memphis Blues*, followed two years later by *St. Louis Blues*. By the early 1920s the blues had become the preserve of black female vocalists, including Mamie Smith, Bessie Smith, and Ma Rainey. Georgia-born Thomas Dorsey, who toured with Ma Rainey from 1923–1926, came to Chicago and incorporated blues into the sacred, resulting in gospel music. Mahalia Jackson, whose voice became the clarion sound of gospel, became associated with Dorsey in Chicago, while the Clara Ward Sisters, also affiliated with Dorsey, became the first gospel group to sing at the Newport Jazz Festival in

1961. Of course, there were many other gospel legends, including Alex Bradford and James Cleveland, who also had Chicago connections.

The early decades of the twentieth century also saw the development of black brass bands throughout the country, especially in New Orleans, where black and colored creole bands competed in "cutting" or "bucking" contests. Out of this interaction came Buddy Bolden, regarded by some as the "father" of jazz. In New York City, James Reese Europe organized a dance band and invented the fox-trot and turkey trot in the process, and during the First World War took an army band to Europe where he, along with other such bands, introduced the music. By 1918, the term *jazz* was common currency and was played as dance music by both black and white bands. Learned through listening to others, jazz came to be characterized by a high degree of improvisation, a call-and-response relationship between two instruments (or solo instrument and ensemble) that derived from the blues, breaks in which the soloist is featured, riffs or short phrases repeated by the ensemble, and scatting, where vocalists often imitate instruments. The following discussion of artists refers to specific recordings, but they represent only a fraction of their vast body of work.

Great jazz innovators include "Jelly Roll" Morton, whose integration of blues, ragtime, and jazz qualifies him as the father of the solo jazz piano and, for some, the first true jazz composer, publishing his *Jelly Roll Blues* in 1915; Louis Armstrong, whose genius in playing the trumpet and distinctive singing qualifies him as the premier jazz soloist, after whom so many have modeled themselves; King Oliver, a mentor of Louis Armstrong who launched King Oliver's Creole Band in Chicago in 1922 following the start of his career in New Orleans; Mary Lou Williams, viewed by some as the "First Lady of Jazz," having profoundly influenced the Kansas City sound as a pianist, composer, and arranger while serving as sidewoman for major bands; Fats Waller, pianist and composer best known for his 1929 *Ain't Misbehavin'*; Duke Ellington, master composer of an unparalleled orchestral style that, assisted by the pianist-composer Billy Strayhorn, resulted in more than 3,000 compositions, including *Mood Indigo, Sophisticated Lady, Tell Me It's the Truth; Come Sunday* (a blend of jazz and sacred music), and *Take the A Train*; Lester "Prez" Young, melodic alto saxophonist who played with a number of legends, including Billie Holiday, and whose style would influence many; Ethel Waters, whose early career as a blues singer (she would later sing religious music) included such hits as *Down Home Blues* and *Oh, Daddy*; Count Basie, whose band incorporated the Kansas City jazz sound into a style copied by many, producing such recordings as *April in Paris*, *Lester Leaps In*, and *Jumping at the Woodside*; Billie "Lady Day" Holiday, a lyricist whose unforgettable vocal quality produced *God Bless the Child* as well as *Strange Fruit*, an attack on lynching and American racism; and Ella Fitzgerald, whose range, articulation, and scatting were incomparable, as evidenced in such classics as *Lady, Be Good* and *How High the Moon*.

Mention of Mary Lou Williams underscores the fact that although black women were prominent in blues and jazz as vocalists, they were also musicians of note. The piano was often the instrument of choice, as demonstrated by the careers of Chicago's Lil Hardin Armstrong and New Orleans' Emma Barrett in the 1920s. But Dolly and Dyer Jones (daughter and mother) were trumpeters, and women playing instruments other than the piano often played in all-women bands. In the 1930s the pattern of women pianists playing with otherwise male bands and nonpianist female musicians playing in all-women bands became more familiar, the latter perhaps best exemplified by the Harlem Playgirls. While the outbreak of the Second World War saw more women incorporated into previously male bands by necessity, groups such as the International Sweethearts of Rhythm, who played before African American soldiers stationed in Europe, continued to perform as all-female ensembles.

The sounds of blues, gospel, and jazz were popularized during the interwar period by the mass production and distribution of "race records," aimed at black consumers but enjoyed (and studied) by whites as well. With the end of the Second World War came a new era in jazz – bebop – led by such giants as saxophonist Charlie "Bird" (or "Yardbird") Parker, whose *Now's the Time* and *Parker's Mood* heralded his genius; pianist Thelonius Monk, a maverick whose unconventional approach to music can be sampled in such works as *Misterioso*, *Straight No Chaser*, and *Round Midnight*; and trumpeter Dizzy Gillespie, com- poser of such standards as *Salt Peanuts* and *A Night in Tunisia*. In part a rebellion against swing, dominated in the 1930s by white musicians Benny Goodman, Tommy Dorsey, and Gene Krupa, bebop joined a flatted fifth of the scale to already existing "blue" or "bent" notes, and it was characterized by complicated polyrhythms, dissonance, and ir- regular phrasing, to which dancing became very difficult. Cool jazz followed next, led by Miles Davis, his minimalist technique exempli- fied in *Birth of the Cool* (1949–1950). Hard bop ensued, as such artists as tenor saxophonist Dexter Gordon (*Our Man in Paris*, 1963) and drummers Max Roach (who together with Clifford Brown recorded *Study in Brown* in 1955) and Art Blakey (*Hard Bop*, 1956) attempted to move the music back to an earlier period when it connected with the audience. The 1960s saw the rise of avant-garde or free jazz, led by saxophonist Ornette Coleman, whose 1959 album *The Shape of Jazz to Come*, followed by the 1960 *Free Jazz*, signaled his new musical direction; saxophonist John Coltrane, who catapulted to fame with his 1959 *Giant Steps*, followed (after other recordings) by perhaps his best-known work, *A Love Supreme* (1964); and bassist Charles Mingus, composer of enormous talent whose repertoire includes *Pithecanthropus Erectus* (1956), *Mingus Ah Um* (1959), and *The Black Saint and the Sinner Lady* (1963). The music became exploratory, decoupled from fixed chord progressions and tonality, and in many ways was in concert with the turbulence of the times. As was true of jazz since its inception, these artists all played with each other at various points in their careers, in ever-shifting configurations.

An important example of interconnections in the African Diaspora was the rise of Afro-Cuban jazz in New York. Led by the great Machito, the African Cuban percussionist, Afro-Cuban jazz (also known as Cubop) was based on African-derived, 6/8 polyrhythms that developed into the *clave* pattern. This form of jazz enjoyed an intimacy with dance, as it was associated with mambo, cha-cha, and guaguancó (a subdivision of rumba), all African-based dances. African-derived musical instruments, such as the conga and Batá drums and shekerés (calabash gourds), are fundamental to the music and are also associated with orisha worship. Cuban-born Celia Cruz would draw upon similar sources to fashion salsa, a five-note, two-bar rhythm also organized around clave. Two other African-based dances, the tango and samba, would disseminate from Uruguay–Argentina and Brazil, respectively, and they would impact dance around the world. Puerto Rican legend Tito Puente (who recorded the classic *Oye Como Va* in 1963–1964) played in both Machito's band and that of Fernando Alvarez, along with Tito Rodriguez. Their music, influenced by the African rhythms of *bomba* and *plena* in Puerto Rico, would affect Dizzy Gillespie, who also incorporated North African, West African, and Middle Eastern elements into his work. Such influences were also embraced by Yusef Lateef, a master of multiple reed instruments; Pharoah Sanders, who plays various saxophones and flutes and is famous for *The Creator Has a Masterplan*; the learned pianist and composer Randy Weston; and McCoy Tyner, longtime pianist for John Coltrane. A number of these artists, such as Randy Weston and Max Roach, were also descendants of Caribbean immigrants, adding to the complexity of their sound. The African Diaspora was therefore connecting in important ways in New York City and elsewhere.

African American musical distinction was not confined to jazz, gospel, and the blues; it was achieved in every genre and expression. Concert artists such as Roland Hayes, Paul Robeson, and Marian Anderson received acclaim from the 1920s to 1950s, while operatic prima donna Leontyne Price soared to prominence in the 1950s and 1960s. Jessye Norman, in turn, began devoting her talents to opera in the mid-1970s. Likewise, black dance was not limited to church and dance halls. The black concert dance troupe began in the 1930s, most famously led by Katherine Dunham's Ballet Nègre. Dunham, a student of diasporic dance forms, especially those of Haiti, drew upon folk music for her performances, and she laid the foundation for the Alvin Ailey American Dance Theater in 1958, followed by Arthur Mitchell's Dance Theatre of Harlem in 1966, the first black classical ballet company in the United States.

Black dance troupes relied upon black composers and various black music for their performances. Black music produced in the United States, in turn, became popular around the world not only because of its power but because of technology. Recordings and radio programs emanating from the United States would enjoy an advantage over those musical forms not similarly promoted. This was especially true of rhythm 'n' blues, a phrase gaining currency in 1949, and soul music, the term of the 1960s. Motown records, founded in Detroit by Berry Gordy in 1959, signed such artists as Smokey Robinson and the Miracles, Martha Reeves and the Vandellas, Diana Ross and the Supremes, the Temptations, Aretha Franklin, Stevie Wonder, and Marvin Gaye. Motown had a distinct urban sound, combining rhythm 'n' blues and gospel with driving beats consonant with the social movements of the time. Competing with Motown was Stax Records and its more bluesy, rural sound exemplified by Otis Redding, Johnny Taylor, and Booker T. and the M.G.'s, and it was not unlike James Brown, the "godfather of soul," who stressed racial pride in some of his music. Motown and Stax were complemented by the Philadelphia sound, a smooth rendering led by Kenny Gamble, Leon Huff, and Thom Bell. But perhaps no artist expressed the tenor of the times better than Nina Simone,

Sam Cooke, and Curtis Mayfield of the Impressions, whose political discourse was straightforward, unapologetic, and soul-stirring.

The political connotations of North American soul music were matched and perhaps exceeded by Trinidadian calypso (or kaiso). Introduced to the broad American public by the Andrew Sisters' 1944 recording *Rum and Coca-Cola* and further popularized by Harry Belafonte's 1956 album *Calypso* featuring the "Banana Boat Song," calypso in fact goes back to the African-born presence in Trinidad, the calypsonian the descendant of the griot turned chantuelle, who rose to prominence through annual competitions at Carnival. The first calypso recording was made in 1914, and by the 1930s such artists as Atilla the Hun, Roaring Lion, and Lord Invader (*Rum and Coca-Cola*'s original recorder) were prominent. Lord Kitchener emerged in the 1940s and dominated calypso through the late 1970s together with the Mighty Sparrow, who first achieved acclaim with his 1956 hit *Jean and Dinah*, celebrating the removal of U.S. troops from Trinidad. The 1940s also saw the rise of pan, or steel drum, another distinctly Trinidadian form. By the late 1970s, calypso was declining in popularity and was eclipsed by soca, a more up-tempo, less politicized version of calypso popularized by such artists as Lord Shorty (later Ras Shorty I). Calypso remains current and is a major vehicle of sociopolitical commentary, while soca has been infused with influences from Indian culture, Jamaica, hip hop, and French and Spanish cultures resident in the island, resulting in chutney soca, dance-hall soca, ragga soca (soca and reggae), rapso (soca and rap), parang soca, and so on. These forms are paralleled in the French-speaking Caribbean by *zouk*, a sound divided into dance (*chire zouk*) and more mellow expressions (*zouk love*).

Jamaica had its own version of calypso, called mento, that in the 1950s mixed with North American rock 'n' roll to form ska. Ska was the major Jamaican musical form by the mid-1960s, but by then the slower beat of rock steady had also taken hold, popularized through Prince Buster's *Judge Dread*. By the end of the 1960s, reggae had begun to make an impression, with its Rastafarian spirituality, critique of government, and lament of poverty. Toots and the Maytals, along with Jimmy Cliff, were early artists, but the genre became an international phenomenon through Bob Marley. His first group, the Rudeboys, later became the Wailers and included Peter Tosh and Bunny Wailer. In 1973 the group became Bob Marley and the Wailers with the addition of Rita Marley, Marcia Griffiths, and Judy Mowatt. The 1972 release of Marley's first album, *Catch A Fire*, together with the premier of the film *The Harder They Fall*, starring Jimmy Cliff, launched reggae into a global orbit.

Black music from the Caribbean, Latin America, and the United States traveled the world over and has been a major influence since the Second World War. In places like Britain, Caribbean forms have mixed with African genres to create new profusions, while in the United States these influences would eventually give rise to hip hop. In the African continent, diasporic musical forms, with their basis in earlier African traditions, were reintegrated into the work of such artists as Fela Anikulapo Kuti, born in Abeokuta, Nigeria in 1938. Joining a highlife band in 1954, he launched what he called Afro-beat in 1968, a convergence of West African music with jazz (and some James Brown). Fela was more diasporically influenced than his fellow countryman, King Sunny Ade and his African Beats, who perform a genre known as Juju. Like Marley, Fela was an outspoken critic of Nigerian despotism and a proponent of pan-Africanism. His own political ambitions were silenced by death in 1997. South African Hugh Masekela, the "father of African jazz," was similarly influenced by his political surroundings. Exiled in 1961, he came to the United States and began experimenting with novel musical expressions, producing his 1968 hit, *Grazing in the Grass*. He eventually married fellow South African Miriam Makeba, the quintessential vocalist, whose exile from South Africa began in 1963. Her former marriage to Kwame Ture (Stokely Carmichael) further underscores the interconnectedness of the African Diaspora and its common struggles.

Of course, music and dance are intimately associated with Carnival, a melange of African and European elements that takes place, for the most part, prior to the Lenten season. The African-descended in the Americas have also celebrated at other times, such as Pinkster in New Jersey and New York during the eighteenth and first part of the nineteenth centuries. The Dutch observance of Pentecost (or advent of the Holy Spirit), Pinkster was held seven weeks after Easter. Other examples include Crop Over in Barbados in late July to early August; June and July festivals in Santiago de Cuba; the Grenada Carnival in the second week of August; Carabana in Toronto in early August; and London's Notting Hill Carnival in late August (these dates are subject to change). Invariably, Carnival provides an opportunity for a variety of African-based cultural expressions, from the samba schools and "blocos Afros" (drummers, in the hundreds) of Brazil to the steel bands of Trinidad. New Orleans has its version in Mardi Gras, but Carnival in Trinidad is rivaled only by its counterparts in Rio de Janeiro and Salvador, Bahia. Carnival has reinforced cultural affinities throughout the Diaspora.

With Carnival and music come food. African cuisine accompanied Africans throughout the Diaspora, constituting its own widespread dispersal. Examples of foodways transferred to the Americas from Africa include rice, black-eyed peas, okra, and palm oil, called *dendê* in Brazil (probably from the Angolan term *ndende*). Akee, a red tropical, bland-tasting fruit consumed in Jamaica, is also of West African origin. Large white yams were brought to Brazil and other parts of the American southern hemisphere, but in the United States they were replaced by sweet potatoes and yellow or orange yams. Peanuts, originating in South America, were first brought to Africa by the Portuguese and then reintroduced to the Americas via the slave trade as goobers (from *nguba* of West Central African origin). Transferred African cooking techniques included deep oil frying, fire roasting, steaming in leaves, and boiling in water to produce soups and stews. Spicy seasoning, such as hot sauces and pepper sauces, was used everywhere. Certain foods remain associated with African deities, so that in Brazil the orisha Ogun, god of metallurgy, prefers black-eyed peas, roasted yam, and *feijoada*, a mixture of black beans and smoked meats that has become Brazil's national dish. *Acarajé*, a popular snack in Brazil, is derived from the Yoruba bean fritter *akará* and is associated with Yansã, goddess of cemeteries and whirlwinds. Rum, a sugar by-product and a major factor in black enslavement in the first place, is not from Africa but is associated with African labor in the Caribbean and remains an important regional beverage. Local and regional preferences have followed the African-descended in their various migrations since slavery's end, from Caribbean cuisine in North America to soul food prepared by North American musicians working in Paris. Not all of these preferences have been the healthiest, some contributing to a disproportionately high incidence of high blood pressure, heart disease, and cancer.

A final realm within which the Diaspora interacted culturally was sports. Baseball, international amateur competitions, and boxing were major arenas for fans of all colors and nationalities, and they were especially important to groups struggling to prove their worth. Baseball, segregated through the first half of the twentieth century, was perhaps the most significant vehicle through which diasporic communities learned of each other. Professional black teams were formed as

early as the 1880s and included the Philadelphia Orions, the St. Louis
Black Stockings, and the Cuban Giants. Through 1920, black teams
"barnstormed," traveling from town to town, playing any team the
town could assemble, of any color. The Negro National League was
founded in 1920, followed by the Eastern Colored League in 1923.
The Negro National League was revived in 1933 after folding two
years earlier, and it featured such legends as Cool Papa Bell, Satchel
Paige, and Josh Gibson. It was during this period that Cuba, Mexico,
and the Dominican Republic emerged as premier baseball venues, as
white and black teams could compete in these countries during the
winter. But in addition to playing in Latin America, American black
teams had also been playing Latino teams since 1900, and in 1910
the Cuban All-Stars were an important part of black baseball, evolving into the New York Cubans in 1935. Only the Indianapolis Clowns
had as many Cuban, Puerto Rican, Dominican, Mexican, and black
American players. The New York Cubans won the Negro World Series
in 1947, fielding such greats as Luis Tiant, Sr. and Martin Dihigo of
Matanzas, Cuba. Jim Crow baseball came to an end with the Brooklyn
Dodgers' signing of Jackie Robinson that same year.

International amateur competitions include football or soccer's
World Cup series, the Pan-American Games, and the Olympics. While
fostering international relations as a whole, such competitions have
played a vital role in promoting an awareness of the African Diaspora
through the emergence of the black athlete. Concerning the World
Cup, probably the most famous example is Pelé, the "black pearl"
who in 1958 led Brazil to the championship at age 17. Scoring some
1,280 goals in 1,362 games, he was declared a national treasure in
Brazil. There are numerous Olympic examples to choose from, but
the gathering of athletes every four years has exposed the world, via
television, to the existence and excellence of black athletes from the
Caribbean, Latin America, Europe, Africa, the Middle East, and the
United States. That black athletes competed from North America and
the Caribbean came as no surprise, but the rise and dominance of black
athletes elsewhere, especially Cuba and Brazil, has been a revelation to
many. Certainly, Jesse Owens' winning four gold medals at the 1936
games in Germany was an historical watershed, and following a young
Cassius Clay's (later Muhammad Ali) victory in the light heavyweight
boxing division in 1960, everyone took notice of the dominance of
Cuban heavyweight Teófilo Stevenson in 1972 and 1976.

Just the appearance of successful black athletes was a source of
pride for fans, as was the case in 1957 when Althea Gibson became

**FIGURE 12.** Group portrait of the Cincinnati Clowns, 1941 champions of the Negro American League. Back row (l. to r.) Buster Haywood, Pepper Bassett, Leovildo Lugo, Aleo Radoliffe, Jesse "Hoss" Walker (manager), Albert Overton, Henry Merohant, Walter "Rev" Canady, Bus. Mgr. McKinley "Bunny" Downs. Centre (l. to r.) Al Lipkins, Armando Vazquez, Fermin Valdes, Antonio Ruiz, Johnny Ray. Front (l. to r.) King Tut, Rafael Cabrera, Harry Jeffries, Henry Smith, Roosevelt Davis. Photographs and Prints Division, Schomburg Center for Research in Black Culture, The New York Public Library, Astor, Lenox, and Tilden Foundations.

the first black tennis player to win the Wimbledon tournament. Stars experienced enormous pressure as their race's "representatives" to live as models of decorum and to avoid political controversy. The 1960s changed all that, as athletes began to politicize the games and relate their solidarity with freedom movements around the world. The medal ceremony for Tommie Smith and John Carlos at the Mexico City Games in 1968, at which the two raised their gloved fists and lowered their heads at the singing of the American national anthem, remains emblematic of the tensions of the period. In 1976, thirty African countries boycotted the games in protest against South African apartheid, a protest actively supported by tennis star Arthur Ashe, who won the U.S. Open in 1968.

Professional boxing was perhaps the most glamorous of the three categories, and if the discussion is limited to heavyweights after Joe

Louis (champion 1937–1948), there is no question that Muhammad Ali is the paradigmatic champion of the entire Diaspora. He is man whose appeal transcended sports, an eminently political figure whose conversion to Islam, announced immediately after his defeat of Sonny Liston in 1964, catapulted him into a rarified atmosphere. Perfecting a pugilistic style featuring circular dance and uncanny speed, his principled refusal to fight in Vietnam, his suffering the removal of his championship title, and his pan-Africanist perspective endeared him to millions all over the world. His identification with Africa reached its zenith with his reclamation of the title in the 1974 "rumble in the jungle" against George Foreman in Congo (then Zaire); his overall career underscores the vital role of international sports in the rise of the contemporary African Diaspora.

## Suggestions for Further Reading

The second half of the twentieth century would see the emergence of literature seeking to treat the African Diaspora as a single subject, or as a series of related subjects. A number of edited volumes have been produced among these works, including Joseph E. Harris, ed., *Global Dimensions of the African Diaspora* (Washington, DC: Howard U. Press, 1982); Darlene Clark Hine and Jacqueline McLeod, eds., *Crossing Boundaries: Comparative History of Black People in Diaspora* (Bloomington: Indiana U. Press, 1999); and Sheila S., Walker, ed., *African Roots/American Cultures: Africa in the Creation of the Americas* (Boston: Rowman and Littlefield, 2001). One of the better, coauthored syntheses is Michael L. Conniff and Thomas J. Davis, *Africans in the Americas: A History of the Black Diaspora* (New York: St. Martin's Press, 1994). One work examining the linkages between liberation struggles not yet mentioned is Imanuel Geiss, *The Pan-African Movement; A History of Pan-Africanism in America, Europe, and Africa*, trans. Ann Keep (New York: Africana, 1974. An important article reviewing the historiography of the Diaspora is Tiffany Ruby Patterson and Robin D. G. Kelley, "Unfinished Migrations: Reflections on the African Diaspora and the Making of the Modern World," *African Studies Review* 43 (April, 2000: 11–45).

Concerning Africans and their descendants in Europe, one could begin with David Northrup's very useful *Africa's Discovery of Europe: 1450–1850* (New York and Oxford: Oxford U. Press, 2002) and should consult Winston James and Clive Harris, eds., *Inside Babylon: The Caribbean Diaspora in Britain* (London: Verso, 1993); James Walvin, *Making the Black Atlantic: Britain and the African Diaspora* (London and New York: Cassell, 2000); Tahar Ben Jelloun, *French Hospitality: Racism and North African Immigrants,* trans. Barbara Bray (New York: Columbia U. Press, 1997); Allison Blakely, *Russia and the Negro: Blacks in Russian History and Thought* (Washington, DC: Howard U. Press, 1986) and *Blacks in the Dutch World: The Evolution of Racial Imagery in a Modern Society* (Bloomington: Indiana U. Press, 1993); Adam Lively, *Masks: Blackness, Race and the Imagination* (London: Chatto and Windus, 1998); and Inongo-Vi- Makomé, *La emigración negroafricana: tragedia y esperanza* (Barcelona: Ediciones Carena, 2000). There is also a wonderful collection of visuals in the multivolumed *The Image of the Black in Western Art* (Cambridge, MA: Menill Foundation, Inc. and Harvard U. Press, 1976–89).

The civil rights movement in the United States has engendered a great deal of research. Just a few include Barbara Ransby, *Ella Baker and the Black Freedom Movement: A Radical Democratic Vision* (Chapel Hill and London: U. of North Carolina Press, 2003); Kay Mills, *This Little Light of Mine: the Life of Fannie Lou Hamer* (New York: Dutton, 1993); Chana Kai Lee, *For Freedom's Sake: the Life of Fannie Lou Hamer* (Urbana: U. of Illinois Press, 1999); Belinda Robnett, *How Long? How Long?: African-American Women in the Struggle for Civil Rights* (New York and Oxford: Oxford U. Press, 1997); Taylor Branch, *Parting the Waters: America in the King Years, 1954–63* (New York: Simon and Schuster, 1988) and *Pillar of Fire: America in the King Years, 1963–65* (New York: Simon and Schuster, 1998); and Vincent Harding, *There is a River: The Black Struggle for Freedom in America* (New York: Harcourt Brace Jovanovich, 1981). On Malcolm X, the best source remains *The Autobiography of Malcolm X, With the Assistance of Alex Haley* (New York: Grove Press, 1965). Also see John Henrik Clarke, ed., *Malcolm X; The Man and His Times* (New York: Macmillan, 1969). An accessible work examining Malcolm X and Martin Luther King, Jr. is James H. Cone, *Malcolm and Martin and America: A Dream or a Nightmare?* (Maryknoll, NY: Orbis, 1991). Read it with Lewis V. Baldwin and Amiri YaSin al-Hadid, *Between Cross and Crescent: Christian and Muslim Perspectives on Malcolm and Martin* (Gainesville: U. of Florida Press, 2002).

Of course, there is voluminous work on black music. One of the most important publications on the topic is Le Roi Jones (Amiri

Baraka), *Blues People: The Negro Experience in White America and the Music That Developed from It* (New York: Morrow, 1963), but not far behind are Eileen Southern and Josephine Wright, *Images: Iconography of Music in African-American Culture, 1770s–1920s* (New York: Garland, 2000), and Samuel A. Floyd, Jr., *The Power of Black Music: Interpreting Its Music From Africa to the Americas* (New York: Oxford U. Press, 1995). A good general source is Eileen Southern, *The Music of Black Americans: A History* (New York: Norton, 1997), 3rd ed. Regarding women in jazz and the blues, see Angela Davis, *Blues Legacies and Black Feminism: Gertrude "Ma" Rainey, Bessie Smith, and Billie Holiday* (New York: Pantheon Books, 1998); D. Antoinette Handy, *Black Women in American Bands and Orchestras* (Metuchen, NJ: Scarecrow Press, 1999), 2nd ed.; Sherrie Tucker, *Swing Shift: "All Girl" Bands of the 1940s* (Durham, NC: Duke U. Press, 2000).

Calypso and reggae and related music can be read about in Kwame Dawes, *Natural Mysticism: Towards a New Reggae Aesthetic in Caribbean Writing* (Leeds, England: Peepal Tree Press, 1999); Chuck Foster, *Roots, Rock, Reggae: An Oral History of Reggae Music From Ska to Dancehall* (New York: Billboard, 1999); Lloyd Bradley, *This is Reggae Music: The Story of Jamaica's Music* (New York: Grove Press, 2000); J. D. Elder, *From Congo Drum to Steelband: a Socio-Historical Account of the Emergence and Evolution of the Trinidad Steel Orchestra* (St. Augustine, Trinidad: U. of the West Indies, 1969); Donald R. Hill, *Calypso Calaloo: Early Carnival Music in Trinidad* (Gainesville: U. of Florida Press, 1993); Rudolph Ottley, *Women in Calypso* (Arima, Trinidad: [s.n., 1992); Louis Regis, *The Political Calypso: True Opposition in Trinidad and Tobago 1962–1987* (Barbados: U. of West Indies Press and Gainesville: U. of Florida Press, 1999); and Keith Q. Warner, *Kaiso! The Trinidad Calypso: a Study of the Calypso as Oral Literature* (Washington, DC: Three Continents Press, 1992).

You can read about blacks in film in Karen Ross, *Black and White Media: Black Images in Popular Film and Television* (Cambridge, MA: Polity Press, 1996), and Michael T. Martin, ed., *Cinemas of the Black Diaspora: Diversity, Dependence, and Oppositionality* (Detroit, MI: Wayne State U. Press, 1995).

The list is long concerning blacks in sports. Just two examples of serious scholarship are Jeffrey Sammons, *Beyond the Ring: The Role of Boxing in American Society* (Urbana: U. of Illinois, 1988), and Kenneth Shropshire, *In Black and White: Race and Sports in America* (New York: New York U. Press, 1996).

# Epilogue

Since the 1960s, reconnections with Africa and within the African Diaspora have intensified. Given the ongoing impoverishment of many in Africa and the Diaspora, such interrelations require deeper and more practical meaning if they are to play a significant role in ending the despair. The incredible beauty and creativity of the African Diaspora, combined with its unbelievable suffering and disadvantage, are contradictions awaiting resolution.

# Index

Made in the USA
San Bernardino, CA
09 September 2016